Praise for *A Daily S...*

Eleanor Hooks has crafted a remarkable gem of a book that relentlessly reminds us of our true nature. It won't take long for you to realize that we are the "spiritual energy" that animates the human form, and everything else in the universe.

-STEPHEN MIDDLETON, PHD
Professor and Director of African-American Studies
Mississippi State University

A Daily Sip of Joy & Peace is an inspired and contemplative call to wise well-being from a gentle provocateur.

-RUTH KING
author of *Healing Rage: Women Making Inner Peace Possible*

A Daily Sip of Joy and Peace is an invitation to enter more deeply into the dimension/origin of Joy and Peace, for oneself and others. There are many names and descriptions of this Space, I call it God. This book allows one to see and know from within this space that "All is well and that this space encompasses the universe."

-MARY ALICE SAUNDERS, MEd, MSN, CNS
Assistant Professor, The Breen School of Nursing
Ursuline College, Retired

Love-filled words that serve to gently nudge towards a shift in perception.

-RALPH HUME, MSW
Clinical Social Worker, Brooklyn, NY, Retired

A Daily Sip of Joy and Peace

Eleanor Hooks, PhD

BALBOA.
PRESS

A DIVISION OF HAY HOUSE

Scripture taken from the King James Version of the Bible.

Balboa Press books may be ordered through booksellers or by contacting:

Balboa Press
A Division of Hay House
1663 Liberty Drive
Bloomington, IN 47403
www.balboapress.com
1 (877) 407-4847

Print information available on the last page.

ISBN: 978-1-5043-6681-6 (sc)
ISBN: 978-1-5043-6682-3 (hc)
ISBN: 978-1-5043-6680-9 (e)

Library of Congress Control Number: 2016915632

Balboa Press rev. date: 01/10/2017

In loving memory of my daughter, Melodie

To all the spiritual teachers who have reminded
me of the joy and peace within

Preface

From a very early age, I have questioned who I am, my purpose in life, and the meaning of events that seemed to happen to me. I say "seemed" to happen, because so often the challenges in my life have been surreal. Early in my life, my intellect was valued more than my appearance, or at least that's the story I have created about feeling not pretty enough or not loved enough. Many of us have similar stories, so when we share them, other people recognize the pain and suffering that dramatizes the story. My story got more complex when I was married and received numerous reinforcements of untrue stories, with new threads and themes. When I became a mother, there were new challenges to my worth as the story became even more complex: Was I a good mother and wife? Was I a good person?

Through a number of racial and gender-based challenges in my career as well as personal challenges – financial collapse, serious health challenges, and personal losses – most recently my two sisters and my daughter – my sense of self-worth has been under attack. Throughout our lives, conditions appear that shake our faith and raise doubts; pain and suffering raise questions about the meaning of life. What has become clear to me is that all the conditions come with a story, one that we have created from a fearful ego. The ego is relentless; it floods our minds with ideas that come from one question – "Am I loved?" That simple question drives our choices, our self-assessments, our religious views, our relationships, and our perceptions of reality. If we feel loved, we feel safe from the threats of the ego. If we feel loved, we live simply, not needing more things or relationships to feel OK. If we feel loved, we have little room for hatred or abusive behavior. If we feel loved, we may experience pain temporarily, but we do not invest in suffering. But even that feeling of being loved is a story that is incomplete. We may still feel dependent on the desires expressed by someone else, or a social system that sets boundaries on our lovability.

As long as we believe that love is something given to us, something we receive because someone or something deems us worthy, we have missed the point. All of our stories are just that, stories, not based in Truth. We *are* love, expressing as love in this universe. The search for love ends when we allow ourselves to just *be* love. In that space of being love, we feel the peace of awareness; we remember who we are, and release our desires for something that we already are. The more complete question is "Am I *Love*? When we realize that the answer is always a resounding "Yes!" we are liberated.

This book is a yearlong testimony to the love that we are. It is a daily sip of joy and peace, the manifestation of love. I sometimes use the pronoun "we" in the daily sips to reinforce the notion of oneness. Even "we" is just an approximation of our relationship. As spiritual energy, we are one, not two or more. When I realize the oneness of the universe, I am aware of the divinity that courses through oneness like electrical currents. There is only one of us – the human beings, the animals, the rocks and trees are all energy, mainly space. I invite you to see yourself in the oneness of love, release your illusions of separation from All-That-Is, and remember that you are love.

There are 366 (one for leap year) daily entries exploring the meaning and experience of consciousness, love, peace and joy. The intent is to open us up to the experience of joy and to position us to experience a life of peace, in the midst of life conditions. The entries are inspired by the nine principles for a joyful life, an inspiration for my writing since 1999.

1. Trust in your relationship with All-That-Is (One Love, One Spirit, our true self)
2. Be kind to yourself and to others (we are one, so what we do for "others" we do for ourselves)
3. Choose to be peaceful (be aware of peace in the present moment)
4. Set aside all worries and fears (quiet the ego, tame the mind)
5. Honor every living thing (one living energy in the universe)
6. Work with integrity (integrate who you are with what you do)
7. Reveal your passion to create (we are creative and evolutionary beings; the universe does not stop moving and creating)
8. Acknowledge love in life (love is all that is real)

9. Know that you already have what you need (there is nothing lacking; we are the universal masterpiece, spirit's expression of love)

Like a refreshing tea that soothes the throat, heart and soul, joy fills us up. The warmth of the awareness calms us with the unmistakable energy of love. Joy is possible every moment, day, week and month of the year. Enjoy the sips.

With great love,
Eleanor "Ndidi" Hooks

Contents

The daily essays are organized into three sections: Awareness; Being in the World; Being Love. Three of the nine principles are addressed in each section.

Part I – AWARENESS – *January 1 to April 30*...................................... 1

- Trust in our Relationship with All-That-Is

- Be Kind to Yourself and to Others

- Choose to be Peaceful

Part II – BEING IN THE WORLD –*May 1 to August 31*................ 160

- Set Aside All Worries and Fears

- Honor Every Living Thing

- Work with Integrity

Part III – BEING LOVE – *September 1 to December 31* 302

- Acknowledge the Love in Life

- Reveal Passion to Create

- Know That You Already Have What You Need

January 1

Silence Before Sound

Silence is the language of God, all else is poor
translation. – *Rumi,* The Essential Rumi

Most of us have never experienced a moment of silence, not real silence.
Our lives have been quiet at times, but never completely quiet. When
we settle down for a relaxed solitude, the sounds of the universe in our
immediate environment soon overtake our consciousness. Imagine that
there was a time when there was no sound. Existence is dependent upon
sound, so we can assume that nothing existed.

Before the existence of anything in the universe, there was silence, voiceless
silence. Out of that profound silence substance emerged, but silence
remained. There is a way to experience that silence, the voice of the
voiceless; we can sit and let silence come to us, embrace us, and remove the
stress that interrupts our joy. When we return to that silence, we are aware
of our being, our eternal existence. In silence, energy exists, spiritual energy;
we come to know ourselves, our true self in that stillness. The energy of
silence is our true strength. When we suspend our preoccupation with the
sounds in our life they recede to the background of our consciousness, and
we remember the true essence of the Self. Imagine how exciting it is to
know that we are that powerful energy; we are the first love of the universe.
Rest this day in that.

January 2

Infinite Universe

We are expressions of the universe, the necessary
evidence of its power. – *Ndidi,* Tea Leaves

If we stand on the banks of a river and look outward to the horizon, we know that we cannot see beyond that horizon, yet we also know that the horizon is not the limit in the distance. It is an illusion to think that there is nothing beyond the horizon. Such a thought is pre-Galilean, an archaic notion that the world is flat.

Almost everything that we experience has a perceived limit; we get assurances from a world of objects that have a structure with boundaries, with a beginning and an end. We are told early on in our lives that we are individuals, so we too develop boundaries between ourselves and others. Because our individual bodies and personalities are expected in our cultural and social communities, we come to see ourselves as separate from others.

We are brief visitors on the earth as expressions of divine energy. Every moment is a transformative experience, an opportunity to feel the joy of being, and to know the interconnectedness of all creation. Our connections are so strong that death does not separate us. If we wonder about life after death, we can rest in knowing there is no beginning of the universe and no end; there is no end to love and no end to life born in love. What seems like a horizon is a limited view; so much exists beyond our conscious appearance here on earth. And we are not bystanders in the flow of life in the universe. We are creating and contributing to the beauty and diversity of the universe through the simple reality of our being, and through the legacy of love we express.

January 3

Sound of the Heart

Deep within the essence of our being is a love that
must be shared. – *Ndidi,* Tea Leaves

A young child ambles along the beach searching for shells. He picks up a conch shell and holds it up to his ear. The sounds of the ocean fascinate him, so he begins to smile. He has stumbled upon the many illusions in life. The sound heard from raising the shell to one's ear is really the noise in the surrounding environment resonating within the cavity of the ear.

The sound in our environment is pervasive, so at times we listen closely; but it is the Self, our divine energy that hears the sounds of the universe. When we are aware of our *being-ness,* we hear the sound of our own heart and within that heart space we sense the infinite nature of life. With no fear of death, we can embrace the moment by moment transformation that is life's unending movement. Just as we breathe in and out, so do life events continue in a constant rhythm of coming and going. The beat of our heart reminds us that we are alive in each moment; and the sounds of our hearts remind us that life is an ongoing, unrepeatable cycle. Every moment is new, existing as a crucible for creativity and transformation. Everything in the universe, like a massive orchestra of sounds and silence, will continue the cycle of change and transformation. We are no exception. Our contributions are part of the symphony as we express love and flow as love in the universe. When we rhythmically allow universal love to flow freely in our life, we play music from our heart space. When love flows from us the entire universe applauds.

January 4

Creation

And the Spirit of God moved upon the face
of the water. – *Genesis 1:2 (KJV)*

Water has enviable power; it endures by transforming itself based on conditions in the environment; it's adaptable. Water is a rolling ocean, a placid lake, a flowing river, gentle rain or escaping steam. It gushes and meanders, babbles, and seeps; it moves. We are partly water, and would die without it. Deep within the water of the universe is the energy of creation. The universe has been a relentless, although nuanced at times, movement of creation. The stunning biodiversity is visual and tangible evidence of a world that is committed to creating more, expanding and evolving. All the elements of creation are here right now—all thoughts, ideas, intentions, and creations – in this moment. As the universe constructs and deconstructs in its expansion, we are the opportunity for those precious elements of creation to appear in reality. Every experience, response or reaction we register as part of our life experience is part of the creation; it is our own compelling story, one that is critical to universal expansion. Every molecule of our being, every thought and every act of love and compassion is an essential expression of the spirit within us. Love is first nature, not second nature to us. When we are being who we are, love flows like a rushing stream that soaks every moment with joy.

January 5

Who We Are Not

Joy is knowing who you are in the unbounded
beauty of now. — *Ndidi,* Tea Leaves

A young woman looked into her mirror one morning and did not recognize herself. Masks had obscured her face, and forgotten diets, prized possessions, past awards and unresolved feelings were plastered across her body like graffiti. She longed for the person she used to be.

When we give up our preoccupations with the body and appearances, we discover who we really are. Just as important as knowing who we are is knowing who we are not. Although we have a body, we are not the body. We are not the masks we wear to fit in or achieve some career goal. We are not what we do or what we have done. We are spiritual energy expressing within us.

We are not what we possess or know or even what we feel. Anything that comes and goes, emerges and recedes is not who we are. We are not a personality, label or a style. Labels and other attributes are empty attachments that do not arise out of the experience of *being;* they are social constructions that separate us from one another. We are not the boundaries we place on ourselves. If we think we exist within a perceived boundary, we miss the expansive opportunity to just be; limits constrict us.

All that we are in any perceived reality is transformational energy; we are not stagnant, stuck or immobile, so disturbing conditions or happy events are temporary stops along our journey. We are the beneficiaries of joy in each moment with no boundaries, no labels and no confinements. Joy is not something we seek; it is already here as who we are.

January 6

Je m'appelle

Love is my true identity. Selflessness is my true self. Love is my true character. Love is my name. – *Thomas Merton,* Seeds of Contemplation

Personal introductions in French often include the expression, *je m'appelle*; a literal translation is "I call myself." Je m'appelle" is the answer to *"Comment appellez-vous?"* What do you call yourself? We are named by someone else, and call ourselves that name. Parents, siblings and others call us names, some proper names and some shorter terms of endearment. We know ourselves, we think, by the names we are called. Names and titles are convenient ways to express our unique identity in the world, but our constructed identities are different from who we really are. As we live our lives, we become comfortable with the monikers that identify us; we think that we are a daughter or son, a mother or a father. We use titles to define our worth or names to define our relationships. Names and titles are given to us, or we give them to ourselves, but they always remain a mere representation of who we are.

Names and labels we give to ourselves in our constructed reality are simply our shorthand; universal energy simply is, and that's what we are. As Shakespeare wrote, "A rose by any other name would smell as sweet." Just as the rose does not separate from sweetness, you cannot separate yourself from universal energy. Without the boundaries we place on ourselves with names and other labels, we are free to be who we are. When we remember who we are, there is no name that can define us clearly; there is no shape to assume that tells the full story of who we are. Universal energy is nameless and formless and we are that. When we are aware of our true self, love is our true name.

January 7

Pure Mind

We are shaped by our thoughts; we become what we think. When the mind is pure, joy follows like a shadow that never leaves. – *The Buddha*

Each morning a man awoke with the same frightening thought; he grew so accustomed to the thought that when his morning reverie was interrupted by a pleasant call from a friend, he became surprisingly angry.

We have had recurrent thoughts that interrupt our sense of peace. These tough thoughts stick to us like sheets of cling wrap so we begin to believe these false ideas. The thoughts are sometimes fearful, but they can also be strong desires for something we do not have, or longing for a relationship we have not experienced. Trauma, tragedy or pain create the thoughts for our stories; we can draft elaborate scenarios written through the tyranny of our thoughts. The stories are rewound in our mind since our fears demand repetitive attention. If we give credence to the thoughts and act on their behalf, we allow negative thoughts, based in fear, to cloud our life experience.

Later, we are filled with regrets because of our behaviors, and blame others for our feelings. Because we are beginning to believe falsehoods, we begin to suffer. But we may not recognize the suffering as our created story, so we ignore the ever-present love that rests quietly in the midst of our suffering. We must not worry. The story is not who we are; it is a story we have created at the direction of a fearful, untamed mind.

As a continuing stream of ideas, images and sensations, the mind is a constructed concept that can shape what we perceive. A tree, river or a flower is *pure mind* without grasping for approval, safety or love; it is being what it is, mindlessly. With the pure mind of a flower, having no judgment of conditions or clinging to false stories, we refuse to give our pain more energy. A pure mind is an allowing mind, but also one that observes the energy of thoughts, and does not focus undue attention on them. Our pure mind does not attempt to control the streaming images and words. We allow thoughts to arise in the mind and then disappear, without giving attention to them. Thoughts come and go in reaction to what we perceive or feel, but when we let them flow, we can also let them go.

January 8

Find Strength Within

Deep within your consciousness you know who
you were meant to be. – *Ndidi,* Tea Leaves

People often refer to Robert Frost's poem about a choice of paths to take. In his poem, "The Road Not Taken," a person walking in the woods arrives at a fork in a road, and is confronted with a choice. Even though he laments the possibilities of the path he chose not to take, and took a road "not travelled by" he realizes that his choice made a difference in his life. The poem has been used to show that choosing a less-traveled road could turn out to be the better choice. All roads lead to the same end; how we get to the end depends on what we choose to experience in life.

We may look outward for support from other people, friends and family. We may also seek help, guidance and information to help navigate the challenging conditions and frustrations in life. In the end, we make choices about what to do, even when the choice is not to choose.

As children we are often told what to do; choices may be limited. Yet, we wonder about alternatives, and sometimes long for the time when we can make our own decisions. We learn to find strength in the answers from parents, family members, mentors and people we respect. We trust their thoughts and take them as our own.

But when we get older, we learn to find the strength to make those choices on our own, and commit to living with whatever outcome emerges. Without attachment to or expectations of a particular outcome, we find the strength to experience our life as it is. We realize that we *are* the path, and that everything is as it should be.

We no longer gain any assurance of who we are from an external source; we look within. The path we choose is choosing us, so we are curious about the road less-traveled and make our way in the world.

Our reliance on an external source of direction denies our own efficacy, that energy to create that is within. When we find that assurance within, knowing that we are the ones we have been looking for all our life, the realization is liberating. We all have a reservoir of ideas, universal intelligence, and eternal love inside. Our only challenge is to remember, then we realize that the choices are simply as it should be.

January 9

Beyond Appearances

The truth of our being is beyond the senses. — *Ndidi,* Tea Leaves

Reports of murder and mayhem in the news of the day disturb our peace and encourage our minds to embrace new fears. Each of our expressions of fear have one enduring theme: the fear of our own demise. News is not new but a repetition of past fears, displayed with a deceptive freshness in order to mask false messages about our world.

When we look deeply into the true nature of our life and realize that when we begin to feel uncomfortable with what we're hearing, seeing or doing, we have entered a shadowy cave. The cave casts shadows like Plato's metaphor, deceiving us at every turn. Our vision becomes obscured with negativity and we begin to look for truth in the shadows.

We may begin to identify with the people who are harmed or threatened, and behave as if it is a rehearsal for our own destruction. The events feel personal because we are participating as an observer in someone else's story. Like ogling a crash along the highway so long that we begin to feel the tragedy and suffering, we look at stories and think they are our own.

We can face our fears without attaching ourselves to them; they are not based on enduring events. We must let them go before those fearful stories begin to feel like the truth. Although we do experience pain in life, suffering is always a choice. When we let go of suffering, we enter a space where even if the pain remains as a reality, the release of suffering frees our mind for healing.

We must stop, be still and remember the power within us. In the present moment there is nothing wrong; appearances are deceiving images from the past or the future and neither time exists now. There is no condition or experience that does not at its core contain the potential for joy. Awareness allows us to recognize that we are potential, ready to experience deep abiding peace.

January 10

The Questions

One of the moral diseases we communicate to one another
in society comes from huddling together in the pale
light of an insufficient answer to a question we are afraid
to ask. – *Thomas Merton*, No Man is an Island

As we hustle along through life being busy with activities and thoughts, we may become aware of simmering questions that seem to be unanswerable. Why do events happen as they do? What do we have to do to change the experience of our lives?

When we ask why or what happened, we are thrust immediately into the past, a time that no longer exists; so the true answers will always elude us. Some will attempt to explain the past, but our existence, in the past or future, is inexplicable. Even though we search for answers, the search continues without end, because answers change with changing times. Those changes create the adventure of life.

Know that the joy is in the questions. It is our curiosity that allows us to express ourselves fully. Intuition stirs in us; a voiceless, causeless mystery unfolds as the temporary answer. Since moments continue ad infinitum, each moment contributes new chapters to our mystery.

Questions are the fuel of our existence; they ensure the world's expansion and creativity. Not knowing is a gift and an opportunity, because curiosity is the bedrock of innovation and creativity. We can turn our attention to what is happening right now, and settle into the beauty of our life experience as it unfolds. Instead of living life in the absolute answers, we can live life in the ever-present, evolving questions.

January 11

Illusion and Truth

Three things cannot be long hidden: the sun,
the moon and the truth. – *The Buddha*

Just when life seems to be working, something happens to disturb our sense of peace. We may say, "If it's not one thing, it's two! or "It's always something." We may eagerly curse the darkness of challenges, and search for the light, but one is not cherished without the other.

The world of contrasts or challenges helps us to make sense of our reality; challenges also help us to decide what we want or prefer as our life experience. We crave a sense of order, but the universe is continually organizing itself as it continues its expansion. Because we feel safer in a predictable environment, we create boundaries in our mind around everything material and natural. The boundaries are a way to maintain sensory and mental order. Living without these boundaries may seem like an insane or unstable idea; but the structure of our lives is not imposed on us; we are creating those boundaries, all of them.

In our desire to keep things separate and identifiable, our awareness of who we are as spiritual beings becomes obscured by fears and anxieties. As long as we see our world as something that happens to us, we are likely to continue feeling uncomfortable with life events. Our discomfort is a sign that we are entangled with illusions; we have given credence to what is temporary.

In silent prayer and meditation, we release all attachments to temporary life challenges and commune with Truth. Our true self is divine oneness expressing in the warm embrace of love; and that truth will not change.

January 12

Stillness

Stillness is louder than the noise of life. Listen
with the heart. – *Ndidi,* Tea Leaves

We may welcome the day with our list of responsibilities and priorities; and focus most of our attention on getting things done – satisfying the expectations for ourselves and others. We may not stop until we arrive home exhausted from the day's activities. If our day included disappointments or seemingly impossible challenges, we may feel heavy from addressing the burdens we've carried.

Beneath the struggles of everyday life is a wellspring of peace and joy. We may not notice it unless we clear a path for it to surface. Under layers and layers of anxieties, we can discover the peace that has been there all along; cutting through the layers requires that we become still. Stillness is not just stopping, but it is quieting the mind, silencing the voices that are constantly directing our lives. Stillness is leaving the sensations of the body where disturbing memories are stored, and meeting our true self in the direct experience of the moment. Stillness is not just becoming peaceful but becoming peace itself. When we clear a space for peace to emerge by quieting the mind, we allow the pressures of the day to fall away.

January 13

We Are Never Alone

The universe is made out of energy, everything is entangled,
everything is one. – *Bruce Lipton*, The Biology of Belief:
Unleashing the Power of Consciousness, Matter & Miracles

A young boy sits on the beach at sunset, and waits for the night sky to show up so that he can see the stars. He is looking at the stars as disconnected blinking lights in the heavens, but he is both the perceiver and participant; his looking with anticipation and awe connects him to those lights, even though they are far away. Because the stars are present in his awareness, they are part of his experience; so as long as we have conscious awareness of life, we are never alone.

If we try to imagine ourselves without our surroundings, atmosphere, or senses, we realize that such a state is impossible. As John Muir, the noted American naturalist, said, "When we try to pick out anything by itself, we find it hitched to everything else in the universe." When you experience the lack of separation from the entire universe, you know finally the joy of never being alone. We are not a separate body we sense and feel; we are "hitched" to everything else.

As social beings, we understand the desire for connection with others, but as spiritual beings the desire is already fulfilled. We reach out to others for emotional and physical connection, but the connection seems at times incomplete or unsatisfying. The interactions are sometimes weak ties, temporary interludes of connection. But there is a permanent connection to the source of being; we cannot be disconnected even for a moment from this omnipresent intelligence. Awareness of our relationship to All-That-Is in spirit is a state of "all-oneness" instead of alone-ness. Connection brings to us a sense of communion with the earth and everything within it. We can begin to see people and everything else in the universe as an expression of our place in the world. Oneness is what Thich Nhat Hanh refers to as *interbeing,* the state of interdependent connectedness of all phenomena in the universe. We come to realize that in the ultimate connection, we are never alone.

January 14

Breathing Together

Thousands of candles can be lighted from a single
candle, and the candle will not be shortened. Happiness
never decreases by being shared. – *The Buddha*

If we explored the roots of the word, "conspiracy," we would find that Old French and Latin roots define 'conspiracy' as literally 'breathing together.' But the word has taken on a newer connotation of gathering to plot some negative action. The original meaning maintains the richness in the idea of breathing together, especially as a conspiracy of love.

One way to breathe intentionally together is group meditation. Being silent together or experiencing a guided meditation together brings a special experience of intimacy. There is beautifully contrasting experience of being in solitude and being in communion at the same time.

Group meditation - silent, sitting meditation and discussion - can be an opportunity to breathe together - a conspiracy of stillness to experience who we are. Breathing is a natural process of inviting in and letting go. It is a model of the comings and goings of our life experience.

Breathing is the essence of life; if we hold our breath deliberately for too long, it can be life threatening. During meditation, we sense the life and death cycle, as we breathe in and out. We are also reminded that life continues as we experience the out-breaths and the in-breaths. The flow of breath is a reminder of the power of letting go of the illusion of control; as long as we live, without illness or injury, our breathing continues without our control.

We know at an unconscious level that we must let go of breath in order to continue breathing; so it is with the process of joyful living. We must let go of many fruitless ideas and old hurts that threaten our well-being, so that we can enjoy the full 'breadth' of our life. When we have embraced the clarity that remains after we release useless ideas, we breathe in awareness of the presence of others. When our breathing awareness is deep and resonant, we breathe in harmony with others, and recognize our true presence. When we share our breath, we share the lightness of love we feel, and become the opening to peace in the world.

January 15

Justice

Truth is a deep kindness that teaches us to be content in our everyday
life and share with people the same happiness.
– *Thomas Merton*, New Seeds of Contemplation

When what we want in life is different from the way it is, we may see
actions as unfair or unjust. We may be critical of those who seem to take
no action against what we deem unjust, and are disappointed in their
apparent silence. Those who agree with our assessments are deemed allies,
and those who disagree become enemies. In these divisions, we create new
injustices - blaming, demonizing, and dehumanizing.

We participate in the creation of our collective reality, including the ideas
we have about justice and injustice. Suppose we are a collection of *tribes,*
groups of people who have made up a story about being separate from one
another. Our views of each other as independent individuals and groups
can create tensions that seem to interrupt the natural flow of energy in
the universe. Divisions give rise to injustice; our belief in our spiritual
separation creates a breeding ground for the defamation of differences.
The tensions and attachments to particular thoughts create a stuck-ness
that leaves us feeling uncomfortable. We begin to believe the story that we
are exceptional and independent, denying our natural *inter*dependence as
one spirit. We then assign separate and unequal worth to humans, animals
and other parts of the world. The story feeds the false self we pay attention
to, the self that creates fear. We place a lock on our hearts to protect our
false self, and are convinced that some of us deserve something that others
do not. We turn away from our essential oneness and commit to the false
ideas of inferiority, superiority, privilege and favoritism. Fear has made us
something we are not.

The truth is that we are love expressing as individual souls in this world. Justice washes over us when we are aware of our interconnectedness with everyone and everything in the universe. Justice appears when our hearts beat as one loving spirit; when we share innocence in equal measure. Justice is possible with compassion and lovingkindness for all; it is not a legal pronouncement, but a commitment to the truth of our being.

January 16

Echoes of Words

There is a way between voice and presence where
information flows. In disciplined silence it opens, with
wandering talk it closes. – *Rumi,* The Essential Rumi

Words are the symbols we use for the images of the mind; we speak and
write with the echoes of mental and cultural impressions. Language is a
reaction to what we have learned, thought, felt and imagined. The impact
of centuries of pain and delusion can turn words into knives, and people
into prey. But we can also smooth the waters of argument with our words,
and support others as they explore what is true for their lives.

Words have power and force; they can be decision points that define
a moment. Words can heal or hurt, soothe or sting, blame or praise.
Our symbolic language can be misinterpreted, misunderstood and
miscommunicated; words can be soft, strong, assertive or aggressive as
they insert meaning into the present experience of our life.

How words are communicated can be just as powerful as the words
themselves. We express beliefs that are based on stories we are accustomed
to hearing. Sometimes opinions dress up in words and prance around
as fact. Spoken beliefs can mask fears and pain, while causing both; the
casualties of speech are well-documented in life experiences.

Our silence can be liberating. In the present moment a wordless voice makes
language unnecessary; unconditional love silences all the echoes of the past,
where opinions, requests, and pronouncements have promoted a false self. In
the present moment the only awareness is joy. We must cherish moments of
stillness inside us; we must listen to the still, small voice that doesn't use words.

January 17

Invisible Force

We are so much more than the mind can conceive. – *Ndidi,* Tea Leaves

Our mind is often murky and sometimes difficult to rely on as the source of clarity. Our ego tries to convince us we can find the answers to our existence in our thoughts, so we begin to believe that the mind is reliable. The original source of thoughts is generally unknown, arising seemingly out of nowhere; thoughts are without substance until we give them our attention. This invisible force shapes what we believe and do. Respect the mind's power, but know that our true self transcends any notion of the mind. The true source of our being is all-knowing, everywhere present, and pure love. Mind is not an enemy, but a stream of consciousness, begging for attention. We can allow its stream to flow onward without getting swept up in the current. When we attach ourselves to a thought, it becomes our own, but often it can possess us even though we try to control its direction.

Who we are is beyond thoughts and ideas of the mind. Any attempt to label who we are falls short of our magnificence, because the depth of our being is inexplicable and invisible. We come to know that who we are is invisible like the mind, so we can easily believe that our mind is who we are. Awareness of the true self is not reliant on the senses. We do not feel, see or touch its essence; but when we take the journey within, we become aware of the invisible presence, the sacredness that is joy. The presence cannot be discovered because our true self is not lost, but always present. The presence cannot be possessed because there is no one to possess All-That-Is. But in that presence "we live and breathe and have our being."

January 18

Calm Center

Peacefulness is the sweet calm center around which our life swirls.
We enter that calmness with every breath. – *Ndidi,* Tea Leaves

Life can be a whirlwind of joys and sorrows, challenges and opportunities, successes and failures. When we look back at what we have been through, we sometimes wonder how we survived. Sometimes we're not certain we will survive what we're currently facing, but we do.

As spiritual beings, we have access to the truth of our existence in the present moment. With each breath we can know that just as we are one spirit, so are all the events we experience, one moment in time. We reflect on past events now, and dream of the future now. In all our thoughts and reactions to thoughts there is a pattern - habitual thoughts and behaviors, or particular ways to overcome challenges.

There is a coherence of experiences that pervades the entire universe, including our experiences of life. Experiences are not isolated, but connected and symmetrical. There is an order even when we sense that the world is chaotic. Like a hurricane's calm eye, within the chaotic swirling of events, the calm center rests in stability. The universe is moving continuously in a hurricane of motion, but the evolving pattern is always stillness. When we align ourselves with that stillness we are able to withstand the battery of our current experience, allowing its fury to arise in our consciousness and dissipate like the winds of the hurricane. The winds of life are strong, but a calm center is the core of our existence. Within the swirling chaos, we can remain rooted in the resilient presence of the Self. The storm will eventually pass, but our true self will always remain.

January 19

Attention

Tell me what you pay attention to and I'll tell you who you are. – *José Ortega y Gasset,* Man and Crisis

Ophthalmologists sometimes ask patients to take a depth-of-field test that tracks the patient's ability to see a flashing light at numerous points on a screen. The person focuses on a light in the center of the screen, but is expected to see flashes within a broad range. Focused attention on the flashing lights is critical to the success of the test; failure to keep the eyes focused on the lights can interfere with the quality of the test results, because the lights exist within a boundary that requires focus.

The true self has no boundary and no edge; it cannot be captured or limited, yet consciousness of its presence is undeniable with focused attention. Because the true self is not locatable with the senses, we may struggle with awareness of it. Consciousness of our being is like an aura we carry around us that cannot be seen. If we're not careful, we can begin to take it for granted, since we cannot see, feel, hear or touch it. Our consciousness of our bodies is always present, but awareness of the essence of self can be lost with inattention, and we may run through life, missing most of what is our true nature. Missing the essence of our being is a way that we miss the fullness of life.

Our first attempts at attention can occur in stillness, often in meditation or prayer, where the primary attention is to breathing or divine presence. If we are meditating, we become aware of the in-breaths and out-breaths as ways to focus our attention, although awareness of our breathing is frequently interrupted by endless, self-centered thoughts. Like random

25

dots on our field of consciousness, thoughts flash through our mind, and beg us to become distracted.

Like murky guides, thoughts beckon to us to follow paths that leads us away from attention to the true self. As we begin to travel down those paths, we begin to plan or review old tapes in our mind about unresolved issues. We begin to worry and allow sadness to throw its cloak over us.

Inattention is not only a distraction from self, it is a fruitless search for answers. The answers we seek are already present, if we attend to the truth of our being. The boundless self holds all answers and all questions; it is too large to measure and to deep to fathom. But when we attend to what is, instead of what we want, think we need, or plan to have, we free ourselves to pay attention. We focus the spotlight of our awareness deep within our soul, then our attention settles us into the present moment and points the way to peace.

January 20

Innocence

From mercy comes courage; from economy comes generosity; from humility comes leadership. – *Lao Tzu,* Tao Te Ching

A young law student decided to participate in the annual Thanksgiving Day student program to feed homeless people who languished during cold weather on the streets just outside of the law school buildings. He and others assembled with cooked meals and started to distribute them. Suddenly, a large black vehicle arrived and parked nearby, with the engine still running. A well-dressed man jumped out of the vehicle, took off his long, cashmere coat and gently wrapped the coat around a man who was shivering. Without a word, the man re-entered his car and drove away. The stunned students began to cry tears of joy.

Most of us believe in the value of service to others and recognize needs in our various communities. We may also envision a time when those who temporarily need our support will become self-supporting, and live a life they dream for themselves. The true service we give to others is to recognize the innocence in them. If we turn the mirror to face ourselves, we will realize that we all have perfection at the core of our being. All of us are potential, ever-changing consciousness, whole and complete in the present moment.

Sympathetic views of others can create out-groups of neediness and in-groups of providers. When we acknowledge our collective innocence, we can discover that our service to others is a way to recognize the divine energy flowing through everyone.

January 21

Meditation Practice

Meditation clears the clutter in the mind that obscures
our deep presence. – *Ndidi,* Tea Leaves

A monk dreaded practice because of the long hours sitting quietly in meditation. He complained to his teacher in private that he was afraid that spending his days in meditation was wasting his life. The teacher looked at the monk and asked, "How much life do you have left?"

When we are successful in letting go, we move to a new *awareness* and appreciation of our inner sanctuary. The awareness can generate feelings of profound peace particularly in contrast to the pain or discomfort we may feel as we make our way through life's conditions.

Some of us may establish a goal for meditation to experience peace and escape the pain. Although the relief from suffering is possible, meditation is not a cure. Instead meditation invites us into a state of awareness; in that state we sense that there is nothing wrong. If we meditate *for* something, we then thrust ourselves into the future, and miss the peace in the present moment. If we think our meditation practice is an opportunity to be a better person, we will judge or measure our progress toward that goal. But there is nothing wrong with us. Without attachments to thoughts, plans or goals, we are free to be who we are.

Often we want to feel better so we meditate with the expectation that our lives will change. Meditation does not change the conditions in our lives; the practice simply improves our response to them. When we become fully aware of our peaceful center, we carry it with us consciously throughout the daily challenges and joys of our lives.

January 22

Nature's Gifts

We are one with the natural world; spirit creates
no boundaries. – *Ndidi,* Tea Leaves

Nature is as much who we are as any part of our body; we are both beneficiaries and contributors in the natural world. Nature is not only around us but also within us. Movement in nature is the unnoticed growth like the slow transformation of a butterfly, or like the changing of the seasons with the colors of Autumn. The natural world is busy *being* itself, just as we are. If we rest our eyes on the green of the trees or the rush of the ocean waves, we experience peace within. In the stillness of the mountains or the waving grasses of the plain, we see no anxiety, no strain or regrets; but when we look at mountains or sway with the waving grasses, we are transformed.

Witness the tree being a tree. Notice the carefree butterfly that has emerged from its cocoon, being a butterfly. Smell the flower expressing itself with its fragrance, unconcerned about whether or not it is attractive or valued. The tree is not jealous of the flower or wishing that the butterfly would not rest on its branches.

The unfettered rhythm of nature is our teacher; we can learn much about ourselves by looking into the mirror of the natural world. If we look deeply at the power, beauty and openness to change in nature, we become aware of our own worthiness, loving spirit and flexibility. As contributors to the ongoing movements in nature, we see things as they are, and know that everything is as it should be.

January 23

Movement

The only way to make sense of the change is to plunge into it,
move with it, and join the dance. – *Alan Watts,* The Way of Zen

Over time we notice changes in our appearance. Babies develop new
capabilities every day and toddlers grow older and test their independence.
Material possessions age and show signs of use, and our tastes in foods
and fashion may change. The days and years plow on day-to-day with
subtle movements. We may notice the changes more readily as we age;
and become surprised by unnoticed changes that ultimately affect us.
Everything moves.

Movement is another form of present awareness; each moment that we
move is an immersion into the present moment. We are self-starting balls
of energy influencing and imprinting our world as we adapt to the changes
that continue our existence. We sit, walk, run, cycle, practice hatha yoga,
or move chi energy with qigong as we move with the rhythm of the
universe. Without resistance, our life appears to move painlessly from one
moment to the next, but with resistance to our life as it is, we begin to
suffer. When we are aligned with life's movements, and grateful for the
adventure of life, we experience peace.

Movement with life allows us to feel the divine energy that is the source
of our existence, but when we're still, our awareness of the continuously
moving energy is heightened. As the wisdom of the Upanishads states,
"Everything that moves, breathes, opens and closes is the Self." As the
universe moves and transforms, we are changing with it, because we *are* it.

January 24

Beyond Hope

Lift the veil that obscures the heart, and there you will find what you are looking for. – *Kabir,* The Kabir Book

In the film, *Back to the Future*, time travelers believe that going back in time can alter the present and the future. This fantasy is a testimony to hope that changes can occur regardless of time and space. If we believe that the present is all we have that is real, hope is a departure from reality. Hope sends us longingly into the future, a time that does not yet exist. In the past, a time that is no longer available to us, we may think about what has happened in life - the regrets and the disappointments we have felt. Our tendency is to hope for a better future, particularly if the past was regrettable. New Year's resolutions and plans are imbued with hope. We may hope that our resolutions will pay off for us, or that our plans will result in a predicted outcome. Believing that happiness is fulfilled hopes, we become dependent on fate or hidden destiny. Since we're willing to face possible disappointment, we continue to hope for the best.

The problem with hope is that it limits our experience; it sets aside the present and gratitude for things as they are now, in favor of a possible future state. We live in a vibrational universe where what we are grateful for now is the blueprint for experiencing happiness in the next moment in time.

There is an experience beyond hope, where desires are released, where we have no attachment to the future, or the past. As the third century BCE philosopher Chuang Tzu said, "Happiness is the absence of striving for happiness." In that field beyond hope, where there is no striving, and gratitude fills our heart, we experience joy.

January 25

One-Pointed Stillness

Strive to still your thoughts, make your mind one–
pointed meditation. – *Bhagavad Gita*

We may miss many of life's events because we're overwhelmed with stressful thoughts. A solar eclipse goes by unnoticed, or the flight of birds in formation may be taken for granted. Life is full of wonder that we may miss along our path. Our continuing stress may convince us that changing our activities, or going away could save us from ongoing despair. If we want to take a vacation from the stress and expectations, we don't need a different activity or a different place. Instead, we can begin our path to peace by stopping; but stopping alone is insufficient, if our mind continues to focus on the complexities of living. We do not have to remove ourselves physically from overwhelming conditions; we can withstand the barrage of events if we refuse to cling to any of it. In the peace of stillness, we can redirect our focus.

In one-pointed stillness, we focus our attention on something, such as a candle flame or photograph and fix our attention on it until the boundary that exists between self and the object begins to dissolve. In this state of *flow*, when time and surroundings disappear from consciousness, we experience one-pointed stillness, a timeless space where no boundaries exist and we no longer see ourselves as separate bodies. Instead we have an intimate and spiritual connection with the universe of ideas, images and energy. It is the ultimate experience of letting go.

One-pointed stillness trains the mind to serve us instead of enslaving us to its false fears. One-pointed stillness allows the mind to slink into the shadows, and to re-emerge when we need it to help us discern the truth of conditions and challenges in our life. We can free ourselves from the inscrutable ideas that walk through our mind endlessly, if we tame the mind. When we practice one-pointed stillness we can appreciate the unbounded nature of the present moment and liberate ourselves from the tyranny of thoughts.

January 26

The Kingdom Within

Neither will they say, Behold, it is here! or behold, it is there!
for the kingdom of God is within you. – *Luke 17:21(KJV)*

There is a kingdom within each of us; it's a world of spiritual neighborhoods: imagination, compassion, forgiveness and awakening. In the neighborhood of *imagination*, we dream of better times and envision peace, but if we linger too long in that neighborhood, we miss the present moment as we mortgage our present for the future. The imagination neighborhood is where our ideas and images reside, where vivid dreams and curiosity come alive. Our imagination has no limits, so we imagine a universe where peace is present.

In the neighborhood called *compassion,* we recognize suffering, our own and others. We see inside the suffering, and know that the release of suffering comes from letting go of hatred, the love of possessions, and false notions of separation from neighbors. We have no strangers in this neighborhood because we are connected to everyone. We choose to express compassion freely to everyone without an expectation of reward, and then we experience inconceivable joy.

In the neighborhood called *forgiveness,* we release our pain and send love to ourselves and others. We heal the wounds laid bare by resentment and anger. But if our forgiveness is an empty expression of prescribed words without awakening to the spirit and innocence of ourselves and others, we are vulnerable to future feelings of victimhood. Ultimately, there is nothing to forgive; we are all on a journey of living and learning. At the core of our being, perfection exists; we are on a steady, though rocky path toward realization of that perfection.

In the neighborhood called *awakening*, we are fully aware of every moment of our lives as a unique gift of presence. Stillness murmurs lovingly to us as we wake up to the present moment in all its glory. In our awakened state, we see with new eyes, experience joy and peace, and participate fully in life. With growing awareness, we live and breathe in all the neighborhoods: grateful for the unfolding life through imagination; the compassionate heart of spirit; the faith in forgiveness; and the awakening to the truth of our being.

January 27

False Rivals

The night is not the opposite of the day; it is the long
breath before the dawn. – *Ndidi,* Tea Leaves

The mind demands an antagonist for each of its stories. Contrived battles
are always evidence that the stories are untrue. An example is the ongoing
struggle between religion and science. Our world religions and sciences are
false rivals; the truth is far beyond the mundane premises of the rivalry.
The universe benefits from the curiosity of the sciences and the faithful
contemplation of religions. As long as science and religion observe their
synergies and respect their divergences, the inherent interdependence is
useful.

If we believe that the world is always a set of opposites doing battle,
everything we encounter will have at least two competing sides. There will
be a protagonist and an antagonist, a wrong side and a right side; but the
two sides always create one, like the union of opposites in yin-yang. In a
competition for the truth of our existence, a false rivalry between science
and religion often creates enemies and infidels. Each side claims greater
access to the truth and attempts to defame the other.

How we close ranks around our values; or how strongly we voice different
perspectives about truth depends on our situations or beliefs. As situations
change, so do our versions of the truth. In attempts to make our views
concrete, we use particular languages, symbols and rituals, and expect
those who take our "side" to adopt the same cultural behaviors. The more
convinced we become that our way is the only right way, the more we
consider others' views to be wrong, and often fail to see where we agree. If

we don't see agreement, we become completely resistant to the possibility of a viable but different belief or viewpoint.

Constructed boundaries keep us from seeing our own boundlessness. When we limit others, we limit ourselves; trapped in our own inviolable way of seeing, we miss parts of our lives. When we embrace our true essence, there is no rivalry and no divisions; we give up judgments and fears that create differences. There is no longer a need to fear discovering that we may be wrong, or seeking to protect our egos. The true self is neither wrong or right; it just is. Beyond our notions of what is right view or wrong view is our true unity, which is love.

January 28

We Always Matter

When you realize that who you are matters, you
do great things. – *Ndidi,* Tea Leaves

On the surface, when we are compassionate, it seems that we present ourselves as just, fair and loving, whether or not we really believe that we are all those things. We may want to experience love from the "other" person, so we extend our loving acts in the hope that the others will return the favor. The compassion is then a transaction of give and take, a kind of quid pro quo. In an effort to matter in some way, we rescue others from their challenges and hope to feel good about our sacrifices. The seed of compassion is love; feeling good is the result of planting a seed that heals and sustains peace in a frustrating reality. Love desires no reward.

With all that we do and say, sometimes we still question whether we matter. We know for sure that we matter when we become aware of who we are. We no longer see ourselves in comparison with others, nor do we seek happiness from what we do or have.

Often embedded in the question of whether we matter is "Am I loved?" That gnawing question causes us to question our life's purpose. No one outside of us can answer that question to our satisfaction, if we harbor doubts about the nature of our being. As Rainer Maria Rilke assures us, "The only journey is the journey within."

We are spirit, expressing as the divine love of the universe in the present moment. If we are awake to our truth, we are also aware that we cannot be anything but love. What we do today, this hour, this moment always matters, because the universe resides in us and we in it.

January 29

Pointing a Finger

Love is the way messengers from the mystery tell
us things. – *Rumi,* A Year with Rumi

When we point a finger towards something, do we focus on what we are pointing to, or do we focus on our finger alone? Throughout the ages, men, women and children have pointed to the truth of our reality and our divinity, and we have worshipped their finger. As guides, they have taught us with stories, parables, puzzles and poetry, and with their experiences of life and death. We study their words and honor their lives and legacies. Some of us derive meaning from the parables of Jesus of Nazareth to live a life of love for God and other people, or the sutras of the Buddha that lead us to the release of suffering for an eternity. The Bhagavad Gita, a 700-verse Hindu scripture encourages the experience of divinity through selfless service, and offers comfort in the midst of struggle. Zen masters such as Bodhidharma, Bankei, Dogen and Chuang Tzu have inspired us with poetry, prose and sutras, and challenged us with puzzles and koans to experience the true self. In an attempt to bring unity to Arabic tribal nations, The Prophet Muhammad revealed the divine recitation called the Quran in 114 suras. With devotion to those words as guidelines and precepts for living, we have devoted our lives to the fulfillment of their assignments. We have attempted to follow their examples, even though times have changed, and the context of their experiences is often part of the past, not the present. We have used the words of the masters and guides as weapons of division and war, and re-interpreted their intentions of love and peace. We have separated ourselves into sects and denominations, tribes and factions as we try to establish our significance. And in our departure from their original intent, we have lost their message of love and peace.

We have become enamored of them as personalities and messengers of love, and sacrificed their message. Each guide pointed to our inner divinity, our oneness with life, and the centrality of love in our life. Each gave a name to our experience of love and has given a glimpse of eternity. Jesus spoke of eternal life, Buddha led the way to enlightenment, The Gita opened up the possibility of happiness now, rather than later, and Zen masters encouraged us to find peace within, to experience enlightenment here and now in the present moment. Each shared a message with contemporaries who understood the power of their intentions, and promised to spread the word to all who could believe the truth.

None has encouraged us to divide and hate, but rather to love one another. None has taught us to choose the deathly option of separating ourselves from others, because of what we want for ourselves. None has lost their true self in the message, but has strongly identified with their source of being. None has been ashamed of who they were or made others wrong because of a need to be superior. None has denied their divinity, their oneness with the entire universe.

Each of our prophets, spiritual leaders and truth-seekers have pointed to love, peace and joy. Each has been a loving, divine spirit, who believed that what they were pointing to in their stories, parables, and poetry was enough.

January 30

Dear Crossing

Celebrate our dear crossing; the journey could not
be the same without us. – *Ndidi,* Tea Leaves

In Australia, indigenous people traditionally encouraged young males
to participate in a walkabout, now referred to as "temporal mobility," as
part of the transition from boyhood to manhood. The walkabout is a rite
of passage involving a journey into the wilderness for a long period to
make the spiritual and traditional transformation into adulthood. Rites
of passage are part of ritual practices among many people. Confirmations,
bar mitzvahs and bat mitzvahs are ritual rites of passage. Many African
people traditionally have five rites of passage - birth, adulthood, marriage,
eldership and ancestorship. Passages during our life can be marked by
acknowledgement of certain stages of development.

If we wonder about our purpose in life, we can look at the journey of our life
so far. Whether or not we are acknowledged for the stages of development
we reach along the way, our lives are treasure maps of joy. We give purpose
to our lives by virtue of how we are choosing to create our reality. We don't
create all the events in our lives, but we create a response to what we sense
and thereby weave our lives into the complex tapestry of the universe. We
have nothing to prove, nothing assigned to us to complete. The freedom
to choose how we cross this life, and which milestones we will celebrate is
up to us. The true self is with us throughout our journey, stabilizing our
existence in an uncertain world of ideas, images and experiences.

Our precious life is a gift from the universe as part of the ongoing evolution
of matter and spirit. We cross this life as interdependent collaborators with
all beings, continually creating fullness in the present moment. Without

the symphony of diversity in our world, the universe would fall apart, flung into oblivion like shrapnel from an explosive. Our crossing is dear, uniquely significant, an expression of the divine energy that drives the universe. We can be thankful that we are here for the journey.

When we realize the extraordinary opportunity to be an expression of All-That-Is, we also realize that love is who we came to this life to be. When we are aware of the magnitude of the universe, we feel simultaneously large and small. We are significant because we *are* the universe, its energy and being, regardless of our placement in time and space. Our energy, like the energy of all beings, is a continuation, not a beginning nor an end. Our journey is a cause for celebration!

January 31

Why This?

Be grateful for challenges. Without the experiences of life up to
this point, we would be someone else. – *Ndidi,* Tea Leaves

We sometimes encounter a number of unfortunate events in our life; these
events can either destroy our faith or make us stronger. We ask ourselves,
"Why is this happening?" If we replace our question, "Why this?' with
"Why not this?" we align with what is and are freed from the attachment
to knowing. Each event makes us pioneers, not victims. Each response we
choose is a possible path to personal freedom.

A major challenge in life is resisting the idea that conditions define us; we
may believe that what happens is unwarranted punishment or bad luck.
We wonder what attracted the pain and suffering, and feel guilty about
what has happened to us. It can be easy to beat ourselves up for mistakes
or behaviors, but the negativity we hurl onto ourselves simply makes us
more vulnerable to continuing stress.

When we see ourselves as mere victims of unfortunate events in our life, we
have surrendered to the falsehoods of the ego. As an overdeveloped reactor
to ancient drives for self-protection, our ego can terrorize us with fears. Our
fears are like beacons for additional pain and suffering, attracting more
of what we would like to avoid. The energy of resistance is powerful since
its intention is to avoid pain without thoughts of an alternative. When we
think about what we want more than what we don't want, our experiences
of life events change. We can train our mind to think more of what gives us
joy even in the midst of pain, and as Joseph Campbell said, "Find a place
inside where there is joy, and the joy will burn out the pain."

We are less vulnerable than our ego tells us, yet we may react not only physically but emotionally to perceived dangers. The universe is malleable and changing; a clear, consistent explanation is elusive since everything evolves. But joy can be found in every moment. When we take the time to find joy in the smallest, most nuanced aspects of our lives, the power of the joy will dissolve the pain like butter in a frying pan.

February 1

Judgments

Isn't it kind of silly to think that tearing someone else down builds you up? – *Sean Covey*, The 7 Habits of Highly Effective Teens

A hard-working man won millions of dollars in the lottery. His co-workers told him that the money would bring him bad luck because everyone else in the company was jealous of him, and that he should be less selfish and naive. They told him they had heard of other lottery winners who were foolish and lost their fortune within months of receiving the money. They suggested that he split the money with everyone on his team, so that no one would harbor resentment toward him. He assured the co-workers that he would make good use of his money and that all would be well, but they continued to criticize his selfishness. When he received the money the man was relieved; he could finally afford to pay for his niece's expensive operation.

When we are trapped in the illusion of separateness, we are free to engage in judgments of others. We may easily resort to criticisms and resentments because we are convinced that others do not share our pain or suffering. We may seek the satisfaction of our own interests, and miss the opportunity to experience the warm spirit of compassion. But if we embrace our existence as mirrors of others, we are hard-pressed to find faults in others that are not our own. We may be oblivious to the full story of another person's life, but when we engage with others, we have an opportunity to know ourselves more profoundly.

Judgments are opinions based on old hurts and fears: unfinished business. If wounds have failed to heal and old hurts remain, we may more readily detect evidence of that pain in others. The suffering person will not finish our own unfinished business, but often we make him a proxy for our pain. The proxy healing never works, but instead stirs up the sleeping hurt.

Giving up judgments is a challenge to the ego - our personal hard drive that professes to know what is real. With courage, we can place a block on that unrestrained ego. The ego does not disappear, but ceases to interfere with our relationships. When we judge others, we are trying desperately to rid ourselves of what disappoints us about ourselves. If we commit to non-judgment of the self and others, we can challenge ourselves to love who we are, and to forgive what we have done, thought or felt, that we now regret. We are not who we were; we are who we are right now. We are spiritual beings, one loving consciousness.

February 2

Is It True?

If you propose to speak, always ask yourself, is it true, is it necessary, is it kind? – The Buddha

After every political debate, fact checkers determine whether pronouncements made or statistics that the politicians used are accurate or not. The "truthiness" (a term coined by comedian Stephen Colbert) of the statements has been shown to have little impact on the choices of the voters. Often objective data are less attractive than opinions or exaggerations. No allowances are given for speaking under pressure or from a defensive posture; and intentions are ignored in favor of the impact of statements.

Understanding another person's words and feelings, particularly during stressful interactions is often difficult to master. Within the reality we have co-created, interpersonal communication can be a primary vehicle for truth. Like everything else in the universe, the reality of our world is ever-changing. As the context of our beliefs about what is true changes, our judgments change. We may debate the truth of a statement, but the truth of our being is constant, unchanging and infinite.

The truth of our being is the only constant, but when we speak, we have intentions that seem important to us in the moment. We could ask ourselves if our words could stand up to scrutiny with a wider audience. Our truth is based on our beliefs and values, and as such is dependent on how we interpret our reality. Any truth that is dependent upon some other factor is not truth at all, but are beliefs developed through repetitive thoughts, learned behaviors or lived experience. We have both an individual, constructed life experience and a collective experience as one spirit. When we begin to question our certainties and allow multiple perspectives to be our experience, we come closer to the direct experience of truth.

February 3

Opening the Heart

Have the courage to embody love.
– *Panache Desai*, Discovering Your Soul Signature

For some of us, opening to others means becoming vulnerable, exposed. But if we open our heart to another, the other person is known. We recognize ourselves in others; and realize that there is one heart beating in this universe. As written in the Upanishads, "...through spiritual wisdom, dear one, we come to know that all life is one." The intense feelings we experience when we have compassion for others is the beating of an open heart, a heart that recognizes both pain and joy in another person. None of us is immune from the pain in life, the unexpected twists and turns that sometimes rock our world. Compassionate thoughts about others acknowledge our shared humanity, while compassionate action offers the support to move through the tunnel of despair.

The arrangement of events that urge us to act with compassion seem random at times, but the universe is continuously reorganizing as we move and connect with each other. Synchrony, the simultaneous occurrence of events, is the essence of divinity. In the space of synchronicity, we experience the organic movements of One Spirit. There are no accidental meetings, nor is there a predestined plan unfolding. The universal spirit is not limited by design or plans. If we open our compassionate heart, the heart of the universe is known. This knowing is much like thinking about someone and then the phone rings; or waking up at an appointed time even when we forget to set the alarm clock. We are always tuned into the unfolding universe. With an open heart we rejoice in the awe of it.

49

February 4

Expectations

Expectations were like fine pottery. The harder you held them, the more likely they were to crack. – *Brandon Sanderson*, The Way of Kings

Relationships are almost always heavily-laden with expectations, because we so often relate to people when we want something from them. We have expectations that somehow we will know happiness if we have a "successful" relationship, but there's no way that seeing people as separate from us can result in a satisfying relationship. We can ask ourselves what we want from ourselves and discover that expectations get in the way of freedom. Relationships become negotiated partnerships for *something,* when they are based on expectations. Negotiations are the reasons that some people think relationships require work to be happy and loved, but there is *no work* to do.

Being in a relationship requires recognizing our face in the face of another, just as our image is the face of divinity. If we are kind in our relationship with ourselves, our kindness in the world is given freely without expectation of reciprocation. Our sense of emptiness creates a craving to be filled. But if we are kind to ourselves we are already filled, so the kindness we share is the divine overflow. If we love with no hidden expectation, there are no expectations of a reward or a fulfillment of a need; we simply love because that is who we are. Divine spirit is alive in all of us; it is asking for nothing except an opportunity to be expressed in the flow of life. Our love is open, expects nothing, loses nothing, and responds with vibrations of joy and peace.

February 5

Go in Peace

Peace is not the absence of struggle; it is the
presence of love. – *Ndidi,* Tea Leaves

Imagine a world where everyone intended to do no harm to self or others, and where the aura of peace surrounds us in all aspects of our lives. When we "go in peace," we experience the deep resonance of the present moment; we can have deep faith in the truth of our relationship with All-That-Is. The expression, "go in peace" is more than a pleasant wish for someone's well-being; it is a summation of their eternal being-ness. In the present moment, we are in peace – immersed in it, breathing it in and out, remembering it as our true state of being.

The daily struggles we experience are like fear-drenched baggage that weigh us down and disturb our sense of peace. The weight of the moments in our lives sometimes makes it difficult in our overworked minds to discern the joy that is always present. When we stop for a moment, look around, and notice what we can appreciate, peace rises. When we "go" into the moment, peace is our pathway to conscious awareness. Peace is inexplicable and timeless beauty; it sloughs off the blankets of fear, shame, frustration, anger, hatred and resentment, and clears the way to contentment. Peace is full awareness of who we are; an identity that is ever-present whether or not we recognize it. As an omnipresent spirit, peace is the ultimate reality of our life, not the frightful appearances of reality we encounter daily. When we "go in peace," we go within to embrace the essence of our true self.

Assurance

At the core of all well–founded belief lies belief that is
unfounded. – *Ludwig Wittgenstein*, On Certainty

A woman arrived at her office on a Monday morning and noticed that her favorite plant was no longer sitting in the corner. When she saw the vacant corner she assumed that she would be relieved of her position by the end of the day. After all, some people had been replaced when new management arrived. She waited for the call for several hours and then decided to inquire about her status. She was pleased to hear from her manager that the artificial plant had simply been removed for cleaning.

Human beings crave certainty and are almost always disappointed by the seemingly random nature of life. Daily activities are taken for granted; often they become routine. We may enjoy the predictability of routine, and become disturbed by any departure from familiar activities, but surprise is the joy of being alive. When activities seem predictable we may begin to believe that we can control them, and may soon become disillusioned when our predictability is challenged by more unexpected events.

Unfamiliar beliefs or people who have different perspectives may also cause a disturbance in our craving for sameness and security. Any departure from our preferred way of thinking, behaving or loving can disturb the sense of order. We continually seek assurances, but our ego warns us to be wary.

With no assurance of control during our life, we may become resigned to the notion that our life choices will control our experience *after* life. We may decide that when we adhere to prescribed rules and behaviors *during* our lives, our eternal reward will be assured. The assurance of joy requires a journey inward; with awareness of the true self, we can experience the peace and joy of *being* now, not in a future state of transcendence.

Peace and love can transform us now, if we let go of the illusion of separation. As individuals, we may follow different paths based on the simple lottery of our birth; but our origins are the same even though our life experiences are different. We have not forgotten the rules or disqualified ourselves with mistakes; we have forgotten who we are. When we feel the quiet presence of love, we can feel the blessed assurance and go home.

February 7

Formless

And don't look for me in human form. I am inside your looking.
No room for form with love this strong. – *Rumi,* A Year of Rumi

A young child enjoys blowing bubbles, but becomes frustrated when he tries to catch the elusive balls of air. He grows older and spends time chasing his dreams, never reaching that time in the future when he thinks all is well. What we see are often false images of the mind.

Try to capture our mind itself and soon we will discover that it is a futile exercise. We want to find the ego and reprimand it for all the times it embarrassed us, but we soon become frustrated with that search as well. Go on a major search to find the inner self and once again we are thwarted. Our sensory abilities – seeing, hearing, touch, taste and smell – are insufficient if we try to locate the origin of our thoughts. The *effects* of these non-locatable ideas are all we have as evidence of their influence. We know that we have a mind; we often equate it with the brain or consciousness, and we know that our mind "contains" thoughts. We know what the mind does and we believe that it exists, but we are perplexed when we try to locate it.

The mind produces thoughts that we often cannot control, while our egos show up either like a burly bull without self-awareness, or like a sneaky impersonator when we are trying to impress someone. The ego promises to protect us, but instead it gets us into trouble; sometimes we are the last to realize that it has reared its ugly side. Like a bodyguard for the mind, the ego protects us from perceived injury, but sometimes goes a bit overboard. The result is suffering because the frightened ego has convinced us to be afraid. As Gandhi said, "We would have nothing to fear, if we refused to be afraid." The formless ego turns simple caution into terror, and encourages us to grasp and cling to ideas of the mind that are as wispy as light clouds floating across the sky. The ego is an idea in the mind whose power keeps us trapped in temporary events that were only intended to arise and pass away.

Does our failure to clutch these ideas of the mind - the mind itself and the ego - mean that they do not exist? If we rely only on the sensory world for truth, we will not be able to locate either of these ideas. Our perception of physical reality is simply one perspective. We think we are looking outward toward the physical world, but the universe is consciousness that looks within us. Senses are accomplices of the mind creating a human experience for us, but they attempt to place limits on a limitless universe. Our sensory creations are like paintings of a reality, and therefore not the truth of our life.

We are formless within, yet we are filled with boundless spiritual energy. In the stillness of the present moment, we are freed from the boundaries of the senses and the mind; we can then know our boundless, formless energy within. In that formless reality, we become aware of the eternal nature of our essential being; formlessness is necessary for an infinite, ultimate reality. We are no longer influenced by the ego or our external reality; instead we have an overwhelming experience of love. With no boundary to possibilities and no end to love, we know that anything is possible.

February 8

Non-duality

He who experiences the unity of life sees his own self in
all beings, and all beings in his own self, and looks on
everything with an impartial eye – *The Buddha*

Wars have been fought over the right to believe in the supremacy of a
monarch or divine being. In most cases, the supreme figure has been set
apart from all other sentient beings, or deemed more worthy of praise than
others. The right to dominate or control has been ascribed to supreme
rulers of spirit, people and land, because of special powers they had to
protect, heal or harm. The arrangement has been a conscious perspective
among many believers or subjects, so the belief that there are those who
control and those who are controlled has informed a constant narrative
throughout the ages.

The idea of separation among leaders and followers rather than union is
not the only conscious belief system. Another concept is that all life is
one, and that nothing in the universe is separate: one, not two or more.
Non-duality is the belief that there is only one Life, and it contains all that
exists, but further that everything in the universe exists in everything else.
In a holographic universe, the relationship is so close that nothing exists
in isolation. As a result of this lack of separation, there is no possibility
of anyone or anything existing outside of our self. Some may say that
the hologram destroys the concept of God or a supreme being, but the
omnipresent, omniscient, omnipotent power of One offers the concept that
God is everywhere and in all things, human and not human.

But even the "God in everything" explanation is incomplete, unless we
acknowledge that everything is in God. As Rumi says, "You are not a drop

in the ocean. You are the entire ocean in a drop." The "You" in Rumi's quote is everything in the universe. The true self is not a separate self; it is all there is, one spirit, one essence, one being. Buddha shared the impact of a non-dual perspective: "one looks on everything with an impartial eye." When we look at others as ourselves, we love others as ourselves. When we have compassion for others, we have compassion for ourselves. When we are being the love we are, we have no need to seek it. When we let go of our view of the world in dualistic terms, we experience peace.

February 9

Illusions

It is the mark of an educated mind to be able to entertain a
thought without accepting it. – *Aristotle*, Metaphysics

Thoughts come and go rapidly, often responsive to our created reality,
but often seemingly arise "out of nowhere." Thoughts branch off to new
thoughts as they stimulate our mind, and continue the barrage of ideas.
Occasionally, we find a thought that is interesting or attractive and decide
to cling to it. Convinced that the thought is not only attractive but certainly
valid, we begin to reject opposing thoughts. Then we repeat a thought over
and over again to ourselves and others, and begin to believe it exclusively.
We frame stories around our thoughts in order to make sure the thoughts
are reasonable to us. If necessary, we will find data and information to
support our stories. The more dramatic the stories, the more we convince
ourselves that our thoughts are true.

Attachments to thoughts we have apprehended can thwart the possibility
of finding what we are seeking: peace of mind. When we are being who
we really are, we do not construct a life around thoughts, but we are simply
entertained by them. If we attach ourselves to persistent thoughts, we will
live in an unreal world of drama. We may consider a thought to be useful,
and become warmed by the sense of comfort that follows, but the more we
cling to the thought, the less peaceful we become. We then begin to defend
our thoughts to establish them as the right view for others, and actively
recruit others to agree with us. Our lives become a creation of the mind.

The uninterrupted flow of thoughts allows for peace. If we want to stay in
control of the power of our thoughts, we must let go of them.

February 10

Sacred Space

Your sacred space is where you can find yourself again
and again. – *Joseph Campbell*, The Power of Myth

Some people are able to see the auras that surround everyone. Those
who see auras are aware of a particular feeling they have in someone's
presence. The auras they see have specific information about the person.
For example, colors of the auras are said to indicate the energetic state of
the human being. An aura is also a special feeling or quality that seems to
exude from a person, or it may be a distinctive aroma. Sometimes described
as a circle of light, a nimbus of well-being, auras are light meters for the
vibrancy of our true self.

When we know who we are, light is our expression in this time and
space; we are a reflection of the space within us. When we are careful to
create a space to live and work that supports our spirit, the space becomes
saturated with our energy. We may establish a special place in our home
or garden where we experience peace; or erect altars or quiet spaces to read
holy writings and engage in prayer. There may be a special path in the
woods where serenity comes to us. We may think our spaces are external
to ourselves, but the space around us is the same as the space within us.
We are not only living, working, praying and meditating in our spaces; the
spaces live and breathe in us. When we immerse ourselves into our sacred
space, we not only find ourselves, we find peace.

February 11

The Middle Way

Our hands are most useful when they are able
to open and close. – *Ndidi,* Tea Leaves

When we are faced with a dilemma, choosing a side can be disastrous. Conflicts often arise from unresolved dilemmas. Managing dilemmas is sometimes the chosen route to peace; we often call it diplomacy. A diplomat may still offer a point of view, much like the egoist mind, but the view is often partial to unchallenged stories or beliefs. The trained mind transcends the battle between "this and that." Peace sees all points of view and chooses none.

Floating on the waters of love, the transcendent mind knows only compassion and peace. Just as moving a canoe requires the steady alternating rhythm of the oars, if we only paddle on one side, the boat will not be balanced in the water. Taking a seated position in the center helps us to maintain balance. In the middle, we can take in a panoramic view of the water: we see both sides. If we want to train the mind, we can do so from the center. The middle way allows us to detach from the tyranny of opinions and positions that leave us stuck within our embedded beliefs. In the balanced, middle way, we can see beyond divisions and opposing perspectives. We are positioned to transcend pettiness and imagined slights, natural polarities and prejudicial views.

The universe sees no divisions and embraces no dug in beliefs. The middle way is the pathway to being the peace we seek. When we realize that our thoughts have led us to a particular view, we can listen with compassion to the embedded thoughts of others, and rise above divisions. As we come together in love, the language of the universe, we also give up the grasping and hatred that can arise on the horns of a dilemma. We understand that we must lose in order to gain; and we can be grateful to others who have different thoughts. When we acknowledge our interdependence, we desire expansion of our views, rather than clinging to our own embedded beliefs. From the middle way, we can change the direction of the canoe, while we invite others to join us. With an opened hand, and an offering of Love, we find peace.

February 12

Imprints

A tree does not know that it is called deciduous, but it freely
allows its leaves to fall just the same. – *Ndidi,* Tea Leaves

Our lives are imprinted with experiences we regard as true. The imprints
become themes for how we live and establish relationships with self, others
and our inherent divinity. Throughout our lives, the impressions ascribed
to us can guide our concept of self, and define us in terms that limit
who we are. Bombarded by societal expectations, political realities and
economic conditions, we try to find our place in the world. Original
imprints of our worth linger despite changes in expectations or conditions;
and then they rob us of joy.

Sometimes the imprint is "good person" or "sinner," labels ascribed to us
often based on projections. An event in our lives can leave an indelible
imprint that influences how we see ourselves and others; our self-
assessments, bolstered by shame or vulnerability, promote a false sense
of self. Some imprints are limiting; they can confine us to labels and
conditions that are supported in our mind and in the minds of others.
Destructive imprints divide people into groups that are either deserving
of love and approval, or not. Societal imprints may define us according to
standards set by those who have either assumed power or seek it.

An imprint is a mark that cannot define an indefinable spirit except in the
mind. We are not the imprints placed on us by others; our true self cannot
be limited by labels or definitions. Our essence is unlimited expressions of
Love without labels or boundaries.

February 13

Stardust

The cosmos is also within us. We're made of star stuff. We
are a way for the cosmos to know itself. – *Neil de Grasse
Tyson,* 'Cosmos: A Spacetime Odyssey' documentary

About 99% of the human body is composed of six elements: carbon,
hydrogen, oxygen, nitrogen, phosphorus and calcium. These elements
are essential in living organisms. Contrast this information with the
composition of the sun, our important star, the center of our world. The
sun is 90% hydrogen and 10% a mixture of other gases. Our galaxy is
composed of other stars, planets, clouds of gas and dust. Every atom in our
body is billions of years old, and those atoms are mostly empty space. The
miracle of the body is that we share the major element hydrogen with the
stars. We are star dust. The universe exists in us just as we exist in it. Our
presence is not accidental or coincidental but essential; we are the dust of
the universe expressing in this space and time.

The interdependence of everything in the universe is poignantly explained
through the pollination of bees. Plants depend on bees to pollinate one-
sixth of the plant population worldwide. They help to sustain the planet's
ecosystems, so without bees, we would not have sufficient quantities of
food to eat. Bees matter. Our reliance on bees and other beings is a
demonstration of the complex nature of the relationships among all beings
in the universe. Our stardust origins are not coincidental. Just as the
universe exists in us, so do we exist in it as interrelated players in life. We
are here to play the infinite game of life, being love in all we do so that
life can continue.

February 14

Forgiveness

I wondered if that was how forgiveness budded; not with
the fanfare of epiphany, but with pain gathering its things,
packing up, and slipping away unannounced in the middle
of the night. – *Khaled Hosseini*, The Kite Runner

If we ask ourselves, "Is there anyone I need to forgive?" after some reflection
we may develop a long list. In spite of the length of the list, we know that
there is only one person to forgive: our self. But, continuing to blame others
for the story we are living can be enticing. Assigning blame gives us time
to deny our role in past events, or gives us a reason to cling to hurt. The
painful or regrettable relics of the past are events we may replay and regret
with no resolution.

Our healing is a combination of forgiving self and releasing blame. When
we face our suffering, we become aware of how strongly we identify with
the pain, and how the initial pain has been extended into suffering through
repetitive thoughts about the events. We repeat the thoughts over the
long term to feed the fear of a reoccurrence, but the nagging thoughts are
attractors of similar events. We unwittingly invite more of what we are
holding in fear.

Forgiving others may be difficult for us, but forgiving ourselves can be just as
hard. Can we be OK with the gullible, desperate and irresponsible moments
in our past, when we searched for love, approval and recognition? The
feeling of being "right" at the time outweighed the dangers of vulnerability,
insecurity and depression. Perhaps we used unsound principles to guide
decisions, and regret the outcomes. When we honestly claim responsibility
for our behaviors, we free ourselves from shame or self-blame. We realize

that each decision crafted our reality as we live it now, and if we want to have a different story of our life, we can create that as well.

Our participation in the creation of the past can be painful to face but freeing when we do. Sometimes we focus on the behaviors that affected our sense of well-being and peace of mind, but we are mainly responsible for clinging to false ideas. The self-recriminations we invest in diminish us and boost the persona of the false self. Until we notice that our responses to events are sometimes more self-damaging than the events themselves, we may continue to believe stories of our lives that do not serve us.

We are perfect spirits engaging in imperfect behaviors that create life stories. When we forgive ourselves and others, we release the fragrance of peace.

February 15

Subtle Discontent

Love is the magician, the enchanter, that changes worthless
things to joy, and makes royal kings and queens of
common clay. – *Robert Ingersoll*, Orthodoxy (1884)

The face we show to the world belies a subtle discontent that lingers in our mind and heart. Attachments to things we don't have – relationships, wealth, success – can cause us to suffer. The pain of not having these things is not always apparent in how we present ourselves to others; it is subtle but persistent. Our pain is expressed in obsessions with meeting the perfect person or keeping a person we have. Pain may show up in our preoccupations with appearances of wealth, or the markers of success - title, connections, and expertise – that we hope will lead to adoration from others. Self-blame, self-doubt and discomfort may fester within our mind in the form of resentment and disappointment.

Subtle discontent is a response to *feelings* of not being loved. We attach ourselves to things because we think we will feel loved and valued. Releasing attachments is possible only when we realize that love is who we are. Love is All-That-Is in the universe and we are that. When the floodgates of love are open within our essence, we feel the flow and know that love is abundantly present. Love is not something we must acquire; it is our essential being. If we express love in all that we do, say and think, the love will flow as who we are. When we taste the sweetness of eternal love, we have nothing to seek and nothing to have.

February 16

Clarity

…when we think we have things already figured out, we're not teachable. Genuine insight can't dawn on a mind that's not open to receive it. – *Marianne Williamson*, A Return to Love

Zen teaching in monasteries often includes a special relationship with a teacher. The teacher gives the student a koan, a paradox to concentrate upon, in order to provide a focus for a one-pointed mind, freed from dependence on reason. The koan is ultimately unanswerable, although the student struggles to make meaning out of it. A famous koan is "What is the sound of one hand clapping?" The questions are a way to empty the mind of the clutter of knowing, the preoccupation with the relentless stream of information that flows through the mind. Students often reflect on "Mu," meaning emptiness, where answers are irrelevant. Our true self is unfettered by complexity; its simplicity is our real identity.

At the core of our evolving world is an incomprehensible presence that is unchanging. We wonder what it all means to us. When we have a strong sense of who we are, we remember the depth of our wisdom, without getting distracted by "facts" that change daily. But if we're struggling to know, our mind lacks the capacity to answer our questions. Unless we can journey deep within to the void that is unchanging, we will continue to have an unsettled feeling about what is unknown in our world. Apparently, changes have occurred constantly leading to advances in understanding the evolution of the universe, yet most scientists admit that there is more to know. Knowing everything would not produce an ounce of joy; the experience of joy is beyond knowing, even beyond the senses.

Clarity is the vehicle of intuition, insight and discernment that makes change possible, yet by its very nature clarity does not accept everything as absolute or forever true. Attending to our clear views creates joyful journeys, when we leave ourselves open for multiple perspectives, uncertainties and simplicities.

If we detach ourselves from outcomes, we give clarity a chance to happen; we express satisfaction with the way things are rather than how we want them to appear. The satisfaction is not resigning ourselves to what is, but looking deeply at what is, without prejudgment.

It seems contradictory, but detachment is the ultimate state of clarity. With a tamed mind, ideas come and go without interference from us; and we allow greater awareness of the energy of the universe. We can be confident that the "answers" are only temporary peeks into a larger reality; but the feeling of clarity is accompanied by unfettered peace and joy.

February 17

Slowness

The butterfly counts not months but moments, and has time enough.
– Rabindranath Tagore, from poem, "I touch God in my song"

A restaurant in a rural part of Swaziland, a landlocked country in southern Africa, boasts a particular aspect of its cuisine: "slow food." The cooks promise that their delicious foods will take time to prepare, but will be worth the wait. While people wait for their food, they laugh and visit with each other. The food is a reason to come together; time is a "friend" that affords an occasion for community gatherings.

The fast-paced society we live in has little use for slowness. We are constantly urged to do more and have more as quickly as possible. In the scurry to complete more and have more, we lose the pleasure of savoring the moment. The lifetime that we live is less about what we accomplish and more about who we are being as we live our lives. In our drive to be significant in our world, or to show that we matter, we say we don't have enough time to do what we must do, or that slowing down to "smell the roses" wastes time. We may speed through life, piling in more and more activities, as if more were inherently better. We may try to make up for "lost" time with overwork or greater speeds. Our relationships suffer since we sometimes regard visiting with others as a "time waster" particularly if we prefer to do something else. We sometimes believe that in order to accomplish something, we have to "fill" our time with hard work and struggle.

Time loses its prominence in our consciousness if we become still. We think we don't have time but time is not a thing; it is just an idea, constructed in our minds to attempt to control our reality. Our dependency on time promotes the concepts of limits, lack and frustration; unless we savor the precious peace of the timeless, boundless, present moment.

The only "time" is now. When we slow down to enjoy our life in all its textures, beauty and relationships, we experience the joy of being. A proverb from the Mandingo people of West Africa is a prescription for living in joy: "Do a thing in its time and peace follows it."

February 18

The Way

The Tao that can be told is not the eternal Tao. The name that can be named is not the eternal name. – *Lao Tzu,* Tao Te Ching

If we establish a destination, many roads will get us there, but if our journey takes us within, there is no path. There is only here, now, not some distant place that is unattainable and mysterious. We are continually in the present, the location of the way (Tao). The expression "the way" may be confusing because it implies a journey from point A to point B. There is no beginning point; the path is an illusion, a veil that clouds the reality of our true self. We imagine that the "I," the personal identity ascribed to us, is traveling from one place to another, but that too is an illusion.

We are tempted to see our life as a struggle to finally get to a place of peace. We are accustomed to having maps to show us the way, so people will provide maps of the route to the way called beliefs; but those maps are their story, their attempt to explain.

Even though we may say we know the way, we cannot know, because the way is not a thing we can conceptualize. When we say we will find the way, we will search with no success, because we will look outside of ourselves for it. The way does not change; it is our constant Self. The way is here, now. Be the way to love, peace and joy - now.

February 19

The Calling

The wave rushes to the call of the shore, and the morning bird answers love calls. Each responds to its true nature. – *Ndidi,* Tea Leaves

A newly retired man sat in his easy chair, dreading the next few years with nowhere to go and no one to see. He had devoted most of his life to work but it was time to leave, so he handed in his notice three weeks before his scheduled departure. Now, the real work began: finding out who he really wanted to be.

We have always known deep within who we were meant to be. From the circumstances of our entry into this world, we find ourselves doing and believing what our social, religious, political and economic conditions and context prescribe for us. In the cloud of confusion and projections, we are told what we are worth and what is best for us, but we can feel the urge to be who we are. The counsel we receive can be well-meaning, but the voice within is a constant reminder of what our life really is.

We make decisions that contrast with who we really are, and our hearts cry out in pain; the ego's fears lay heavily on our spirit as we go through the motions of commitment to someone else's dreams. But within our awareness, lies an invitation to just be, to allow the still, small voice to be heard. The pull is intense, but we hesitate and wonder what others will think of us if we respond to our true self. We may reject ourselves because we think the risk of rejection from others is too great, then we settle for believing in what we are not.

In spite of denying our truth, we continue to trudge along a narrowing tunnel, hoping that the light at the end is real; and that we will escape the terror of not being all that we know we were meant to be. The tunnel is a delusion; the loving voice within is reality.

The voice will not be silenced, even though we sometimes stop listening to it because we fear that we will fail. We look for ways to express who we are, and the mind cautions us to be practical and reasonable, so we postpone the strong pull of who we are in favor of satisfying others.

The universe is here for us and as us, whispering silently into our ears that we matter to the world. We must listen to the call of the universe; it is our voice, our spirit, our one loving response as Ultimate Reality.

February 20

Knowledge

The only true wisdom is in knowing you know
nothing. – *Socrates,* In Plato's Apology

Our discoveries are fascinating, even illuminating, but they are incomplete
views based on our myopic view of reality. Yet, we hold onto the opinions
and inferences we call facts and data, and hoist our new knowledge onto
the world as truth.

We are still on the road to eternity; our destination is infinity. Knowledge
can delude us into thinking that we have arrived. We can insist on our
facts as truth, but their existence is both entertaining and incomplete.
Facts are entertaining because they stir us to create new views of reality,
and incomplete because we get stuck in their allure and believe that they
are final. Everything is in flux in the universe. Knowledge can be a stop
along the way to truth, but if we rest too long at the stop, the car may
continue without us, and drive on to new vistas. Rest in knowing that we
do not know.

February 21

Wisdom

I am convinced that the act of thinking logically cannot possibly be natural to the human mind. If it were, then mathematics would be everybody's easiest course at school and our species would not have taken several millennia to figure out the scientific method.
– *Neil deGrasse Tyson*, The Sky is Not the Limit: Adventures of an Urban Astrophysicist

It is easy to believe that using logic can ensure that we know what is true. We may even complain that many people do not think critically, a code for using illogical reasoning. But if reason deserves respect, how do we explain the human tendency for bigotry or prejudice? Why do we attempt to justify aggression or our judgments? Is there a lack of logic or heart?

We may say factual premises are important in order to reach a logical conclusion, but there are always influences on those premises, handles on the blades that seem to prevent the bleeding. But the blade still cuts; the raw, impersonal conclusions that ignore our humanness and lack compassion can mislead us. When we understand that reason depends only on what is externally sensed or known, we discover that our internal wisdom tells us more.

Unlike reason, wisdom is humble. The humility is not a pretense, but a necessity. Wisdom is listening deeply for the essence of what is true, and then questioning whether what has been heard is complete; it is a continual voyage of discovery. Wisdom requires continual reflection, pointing to what we have seen or felt in the heart; it is a salve we use to soothe our wounds, when our life story becomes tragic. Wisdom is our gift to one another; it has power when we receive it or give it away.

In the present moment we are wise beyond imagination; we are connected to all that is true, and if we know who we are, what we express will be based in a deep awareness of our being. We may give credit to our experience when we express our wisdom, but experience is based in an external reality. Wisdom comes from our journey to awareness within. Arising in the present moment, with an uncertain source, wisdom is alive in truth, and that truth is alive in us.

February 22

Beliefs

Bigotry tries to keep truth safe in its hand with a grip
that kills it. – *Rabindranath Tagore,* Fireflies (1928)

A belief is a fence. Those within the fence think they are protected by their righteousness. They imagine that people who exist outside the fence are in danger, and those within the fence will have protection from the unpredictable and erratic nature of life. In order to enter the protected grounds within the fence, outsiders must know the password, and obey the rules within the fence.

There are many fences. We can easily believe that being inside a fence keeps us from passing through "death's door." The fear of death encourages us to cling to our beliefs, to believe in the illusion that we are separate from one another, and to kill, maim and defame in the name of those beliefs. The beliefs are often in direct conflict with the actions perpetrated to protect the beliefs. And people within the fences soon voice their disagreements in an effort to make their version of the truth the standard belief.

Kindness and compassion are sometimes sacrificed on the altars of perfect rules and unquestioned wisdom. The messages are retold and embellished to fit the times, and used to fortify the fences. Despite changes over time, the fence remains as a barrier to any other truth.

The ego may demand the restrictions to conserve its fears of a precarious life, but the loving heart knows no boundaries, no strangers nor infidels. The heart cannot be contained in a fence, because the loving heart is too big to love selectively or to live life from a place of judgment.

When we open our hearts, we unfasten the gates that make us place conditions on lovingkindness. We listen and open our hearts to the joy in communion with others; our new awareness is that the fence is an illusion and real freedom is breathing freely without boundaries in the relaxed presence of All-That-Is.

February 23

Meaning

Life is like arriving late for a movie, having to figure out what was going on without bothering everybody with a lot of questions, and then being unexpectedly called away before you find out how it ends.
– *Joseph Campbell*, Creative Mythology

Viktor Frankl's *Man's Search for Meaning* is a classic book because of its insight into the context of his writing: the systematic destruction of human beings during the Holocaust. We are observers and co-creators of context; nothing has meaning unless we ascribe meaning to it. We could simply call off the search for the meaning of life and settle into the present moment with humility and peace. Our curiosity and the small inner voice that wonders about what we must accomplish while we live, gnaws at us in a persistent way, and encourages us to search for an answer. We try to make sense out of the world – the tragedy, sudden disasters and deaths, the illness, greed and violence. We wonder what it all means. If we could know the meaning of life, would we be satisfied to live out our designated purpose, or would we doubt the meaning and keep searching? If we believe that it has no meaning, what gives us strength to go on? Because we exist and create a story, life has meaning. We are the latest expression of life in the infinite evolution and history of the multiverse. Our ancestors, human, plant and animal created a reason for us to exist. We are being that purpose in preparation for the next generation. As we play out the meaning we choose, the universe embraces our presence as its continuation.

February 24

Grace

For me every hour is grace. – *Elie Wiesel,* author of Night

The original Greek meaning of the word "grace" was to rejoice. When we give full appreciation to the amazing life that we live in each moment, there is cause for rejoicing. When we are aware of our inner divinity, the kingdom within us, the reality of our being, we can see grace as the essence of love. Within the essence of our being is the grace of gratitude, forgiveness, and peace. The grace of gratitude expresses our recognition of the magnificent universe. We can be grateful for everything that we experience, observe and feel.

The grace of forgiveness opens our hearts to the vulnerability we can all feel. When we forgive, we let go of the tired resentments that continually weigh us down and close our hearts. Without the burden of resentments, we become aware of joy and acknowledge it as our natural way of being. Grace fills us dramatically in each moment that we live and breathe, so we can rejoice in our divinity for an eternity. We are the universal opportunity to be grateful, loving and peaceful. No one is exempt from it unless we intentionally see only the suffering of distress. We can rejoice in our awareness of our ultimate reality as one spirit, rejoicing in grace together in every moment.

February 25

Emotions

When the lips are silent, the heart has a thousand tongues.
– *Rumi,* A Year of Rumi

Our silence is an opening, a clearing that makes space for an opened heart. We not only listen but also see the other as ourselves, feel what others feel as our own longing to be recognized, and reach out to others as we fall inward toward ourselves.

It is easy to regard emotions as the antithesis to logic, just as spirituality and science may do battle in our minds. The sharp edge of logic devoid of emotions sacrifices our opportunity to be fully aware of who we are. It is all too easy to become objective in our view of whatever we observe, and ignore what we regard as suspect. Often we have learned early in our life to set aside emotions as untrustworthy and unpredictable.

If we swing the pendulum of experience in the direction of emotions exclusively, we will once again sacrifice the clear view of our life conditions, and run the risk of feeling uncertain and confused. We function best when we do not lean in either direction exclusively. The knife of discernment is only usable with both the blade and the handle. Both clear the way to peace and clarity. There is room in our perceptions for the blade of logic and the guiding handle of emotions-- science and spirituality. Just as logical conclusions become incomplete when new information is presented, emotions come and go. In the present moment, we experience our logic as ideas in the mind, and emotions as the vulnerability of an opened heart. Peace is a balance of both logic and emotions; it is a silent endorsement of a dynamic universe.

February 26

Rest

Be still. Remember your deep longing for peace.
– *Ndidi,* Tea Leaves

A young child may resist going to bed for the night, since she has become afraid of the darkness of sleep. Although just a few years before, she existed comfortably in the darkness of the womb, she has learned to fear the surrender to sleep. When we become older, we understand intellectually that sleep is essential to our well-being, and often look forward to sleep and rest. During periods of sleep, our minds continue to function but at a level of consciousness that has been studied for years by neuroscientists and others. Through numerous sleep cycles called non-rapid eye movement (NREM) cycles we have brain activity as well as changes in our physiological systems. Only a small portion of a night's sleep is at a level of deep rest. The brain "cleans house" filtering out details and information it won't need, and cements memories for access in the future. Even with closed eyes and in a relaxed state of being, we continue to live and breathe – and remember.

During meditation and prayer, the mind also rests but with a level of awareness that can be heightened with practice. The deep relaxation of prayer and meditation, with the falling away of the daily activities and perceived reality, allows us space to just be, the ultimate rest. The rest in being illuminates our spirit, thrusting a spotlight on the hidden corners of awareness that we have stowed away in inattention. Rest allows us to remember what we have always known – that we are magnificent beings, basking in love and abundance.

February 27

Breathless Beauty

A vibrant rose is appealing to the eyes, but its essential
nature creates its beauty. – *Ndidi,* Tea Leaves

John Keats, the Romantic poet wrote, "Beauty is truth; truth beauty - that
is all ye know on earth and all ye need to know." Keats' *Ode on a Grecian
Urn* is a remarkable, romantic description of the beauty in our lives.
Using the urn as an object for the description, Keats has an appreciation
for silence, the story that beauty offers to us, and the limits of objective
experience. We are introduced in his poem to the eternal nature of beauty
even in what seems like lifelessness. He sees the forever aliveness of truth
that although we will leave our bodies at some point, truth lives on forever.
Keats leaves us with the reminder that we are both an audience to the
beauty of life and that beauty is life itself.

Keats offers an explanation of beauty in life that is a sharp departure
from contemporary notions of beauty. Everyone is inherently beautiful,
but our superficial and changeable appearances are often evaluated and
compared to determine who is the most beautiful. The real beauty in us
is our essential true self; it is unchanging and incomparable. Beauty is
All-That-Is in the universe – it is powerful, wise and everywhere present.

February 28

Singing Joyfully

Joy is the holy fire that keeps our purpose warm and our intelligence aglow. – *Helen Keller,* The Story of My Life

Without thoughts or interpretation, judgments, comparisons and repetitive, unsettling memories, we are free to uncover our core self, the oneness of the universe. The mind will try to convince us that there is no universal music playing and that all is lost, but that is a misguided thought. As long as we breathe there is a reason to sing loudly and dance beautifully to the music. Life conditions can shake our faith and flood our thoughts with doubts. The conditions may be temporary, but the emotions stirred by the conditions linger. Sometimes we keep hoping that we'll find some reason to dance, but our search is for something outside ourselves. We look to others to change the conditions to make them more conducive to the dance we are accustomed to. We remember how we enjoyed our dance years ago, and long for the company of all the people who danced with us. We cling to the memories and suffer regrets. When we journey inward, we remember that we are love and joy, and that the song is abiding peace. Right now, the dance of life continues and the song we sing gives it rhythm. We will never dance alone, because the universe is alive with joy.

February 29

Essence of the Divine

There is very great virtue in the cultivation of silence, and
strength to be found in using it as a door to God. Such a door
opens within. – *Howard Thurman*, Meditations of the Heart

There are thousands of words for the Divine if we examine religions around
the world. Some of the names are considered so sacred that they cannot
be spoken. In some cases, the different experiences of the Divine make it
necessary to assign different names to different aspects, creating a pantheon
of beings. Some spiritual leaders and their scriptures or texts believe in one
incarnate, all powerful Spirit. Others see the Divine in everything, diffuse
and interdependent. In many cases, a hierarchy of divinity maintains the
separation of the Divine from all other manifestations in the universe. In
some belief systems the beasts, plants and rivers are regarded as background
materials with no spiritual essence, while in others, animals are sentient
beings.

The essential nature of being is hidden or inconceivable for human beings;
we humans are left to devise our own ideas about what is true about
our lives and purpose on this earth. We may struggle for years trying to
discover our purpose or potential and often remain largely unaware of the
power of our existence. Each of us must find our own way to truth, some
of us in community with others and sometimes in the sheltered space of
solitude. Through many paths, the door to our essence is flung open.

March 1

Loving Reflection

Let us always meet each other with a smile, for the smile is the beginning of love. – *Mother Teresa,* No Greater Love

A woman woke up one morning with a smile frozen on her face. She tried to remove it by thinking horrific thoughts but her face refused to budge; the smile was immovable. She tried to remember her pain but the smile made her feel foolish. She needed to leave the house to attend a meeting, but she was afraid people would think she was insane with such a broad, fixed smile. She was surprised when people she passed on the street or in the office building smiled back at her but she could not stop to explain her predicament. Over time, she noticed that people smiled every time she approached them.

From a position of relaxed calm, a person can smile and experience happiness. The simple act of smiling releases endorphins that produce a pleasant feeling; and then joy rises from underneath the frustration, anger and sorrow. Even though we are hard-wired to either fight or flee if we sense that personal injury or harm is imminent, we can also choose to smile or frown when we want to respond to life conditions. For some time, many have believed that it takes more muscles in the face to frown than to smile. Recent research attempts to confirm that smiles generate a happy experience physiologically, but frowns lead to negative feelings. As interconnected spiritual beings, our smiles influence others. Whether or not the scientific evidence is compelling, the truth of our lives is that we create our reality, influence the life experience of others and offer a glimpse of peace.

March 2

Noticing

I am out with lanterns looking for myself.
– *Emily Dickinson,* The Complete Poems (1955)

We are all responsible, i.e., response-able, but so often that response is in hindsight. Our creative minds catalogue small things and file them under "not important" or "I've seen this before" or "it will have no effect on my life right now." In hindsight, the unimportant, predictably repetitive, and nuanced events take on a haunting significance. In times of loss – death of a loved one, destruction of property, poor health, or emotional distress, our memory files open to remind us of those aspects of our lives we did not notice. We notice in hindsight the smiles, the humor, the tilt of a person's head; we hear the questions of a child or the way a loved one expressed emotions with her eyes.

We may call it memories, but we are just noticing our responses for the second time. We are able to respond now, to listen now, and to love now. When we remember, we often see our situations in a new way. So it is when we remember who we are, and realize how liberating it is to be spiritual beings. Knowing who we are brings us into direct awareness of our ultimate reality. We don't just find a mental image of self, when we remember; we come home to our essential nature.

March 3

Water Everywhere

You will always find an answer in the sound of water.
– *Chuang Tzu,* The Way of Chuang Tzu

Most of the human body is space and water, yet we see each other as solid bodies moving around. At the quantum level our molecules are vibrational energy. Our egos need our molecules to spin wildly, so that we will believe in our own existence in space-time; but our *being-ness* needs no place and no movement. As so often is stated, we are spiritual beings having a human experience. But as spiritual beings, our bodies are expendable.

But the continuation of our physical existence is dependent upon water. With the discovery of a "hidden ocean" of water deep below the earth's surface, there is a likelihood that we will survive for some time. Reportedly, the hidden ocean is three times the size of oceans on the surface of the earth, and believed to be the source of our visible oceans.

The hidden ocean could be a metaphor for the reservoir of truth hidden just below the surface of our everyday lives, deep within our consciousness. When we become aware of who we are as spiritual beings, we no longer thirst for significance or attention, or even love; we know who we are, and always have an endless flow of abundant love and compassion, ready to express itself. Within the deep waters of our lives, we taste the truth of our existence.

March 4

Religious Experience

Relax. Nothing is under control. – *Anonymous*

To many, religious experience is the commitment and loyalty to a belief system. Either we are accepted and believed as a member of the group, or we are not. Communities of followers are necessary groupings of people on a certain path toward realization of the divine. Every path meets the needs of the followers; but the needs change over time and reflect the social, emotional, cultural and even political contexts when changes are made. Religions are living, breathing organisms that influence individuals and global communities. In a frightening and uncertain world, religions offer a sense of purpose in living, as well as some solace in our eventual passing away. We want to have a sense of what to expect, or how to live with the greatest chance of happiness. With no apparent control of events, we want guidance for some peace of mind.

When we begin to follow the thinking of the world's major religions, we respect the revelations and teachings of venerated sages and prophets. We worship or hold in high regard those whom we believe give the highest likelihood of truth. In our quest for truth and happiness, we become aware of the thread of love that weaves itself through religions and communities of faith. That thread is the glue that hold our communities together, but our thoughts about what it means to love, ironically can tear us apart. Our quest for the semblance of exclusive control of the truth can sever the thread of love.

The true experience of love transcends our notions of separateness. Love has been secularized to mean different things: romance, intimacy, physical union, partnerships. Love is not just a feeling, a relationship or an action.

Love is the transcendent awareness of our own divinity. It is not something we seek; it is the essence of who we are. Life is one essence, one love. Religious experience is more than a trek along a path. The path is in our minds, but the destination is the present moment, and the place of worship is within our own consciousness.

March 5

Forgotten Joy

The present moment is filled with joy and happiness. If you
are attentive, you will see it. – *Thich Nhat Hanh,* Peace Is
Every Step: The Path of Mindfulness in Everyday Life

Joy is not something we must discover but rather the essence of a moment
to remember. A baby's smiling face and bright eyes, a hug from a friend,
or the flavors of a delicious meal can be a source of joy in the moment.
No matter how difficult the circumstances of our lives may be, joy is here
now, showing up each moment, holding us together like invisible glue.

Sometimes the suffering becomes habitual, so we miss the joy that is
always available to us. We may be willing to endure our pain hoping that
in time it will subside, but joy is always here, ready to relieve us of the
heaviness of suffering. The memory of joy can be released in aromas from
a delicious meal, the rhythmic chords of a guitar, the soulful notes from a
jazz saxophone, the fragrance of a flower, or the innocent crayon drawing
of a 3-year old child.

When we remember, the heart relaxes into the forgotten joy and brings us
peace. Joy is everywhere; we just have to remember it and cherish it in the
meditative presence of the peace.

March 6

Now is Good

Forever is composed of nows.
– *Emily Dickinson*, The Complete Poems (1955)

At times a person we love enters our thoughts, sometimes with concern and at other times with joy. We may feel the urge to connect with that person by phone or another medium. As the feeling comes into our awareness, we are stirred to action, but if we hesitate, the feeling subsides, and we proceed with our day. The momentary sense of the closeness of another that was felt in the fleeting experience of life has now passed away. But if we pause and reflect on that sense, we realize that the "visit" from a loved one is inexplicable and often unexpected. We may wonder what it means to experience the presence of another in the present moment; and to examine the joy derived from acknowledging what comes to us now.

When the person enters our mind in the moment, she is essentially here, now. When the loved ones we have lost enter our consciousness, essentially they are here, now. When we feel love for another being, even when that being is not present in our real-time space, the person is here, now. Now is not a thought, it is not a feeling, it is conscious awareness of joy. We could say that Now is good, because Now is the presence of God.

March 7

Trusting

I shall not waste any effort in trying to reduce God to my particular logic. Here in the quietness, I shall give myself in love to God. – *Howard Thurman*, Meditations of the Heart

Many of us may recount times when we believed that God spoke to us. We may have taken action based on that instruction or message. We try to explain an inexplicable presence in those experiences; and attribute personal qualities to an incomprehensible presence. In the absence of an explanation of the presence we feel, we call upon our existing beliefs for help. We seek assurances that what we experience in the silence is a shepherding voice toward peace; a small, inner voice of inspiration may convince us that our choices in life are requested by our constructed image or the demands of God.

Our intuitive inspirations may lead us to make decisions or to solve problems, but the essence of our being-ness is voiceless. When we go inward, no sound guides us; the presence of the divine is beyond what we consider infinite reality and therefore is unknowable in the mind and in the senses. Silence within us is a reservoir of divine presence that is always accessible to the spirit; that endless silence comforts us with familiarity because it is our own voice. When we immerse ourselves in the silence, we open to that reservoir. An example of the fullness of silence is when we engage in apophatic prayer; we do not ask or listen, but sit in silence, and face the essential nature of our being. Time passes quickly, because as we embrace the silence, time disappears as the mental construct that it is. Without preconceived notions of what we must do or say, we are laid bare to the ultimate reality of the divine.

March 8

Unlimited Potential

Everyone is aware of the experiences; no one
sees the experiencer. – *Upanishads*

For many of us, it is less burdensome to imagine that someone or something outside of ourselves is responsible for what we sense – what we see, hear, feel or physically experience. If the reason for the unfavorable events we experience are someone else's fault, we then bear no responsibility for the results or impacts. We absolve ourselves of the creation and the blame, and deny our own complicity in the events. When we believe that in order to control something it must exist outside of us, we take action against it to force a change. If we remember the depths of our creative, spiritual potential, we consider not only how we act, but also how we think. But if we deny our ability to change ourselves, we deny our potential; real control is self-control.

We are co-creating everything that we sense in our world, so it seems paradoxical that what we are creating we also cannot fully control in our thoughts. If we believe that what we *think* we become, or that our thoughts create our reality, we can use our power to think useful thoughts. We cannot control the appearances of challenges, but we can control how we experience them and respond to them. The uncomfortable truth is that we are co-creators even if we see our world as flawed; we bear some responsibility for the arising of challenges in our lives. The comfortable truth is that we have unlimited potential to change ourselves, not only in how we respond to challenges, but also in our discovery of joy and peace even within the discomfort. Our change within has the potential to change the world.

March 9

Awake

With an eye made quiet by the power of harmony,
and the deep power of joy, we see into the life of things.
– *William Wordsworth*, Written a few miles above Tintern Abbey

We may find it difficult to truly know the essence of life if we are not "inside" our life experiences. To be inside an experience means opening to what appears in our lives and witnessing life using all our senses. We may eat an orange, but have difficulty describing the taste of an orange to someone who has never tasted one. We visit zoos, game preserves and aquariums to see the animals and sea life, and marvel at their behaviors and sizes, but are we simply observers? In their animal confinement, we stop to see who and what they are. We marvel in the diversity and beauty of life – the waterfalls and oceans, the forests and flowers, mountains and plains, but do we actually experience life mindfully? The more we fully experience life, the less likely we are to fear the unknown. Without fear, we can wake up to the loving divinity in our changing reality.

When we are awake to life, we see it differently, hear deeply the sounds that fill the space of it, and open our hearts to it. We are here to experience our lives now, loving every smell, taste and sound. We are here to experience ourselves in the reality we have created. We want our life to be a peaceful adventure, with enough excitement to stimulate the expansion of the universe, and enough joy to soothe us in each moment. All phenomena are our experience of life. Our daily experience of "ordinary" life is not so ordinary if we look into it deeply. When we look into our lives, we can become fascinated with things as they are, and release our desires for something else. We wake up to life.

March 10

Allowing Awe

There is so much to love and admire in this life that it is an act of ingratitude not to be happy and content in this existence. – *Lin Yutang*, Pleasures of a Nonconformist

A first glance into the Grand Canyon will cause our mouths to open in amazement, just as the magnificence of a live birth may bring tears to our eyes. In those moments of magic, we are both appreciative of the beauty and reminded of the possible dangers that lurk nearby. We want the small baby to survive and we want to remain safe at the canyon's edge.

How often have we experienced awe, the emotion that is a combination of both fear and appreciation? After several experiences, we become awe-prone, so we look for experiences that expand our imagination and excitement. When we experience awe, we align with the experience; we accept the awe-inspiring event into our consciousness. There are countless opportunities to allow awe in our life, from basking in the brilliance of a sunset to watching the grateful flowers in a garden turn their faces toward the morning rain. Nature is a relentless source of awe, whether it is the stoic growth of plants and trees or the gentle complementarity of land and sea. We can connect with their beauty and power naturally because we share DNA with all in the universe. If we see and feel our oneness with nature, we cannot escape being in awe; it is a communion with all of life, deepening our sense of the complexity and diversity of life. If we want to see the fullness of the present moment, awe is the lens. When we allow awe to disrupt the illusion of certainty, the routine nature of a life of doing and activity, we move deeply into being and thriving as the spiritual beings that we are.

March 11

As It Should Be

Healing energy transforms us from the inside out. – *Ndidi,* Tea Leaves

A woman cut her finger while she was preparing a meal for guests. With guests arriving within the hour, she drove herself to the emergency room for help. Later, bandaged and embarrassed, she welcomed her guests. A few months later, after the finger had apparently healed, she noticed that a twinge of pain remained when she accidentally struck her finger on the corner of a counter. Although the surface of her wound was healed, the internal healing was still in process.

We may strive to recover quickly from hurt, pain or sorrow; society prefers that we return to a state of calm. We sometimes accommodate the wishes of others, even though we would rather remain inconsolable. We realize that the internal healing will take time and that we must be patient with the process, because everything is always as it should be in life and healing. Apparent healing starts quickly from the outside in, but deep hurts are slower to heal on the inside. As we manage the impressions we make on others, we sometimes conceal the pain with smiles and avoidances, but with a steadfast belief in the inward sanctuary, the inevitable healing occurs. The pace of internal and external healing is a metaphor for change. We cannot hurry it along, believing that because it looks good on the surface, the internal workings are moving in perfect symmetry. Everything is as it should be, even if our perceptions and stories try to convince us that the world is broken, damaged or unsafe. The slowness of the change helps us to savor the present moment, to allow the asymmetry between who we are and what we are experiencing to come into alignment with each other.

March 12

We are Energy

The most strongly enforced taboo is the taboo against knowing
who or what you really are behind the mask of your apparently
separate, independent, and isolated ego. – *Alan Watts,* The
Book on the Taboo Against Knowing Who You Are

We are energy, not separate physical bodies moving around until the music
we are dancing to stops. We do not have a life, we are life. We do not lose a
life; there is *nothing* to lose. We bring essence to our life experience in the
energy of who we are. Energy is everywhere, in all things; the universe is
alive in us and we are alive in it. We live in a dream of separation, seeing
our life as distinctly different and separate from everything else in the
universe, but that dream keeps us asleep, not knowing who we really are.

Although our sense of separateness creates feelings of loneliness, isolation
and vulnerability, we cling to the notion that we are alone. Being alone
and feeling lonely are different experiences. Feeling lonely is an emotional
response to a sense of having no friends or someone as a close, intimate
partner. Being alone is a false sense of existential isolation; we are never
existentially alone because we exist in an energetic, relational universe.

Energy has no boundaries; it is all-encompassing; it lives in form, all form,
so we are expressing in our individual forms as energy. Human beings are
inextricably connected to one another, and to everything in the universe
through the powerful energy that courses through us. If we look around
us carefully, we see that the space we occupy sits inside other space. We as
humans cannot be siphoned off to some special space in the universe, but
can exist only in connection to everything else. We are more than a body;
we are eternal energy in a body.

Enjoy Small Wonders

Art enables us to find ourselves and lose ourselves at the
same time. – *Thomas Merton*, No Man is an Island

Ben Zander, conductor of the Boston Philharmonic Orchestra says that he
wants his musicians to be "one buttock" virtuosos. He wants them to be so
'at one' with the undulations and rhythms of the music that they cannot
sit flatly and technically in their chairs. Instead, Zander wants them to
lift one buttock in synchrony with the textures of the music. We have
seen excellent musicians move with the music, but the ones that speak to
our heart, seem to be unable to contain themselves. They merge with the
sounds and embrace the spirit of the silence. Like a romantic encounter
where two lovers connect with each other's spirit, these music lovers remove
the boundaries between the player and the played, the music and the
musician. The instruments perform as enthusiastically as the hands that
lovingly commune with them. The instruments are alive and the musician
honors that spirit that is waiting to be expressed.

As observers, our energy and enthusiasm inflame the already ignited
enjoyment. The sounds are our sounds; and the silence is our silence; we
become one with the music we hear. We are as responsible as the musicians
for the enjoyment of the "one buttock" masterpieces. The experience is a
metaphor for our wondrous lives. We *are* the music of our lives. When we
enjoy small wonders in life, we live and move and have *our being*.

March 14

Inconceivable Joy

There must be always remaining in every life, some place for the singing of angels, some place for that which in itself is breathless and beautiful. – *Howard Thurman,* The Inward Journey (1961)

A writer is awakened one morning with an idea that consumes him. He rushes to the computer to record his thoughts, and loses track of time. At three o'clock in the afternoon, he realizes that he has been sitting at the computer all day, but he still feels exhilarated.

If we are wandering in a forest of many paths to choose, particularly career choices or directions, we can reflect on what we have experienced that gives us joy. We may know what it feels like to lose ourselves in the moment, and to forget what needs to be done in favor of the experience of flow; we feel "called" to reveal our spirit. It is a pull that sends us deeper into joy even if we cannot adequately express the pull in words. It's an invitation to remember who we really are; a compelling attraction to an ecstatic dance. Our heart opens and what we say or do is less important than taking pleasure in the inexpressible peace that we feel. Some would call this experience mindfulness or insight, but another name is inconceivable joy: pure, boundless joy. During those experiences, we forget the self, because no self is present; and any physical pain or discomfort, self-consciousness, or attachment to approval or outcomes melts away. We feel whole and indefinable, with both a visceral and spiritual consciousness. We celebrate the "breathless and beautiful" experience of authentic existence, the inconceivable nature of joy.

March 15

Mustard Seeds

Loss is nothing else but change, and change is nature's
delight. – *Marcus Aurelius,* Meditations

A young Indian mother frantically seeks help for her baby whom she cannot accept as dead. She asks for help to heal the child, but since the child is already dead, there is nothing anyone could do. A man referred her to the Buddha for help. The Buddha suggested that if she wanted healing, she must collect mustard seeds from houses in the village, but only from houses where no one had died. She went to many houses, but as she went from door to door she could not find a single house where a loved one had not died either recently or long ago. The young mother returned to the Buddha and asks for guidance in surrendering to the reality of birth and death.

This well-known Buddhist parable reminds us that life is temporary and that the experience of life and death is shared by all that exists. We must realize that when we release the idea that we can hold onto anything that is temporary we release ourselves from suffering. We must let things come as they come, and allow them to go as they go, to experience peace. If we insist on clinging to an experience of loss, we sacrifice moments, perhaps days of our life that could be washed in peace.

We cannot grieve enough to redo the past, because it no longer exists. We cannot control the future by re-writing the past, because both are inaccessible to us, except in the mind. Our mind is fickle: both assuring and deceptive. Our clinging comes from false assurances from the mind that the past could be changed, even though we know logically that such a change is impossible. The mind is deceptive in that it cajoles us with promises it cannot keep, and encourages us to believe that just the right action will change everything. It is true that everything changes, but not through our control of circumstances, but rather through our allowing conditions to change in our mind. When we release our grip, the seeds of change take us to new, exciting places, where the only experience is peace.

March 16

The Promise

There is not one big cosmic meaning for us all; there is only
the meaning we each give to our life, an individual meaning,
an individual plot, like an individual novel, a book for each
person. – *Anaïs Nin*, The Diary of *Anaïs Nin*, Vol.I

A potter produces three clay pots from the same clay. The first clay pot
holds vegetables. The second pot holds broth, and the third pot holds
boiled potatoes. She dips from each pot to create the soup that is life. The
clay pots do not know their purpose until they are filled; what lies within
them makes all the difference in the enjoyment of the soup. The original
emptiness of each pot is an opportunity; each of the ingredients they hold
is essential to the soup. As their ingredients blend with each of the other
pots, a delicious life experience is created. When they share from their
center, the world is nourished.

The purpose of life is not something outside of ourselves that we have to
do or show to others. We exist as containers of truth in different forms;
each of us has substance, even though we have varying life experiences.
Although we spend time seeking our purpose in life, we can also reflect
on the promise of life. We have much to share from an endless center.
What we hope to accomplish is already given to us, when we honor who
we are. We are filled; we need not ask for anything; it is already given to
us as complete beneficiaries of life eternal. We need not seek anything, we
are complete within; like breathing beings looking for air we only need to
breathe in. We need not look for doors outside ourselves to open, because
there is no door that prohibits our being-ness, and the world is open to us.
In the present moment, the promise is love, peace and eternal life; if we
are aware of that promise, the purpose of life becomes clear.

March 17

Training the Mind

Our role in contemplation is essentially receptive, in that when we are in engaged in contemplation we receive a gift of divine awareness. – *Dr. James Finley*, Christian Meditation

A man experiencing hysterical blindness is certain that he will never see. He surrenders to the thought that his vision is lost. He takes a walk into a park nearby with a thermos of water in his hand. Even though he cannot see the sun, it warms his face, and the heat of its powerful rays soon make him warm within. He sips water and appreciates the cool liquid that slips down his parched throat. He touches a flower and the soft petals draw him closer to its fragrance. Over time, if his sight does not return, his direct experience of the world will be heightened by all his senses.

Our blindness to the false messages in our daily life, makes us blind to the truth of our being. If we attach ourselves to the stories of grief, shame and suffering, we attach ourselves to the falsehoods of the mind. Non-attachment is the condition for liberation. Without attachments in the mind, peace and freedom are possible; we are free to experience life as it is, without fear. The tendency to attach to ideas in the mind is a natural occurrence in our life, but if we are aware of this tendency, we can begin to train the mind. We can choose what to pay attention to and what to believe. We can be aware of our desires and fears as ideas, instead of allowing thoughts to control us stealthily. We can take action knowing our intentions instead of realizing our motivation after we have made a misguided decision. If we do not tame the mind, we become its servant.

March 18

Pride

False thinking demands an opponent. – Ndidi, Tea Leaves

An impatient man driving on a rural, two lane road blows his car horn angrily because the driver of the car in front of him hesitates to make a left turn across traffic into oncoming vehicles. The hesitant driver finally makes a left turn onto another two lane road. The angry driver boils as he raises his fist to the driver and passes her yelling, "Pig!" He zooms past her and runs into a pig crossing the road.

The destructive impacts of anger are legend; most people would agree that it's not a good thing. But the truth is that life is rarely anger-free. When we humans don't get what we want, when we want it, in the way that we want it, whatever "it" is, we become angry. Anger thrives on our attachment to an illusion of spiritual separation from all others, but the true origin of that anger is pride. Pride, based on the illusion of separation, is the mother of many strong emotions like anger, resentment or rage. Pride drives us to say and do things we'd often like to forget later. Pride lies to us and insists that we are better than others, and that we must protect ourselves from their threats or inadequacies. Conversations and relationships become battlegrounds, instead of spiritually guided experiences. Because of the rampant indiscretions of pride, sarcasm and demands, accusations and other judgments spew from our mouths or electronic communications like erupting volcanoes. The illusion of separateness is the real danger, because in our desire to control others we lose control of ourselves. We are not separate, but one spirit. When we injure others with our words, we also injure ourselves.

March 19

Self-Healing

Deep at the center of my being there is an infinite well
of love. – *Louise L. Hay*, You Can Heal Your Life

Medical science has advanced remarkably over the thousands of years
of healing practices. Human beings are living longer and medicines are
abundant to sustain life. Botanists and herbalists express confidence that
there is a plant or herb on the earth that can cure any disease. To many, the
only barrier that exists between disease and herbal antidotes is knowledge.
Interests in the relationship between the mental, emotional and social
aspects of healing have intrigued progressive medical professionals and
researchers. Cellular biologists and medical intuitives know that our bodies
participate in the healing process, and can dramatically affect the pace and
quality of healing. The biologists can describe the process that occurs in
healing, and medical intuitives uncover the power of our thoughts in the
healing process.

At the core of our being, at the soul level of awareness, healing is possible.
The divine power of the universe in us, through us and as us, can heal
and restore us. The restoration is not a retreat to the past, but an evolving
newness, a fresh cell, body and spiritual expansion. We not only heal we
change in divine alignment with All-That-Is. What impedes our healing
is the idea in the mind that we must do something, be different, repair
something in the past so that we can be free of pain now. We are always
whole, loved and enough; when we quiet the mind, we allow peace to
supplant pain, silence to surround us and soul healing to occur.

March 20

Holy Ground of Love

We are living in a world that is absolutely transparent, and God is shining through all the time. – *Thomas Merton*, Seeds of Contemplation

Challenging conditions may appear in our relationships: lack of integrity, impatience, physical and emotional rejection or violence and mental battery. We may dismiss the power of these challenges and simply focus on a meaningful response to them or we may deflect attention from them in an attempt to minimize the stress of rejection. Some people in our societies or cultures may expect us to simply endure the challenges in our relationships. Deep within, we know that who we are is being obscured by our fears and anxieties. We fear not being loved, being shamed, being hurt, and being abandoned, so we avoid conflicts that we think would provide reasons for what we fear. We push down the anxieties that flood our minds, until we have become numb with despair.

The holy ground of love is not contingent upon worthiness or appropriate responses to someone; it is unconditional. Love that is unconditional releases all boundaries on experience, and is joyfully present every moment of our lives. When the conditions of our life story describe tales of our unworthiness, the holy ground of love is there, removing the false veils to expose the truth. The holy ground of love is the essence of who we are; it is indestructible and eternal. Love is the powerful presence that always simply is. There is no abandonment, no demands, no unrequited affection; those are ghosts dancing in the mind. Love is All-That-Is.

March 21

Humor

A smile is the shortest distance between two persons.
— *Victor Borge*, Smile is the Shortest Distance (autobiography)

Laughter is healing, a balm for the soul. Comedians understand the release and contagion of laughter. The ones who connect most with the audience are those who show up authentically, not trying too hard to be something outside the self. The humor creates new ways of seeing familiar life events, and brings together different experiences of similar events. Humor is a special connection with our spiritual essence.

A life of joy is a continuous inner smile that radiates. If we are smiling inwardly, we are smiling for the world. Humor highlights mistakes or points to desires; but when humor invites us to see the challenges or frustrations in life as mere stories, it has given us the greatest gift. We laugh and we are relieved, because we recognize the story as our own. We no longer feel shame or embarrassment for what we want or who we are. When the veil is lifted from our hidden desires or perceived imperfections and embedded in the stories, we can accept the morals of the stories without moralizing. We can finally admit to ourselves that our lives are a continuous, often humorous story.

March 22

One of Us

I am all orders of being, the circling galaxy, the evolutionary
intelligence, the lift, and the falling away... You the one in all,
say who I am, Say I am You. – *Rumi*, The Essential Rumi

Yoga, qigong, swimming, running, walking and dancing are some of the
activities we may enjoy that energize us for the day. Even though we may
start the day with enthusiasm, the initial euphoria may fade as the day
progresses, and the continuation of joy will elude us. The culprit is often
our return to the notion that we are separate persons with different needs,
wants and expectations. We see our needs and wants in conflict with those
of others, and become frustrated with the slow pace of gratification. We
temporarily forget our usual sense of community, our spiritual connection
with everything on the planet and beyond, and focus on what we desire.
We are committed to thinking that we can only survive in this life by
conquering or competing with "others," even when one conflict simply
leads to another.

We cannot effectively disconnect from one another without altering our
sense of self; we forget that we are just one spirit. We are breathing air
recycled from eons of the earth's atmosphere, but we forget. We forget that
the entire universe resides within us and that "the bad and ugly misguided
behaviors" are manifestations of our fears and our amnesia. We have
forgotten who we really are. We experience relief when we remember that
there is only one of us – one divine ocean with many waves.

March 23

The Answer is Always "Yes"

Ask and it is given you; seek and ye shall find; knock, and
it shall be opened unto you. – *Matthew 7:7 (KJV)*

"No" is a word we have used to voice our displeasure with what is happening, or what will happen. It is a powerful recognition of the discomfort with what is. The pain is real for us; the "no" is our silent or verbal announcement that pain is present; but when we cling to the "no" it takes on a new meaning. If we're not careful, "No" becomes a fixture in our minds, a constant response to discomfort. We live in a "yes" universe, so our defensive "no" is often out of alignment with universal flow. Sometimes the "no" is "not yet" or "not me." We hesitate to own or remember our ultimate reality or true selves. We place limits on our potential and resist accepting the abundance available to us each moment.

The evolving universe is always flowing with "yes." When we are aligned with that flow, our experience of life is always "yes." When our hearts open to what is, we are flowing with "yes." When we ask from the depths of our being, that expansive reality opens our third eye to what is possible. Our true selves know the voiceless positive power of the universe. We are love made visible, and the answer is always "yes."

March 24

Never Full

A crust taken in peace is better than a banquet
taken in anxiety. – *Aesop,* Aesop's Fables

The rabbit was good friends with the elephant, in spite of their obvious differences. After all, the rabbit's tail was bushy and the elephant's tail lacked long hair. As the friendship continued, the two began to compete. The rabbit hopped faster than the elephant, but the elephant could run further in spite of his weight. Both of the friends had an appreciation for food, but the rabbit seemed to constantly nibble. One day, the two friends were walking through the grasslands when they spotted a pile of tree bark. They happily began to consume the bark. Growing full, the rabbit continued to eat as long as his buddy the elephant did, until he could no longer stand. Miserable from overeating, the rabbit still craved the piece of bark hanging from the elephant's lips.

Craving is based on an idea that we are enhanced by what we crave; we think the satisfaction of our craving will bring us joy and completeness. We are never full as long as we think we need to be filled. That empty feeling is an idea in the mind that we need one more new thing to be whole. Wholeness is just an idea, since we cannot with clarity describe what a whole human being is. We may ascribe our own meaning to the concept, but we can never capture the experience of being whole. We can never get the full meaning without direct experience, and we cannot experience wholeness directly. Our confusion may arise from filling up with food; we know that experience. But fullness is not wholeness. Unlike refilling the body continually, spiritual fullness requires no refill. There is no cavity of spirit that needs to be filled. Peace is knowing that spiritual fullness is our ultimate reality. We experience peace when we know our *being* is enough.

March 25

Reflection

You've got to drop illusions. You don't have to add anything in order to be happy; you've got to drop something. – *Anthony de Mellow,* Awareness

A woman had a recurrent dream about looking into her mirror each morning and seeing a different relative looking back at her. When she asked each relative why they appeared, the answer was always the same, "I come to offer my forgiveness."

Reflection among human beings is the capacity to examine the stories with full consciousness of thoughts and feelings. Whether the past is regarded with horror or with happiness, reflection creates stories in the mind. Our understanding is colored by the light that we shine on our past. We piece together impressions, dark memories that wither and change as time moves on, leaving only the feelings to bolster the pain and make victimhood noble. The details of events may fade, but our feelings remain.

Our past, present and future times, although constructs, help us to create new stories. As long as we are conscious of their lack of truth, the stories entertain us. When we reflect on the past, we can do so mindfully, paying attention to all that appears to us in the mind, remembering joyful moments, and allowing all thoughts of the past to pass through the mind without clinging to them. When the past is shed like a snake's skin, a new past emerges, once again competing for the light that either opens or closes our heart. If we are given the opportunity to create new stories, let them be joyful ones, created for our enjoyment. No matter what has happened to us, the present moment will always provide the opportunity for peace. We could let peaceful stories be written in our hearts.

March 26

Just for Today

Write it on your heart that every day is the best day of the year. – *Ralph Waldo Emerson,* Society and Solitude (1870)

The expression, Carpe Diem, seize the day, was made famous in a 1989 film entitled *The Dead Poets Society,* starring the late Robin Williams. Every 24-hour period of time in our lives, a banquet of treasures is presented to us; thinking a negative thought during those hours is like inserting a fly into the soup; the fly is small but it spoils the soup. Each moment of each day we get a new chance to experience joy; we have a possibility of enjoying a day without spoiled soup or polluting the banquet with the mind's disturbances. If we regret the day, we have ignored the entire banquet; we have colored the day blue even though most of the treasures remain a golden treasure of joy. When we paint an experience with such a broad stroke, we miss the beauty of the gifts of joy in each moment. Just as each hour is a treasure, so is every moment. If we immerse ourselves into the present moment and just be, all the hours collapse into one perfect time. Find joy in the present moment and have no regrets.

March 27

Billions Before Us

Our history begins before we are born. We represent the hereditary influences of our race, and our ancestors virtually live in us. – *James Nasmyth*, James Nasmyth engineer (1883)

Although the current human population of the earth is more than seven billion people, many more have lived before us. Our current existence is possible because of the lives of ancestors; we are because they were. If we look carefully at our life, evidence of previous lives will be obvious reflections. As carriers of history and promises made, we have an awesome responsibility to build on the joys of their creations. Each of their lives was an opening, a statement of infinite reality and the awesome opportunity of life. We could trust that life is here for us, like unformed clay that we can mold into a life of fulfilled dreams and joy. If we could just let go of our self-imposed chains, we could keep the promises of our ancestors. We could believe in our inherent worth as progeny of a billion souls who have paved our way. We could bow to the earth, and lift our eyes to the sky in respect for the limitless boundaries of the universe. We could give praise to the animals that model for us the drive to thrive, and celebrate their willingness to sacrifice all for the sake of the continuation of life. We could know that all is well, and that life goes on in spite of the mind's insistence that we are doomed. We could remember that the ancestors outnumber the currently living, and therefore can make a compelling case for the continuation of life. We could know that we are the universe, living in the flow of spirit; immersed in the joy of living. We could remember that we live on forever in this evolving universe as billions before us.

March 28

Communion

...the deepest level of communication is not communication, but communion. It is wordless, it is beyond words, and it is beyond speech, and it is beyond concept. – *Thomas Merton* (Speech to monks in Calcutta 1968, as reported in The Asian Journal of Thomas Merton, 1975 edition, p. 308)

We live in a collection of communities, with different expectations and rewards. Relationships within the communities assure us that we are recognized, connected lovingly to others and valued for what and who we are; we exist within each community to belong to something larger than our individual selves, and find refuge in the comfort of being accepted. Our communities have layers of meaning that are important to our sense of peace; we are remembered for what we contribute, respected for our devotion to shared beliefs and reassured that we will not be excluded. We want to be a part of solid bonds with others, and have faith that cultural and social similarities will provide a sense of belonging. We hope that communication in our communities will be easy, and that we'll be readily understood. The glue that ultimately holds a community together is a sense of communion, the sharing of our loving spirit.

Communion is like a fire that never extinguishes, an eternal flame of commitment and presence. In the fire of communion, we feel the presence of love and the warmth of its glow, because it lives within us. Communion reminds us of our value and the brightness of our light. In communion with All-That-Is, all our communities collapse into one. We cannot be excluded, because there is no other place to be. We cannot be misunderstood, because the true self cannot be defined. Communion is the experience of Love.

March 29

Eternal Present

Lose yourself in the eternity of the present moment and
finally find what you are seeking. – *Ndidi,* Tea Leaves

Eternity is a rejection of endings in favor of continuation through change
and transformation. The return to the source of our being, the energy
of the universe, is not a prodigal punishment but a reunion. Unlike life's
reunions, there are no memories to qualify the experience of being; there
are no surprises that lead to judgments or unsteadiness. The changes are
not physical, but evolutionary; we are divine energy perfectly unfolding.

We experience eternity each day, each moment. In the momentary splash
of Now we are in an eternal moment. Our reunions are continuous if we
allow ourselves to settle into the joy of just being. The miracle of our life is
that each moment begins and ends in a flash of time, but as we breathe in
the next moment, we experience a rebirth of joy. The river of life that flows
through us, around us and within us also embraces us with love. When we
show up for life in the moment, we discover our true self.

March 30

Centering Prayer

As we sit in Centering Prayer, we are connecting with the divine
life within us. The sacred word is a gesture of consent to the
divine presence and action within. It is as if our spiritual will
turned on the switch, and the current (the divine life) that is
present in our organism, so to speak, goes on and the divine
energy flows. – *Thomas Keating*, Intimacy with God, p.168

Traditional prayers are supplications, requests made to a higher power or
deity to grant a favor in response to continued devotion and respect. There
is a belief among supplicants that they can influence conditions in their
lives by the power of their beliefs and faith. When outcomes appear as
expected, supplicants give praise to the Power and feel that they have had
a role in the changes in conditions. Some feel that they have been blessed
or chosen to experience the requested result. If the result is not as expected,
the supplicants are disappointed, sometimes angry, but gradually accept
the result as divinely ordered.

When we surrender to the best outcome, we enter a space of stillness and
peace, not in defeat but with trust that the universe is unfolding perfectly,
even if we cannot know the intricacies of its unfolding. Centering prayer
encourages us to be in stillness, present moment awareness, and to return
to the sacred, not in supplication but in communion. In a space of non-
thought but abiding peace, the Self is known. As stated in the Upanishads,
Vedic scriptures that deal with broad philosophical problems, "Bright but
hidden, the Self dwells in the heart. Everything that moves, breathes, open
and closes is the Self. And may be known through love but not through
thought." Centering prayer is a method of non-vocal prayer that seeks a
closer connection to the ground of being, the essence of the divine. In

quiet contemplation we can experience peace that we can be conscious of throughout the day. In all that we do or experience in our lives, the sense of abiding peace stays with us. Through the practice of centering prayer, sometimes called contemplative prayer, just below the surface of our ordinary lives an extraordinary connection with our own inner peace is continually available to us. When we release our need to comprehend the incomprehensible, we settle into our life as it is. We then release our desires for greater understanding and open our hearts to the restfulness of peace and the direct experience of the divine.

March 31

Seeing Truth

Something opens our wings. Something makes boredom
and hurt disappear. Someone fills the cup in front of us.
We taste only sacredness. – *Rumi,* A Year with Rumi

The physical heart pumps blood throughout the body; without obstruction,
it will continue to function as a distributor of necessary oxygen for the rest
of our lives. On the other hand, the metaphorical heart, the spiritual center
of love and joy, can be clouded with fear and the illusion of separation.
Spiritual awareness is the oxygen we need to find joy and love in our lives.
We are not blind to the possibility of joy, but we can acquiesce to the false
stories from the mind in response to conditions in our lives that challenge
our faith and sense of safety. When the murky details of the mind's story
consume our thoughts we close our hearts; lovingkindness is abandoned
and replaced with futile attempts to survive.

All of the thoughts either grow from stories of the past or expectations
of trouble in the future. Each moment can discount the false reality, if
we immerse ourselves in the serenity and clear awareness of right Now.
Immersing ourselves in the present moment does not mean that we are
blinded from reality, but rather that we see the truth of our life clearly,
without internal auditing and evaluation. To be in the present moment is
to have heightened awareness of what is, to see with the purity of the open
heart with no thoughts in the mind to blur that vision. We become open
to greater awareness of who we are. Our thoughts that fuel our anxieties
and hurt begin to recede to the background of our life experience. When
love moves to the foreground of our life story, "we taste only sacredness."

April 1

Light and Darkness

Yin and yang are both one and two. – *Ndidi,* Tea Leaves

Opposites are artful products of our creative mind; they are contrasting ideas or opposing concepts in our consciousness. Opposites are illusions of contrast but the reality is that events in our life are always one unitary spiritual force. We cannot recognize one aspect of a duality without the other.

For example, when we experience hatred we crave love. Sadness recognizes the absence of happiness; but it is the sadness that makes happiness as a concept possible. If we experience the exhilaration of gaining some reward or desired object, we may for an instant also imagine the pain of losing that same prize.

Like the well-known yin-yang symbol, each aspect of one part of the symbol is present in the complementary part. Yin encompasses yang; yang also encompasses yin. Loving relationships are no exception. As the mystic poet Rumi helps us to understand so artfully, lovers are in each other even as they seek each other. We are what we seek, but the illusion of separation keeps us thinking that we are incomplete when that is never the case.

There is only one of us, one life we are living; knowing this allows us to see into the nature of consciousness. There is nothing outside of the Self - "no thing." In the Ultimate reality, there are no boundaries, no divisions, no separations. We can see perceived opposites for the messengers that they are — behind every shadow is the sun; within every challenge is an opportunity; and in the midst of every chaotic story is abiding peace. We divide the world into polarities – left and right, soft and hard, light and dark, because it is a convenient way to organize our reality. When we pay attention to only one of the poles, the other does not disappear, except in our perspective. One aspect helps us to get clearer about the other, but the view that encompasses both "sides" is the real opening to freedom.

Light energy is electromagnetic radiation, speeding along in high frequencies through the darkness. Our energy is light energy, moving from moment to moment, speeding toward infinity. When we shine the light of love in our lives, we acknowledge the darkness as part of life. Without judgments, we embrace others as whole and divine. If we choose to love others only when they reflect our own light, we become blinded by our own righteousness. But if we allow ourselves to look for the light of others even in their darkness, we can define our own darkness more clearly. We say that no one is perfect, but actually we are perfect spirits. Our darkness is part of who we are, and although we are not defined by our darkness, without it our light cannot exert its true strength. There is no place that God does not exist, whether the space is in the bright light of love or in the movement of transformation. Darkness is the complement to light, not the absence of it. When we embrace wholeness we embrace all of who we are.

April 2

Resurrection

Only after disaster can we be resurrected. – *Chuck Palahniuk,* Fight Club

Phoenix rising from the ashes reminds us of the necessary cycle of dying to self and rising to new beginnings. Like the Hindu god Shiva, the destroyer of the ego, Phoenix overcomes adversity in his insistence on living.

We may feel compelled by society to give up when challenges come our way but all endings are simultaneous beginnings. The universe must continue, so the endings are pauses to prepare for a beginning. Without destruction, nothing in life could emerge as newness. Without beginnings, the death of life would be our only reality. But when endings are beginnings, everything in life lives, breathes and continues.

When we know who we are, we do not lament the ashes, or pine for only the desired conditions in life. We know that our essence is indestructible, so we witness the changes as they come into being and disappear, as conditions always do. In that space of allowing, we no longer experience the heaviness of the limitations in life, but rather we embrace them as harbingers of new creations. We are then free to see things as they are, and to be aware of the peace in the midst of change that pervades our existence. We then know that life will go on forever, and we are that life, as we freely move toward eternity.

April 3

Quiet Power

The inner secret, that which was never born, You are that
freshness, and I am with you now. – *Rumi,* A Year with Rumi

When a storm rages, the first thought is to find a safe space to survive
until the storm has passed. The rage of the wind and rain makes our
heart pound with excitement and fear. Our mind can be a raging storm
of thoughts, sending fearful messages to us of impending disaster and
destruction. Sometimes the messages are less dramatic; the mind warns us
about repeating past failures or trusting people who should not be trusted.
We hear messages of encouragement as well; and tell ourselves that we can
do anything we believe in, so nothing can stand in our way. These ideas
of the mind, whether we regard them as negative or positive, are a steady
stream of thoughts and images that continually define our sense of being
loved or safe.

Beneath the rubble of our active minds is a presence that is like a gentle
breeze. It is the quiet power that pervades the universe, always present
for us and as our core being. Some may call it spirit, others may call
it infinite intelligence, but we know that wherever we go, there it is;
whenever we love, there it is. When we become aware of our true self,
we see the face of quiet power, the end of painful thoughts and needless
suffering. We may not always acknowledge the Presence of the power,
but it lives within us. We may try to name it, but naming limits it, so
it cannot be named. We may try to relate to it as exclusively our own,
but the power is moving in its own way, regardless of our desire to
possess it or even learn from it. We believe that it speaks to us, but the
language of our heart does not use sound. We believe that the quiet
power is our benefactor, and then we realize that nothing is lacking,

and there is nothing we need. We wonder about our purpose in life, and then through the voiceless presence we turn inward and find our answers in just being. We are not separate from quiet power; we often know it as ourselves.

April 4

Solitude

Our language …has created the word loneliness to express the pain of being alone. And it has created the word solitude to express the glory of being alone. – *Paul Tillich*, The Eternal Now

Solitude is more than being alone; it is a state of meditation that makes the concept of time withdraw into the background. We are never really alone, since love is always sustaining us. Solitude is an opportunity to be still, and to know the sound of our own voice, our own heart, and our own thoughts. It begins with a heightened awareness of what we are experiencing, and then moves to what we are feeling about the experience. Solitude opens us up to who we are as glorious beings. When we see ourselves as experiencing something, we still believe that what we are experiencing is reality. As we continue to experience solitude, we settle into the present moment, and lose the sense of separation from what we are experiencing. There is no background and foreground to our experience; life just is. Instead of feeling profound aloneness, the sense is that we are connected to everything. We know at the essential core of our being that the boundaries we have established in our lives are more a convenience than a necessity. With this new sense of the purity of life, we can live joyfully knowing deeply that we have never been alone, and never will be.

April 5

Contentment

The best remedy for those who are afraid, lonely or unhappy is
to go outside, somewhere where they can be quiet, alone with the
heavens, nature and God. Because only then does one feel that
all is as it should be. – *Anne Frank,* The Diary of Anne Frank

As conscious beings, we often express desires for more, better, different
objects, relationships, or experiences in life. Sometimes our desires are
insatiable. As our desires continue to be our focus, we become more and
more frustrated with the absence of what we want, and devise plans and
strategies to get them. We are often disappointed when we finally receive
what we grasped for, so we launch new plans for new things or relationships.
We sometimes look inside our collection of talents, things and people to
find our signature, our meaning in life, but this too disappoints us. While
we struggle with our desires and their disappointments, we miss the beauty
of the present moment that life offers as a gift to us.

When there is an absence of striving and grasping, we experience the
perfection of peace. The absence of something usually means that there
is a void that needs to be filled. We often think of the world in zero sum
terms -- if one thing increases, the alternative thing decreases; but the
universe has different rules, so it continually expands.

The more we are satisfied with what we experience now, the more the
universe changes, attracting to us more of what we imagine will make us
happy. When we are still, the universe moves, but when we push or try
to hurry the process, we misalign with the natural changes that lead to
expansion.

Contentment is alignment with what is, because everything we experience is as it should be. The irony is that when we let it be, we are letting ourselves be deeply fulfilled. Some may say that contentment is simply the act of loving what we have, but contentment is loving who we are in the moment. If we embrace contentment every moment, we experience peace. There can be no time when joy is not present, no time when we are not our true self. But in order to experience contentment we must remember who we are.

April 6

Healing Words

Unable are the loved to die, for love is immortality.
– *Emily Dickinson,* The Complete Poems (1955)

When we connect with people who are grieving a loss or coping with deeply disturbing life struggles, appropriate words to express our feelings may be difficult to find. We may say we are sorry for their troubles, or that everything will be fine. We may rely on traditional statements to smooth our awkwardness. We are both sympathetic and concerned as we see our own lives reflected in the lives of others. Their struggles are a grim reminder of the struggles we have faced or may face in the future. When we feel 'for' someone, the sympathetic tone is helpful, but it enforces the notion of victimhood or powerlessness. When we are empathetic, we feel 'with' someone, and enter into communion with the pain. We acknowledge the shared experience, but we must surrender to the pain and not the suffering.

Only when we can be in the pain with another can we walk heart to heart out of it. We can listen and breathe in that pain of grief and struggle, and breathe out the words of peace. Healing words transcend the conditions of our lives, and transform the fear and struggle into the positive energy of love. Healing words are transformative, opening the heart to divine energy that is the source of our being; the words are kind, positive and inspired like a balm especially prepared for the soul. When we take away the sense of isolation that arises in grief, we enter a place of compassion and healing with another person. The loneliness of grief and struggle are overcome, and the panic of pain moves on with the changing moments.

April 7

Perfection

I exist as I am, that is enough. – *Walt Whitman,* Leaves of Grass

An intuitive sculptor releases an image from wood; the image that emerges has existed in perfection inside the wood even though it has been obscured by the "ordinary" covering of the substance. The intuition of the sculptor is an ability to see into the wood, to imagine the treasures that lie within its rough exterior. As the poet William Wordsworth so beautifully writes, "While with an eye made quiet by the power of harmony, and the deep power of joy, we see into the life of things." Our own perfection is smothered under layers and layers of perceived imperfections that we must release in order to become aware of it.

With a sculptor's eye we can be still and see into our own core essence and release the truth of who we are. We must chip away at the negative self-talk we have grown accustomed to voicing when we feel unworthy or vulnerable. We could throw off the covers of secret indiscretions that we think have made us unholy or imperfect. We could see conditions in our lives as ways to smooth our corners and not ways to damage us. We could remember that the key to our joy is not so much that we are becoming something better, but simply more of who we already are. We could look at the dust or shards of past situations and realize that every moment is a beginning. When we realize our perfect essence, we become aware of all that we have always been, not all that we have done. Our essential being is love, and love is the essence of perfection. When we are being love in all we do and say, we are remembering who we are.

April 8

Source of Suffering

You were born with wings, why prefer to crawl
through life? – *Rumi,* in Wisdom for the Soul; Five
Millennia of Prescriptions for Spiritual Healing

A woman volunteered at a shelter for homeless persons, but felt uncomfortable after a few weeks because she was experiencing critical financial difficulties; no one at the shelter knew of her predicament. Because of her embarrassment about her own financial struggles, she found it increasingly difficult to face the homeless people at the shelter. She confided to a friend, "I tried to deny my financial distress by volunteering, but I only felt like a hypocrite." The friend listened and then asked her to consider something to find peace with her predicament. The friend reminded her that we cannot solve our problems through other people, even if they reflect our own struggles. She suggested, "Create a vision of abundance inside of you, a place where there are no boundaries and no limits," she said. The friend added, "When you find your own center, you can then share the peace of abundant reality with others."

Sometimes we have to go inward in order to find ways to reach out to others. When we center our attention on our self-interests and needs, we ignore the changes that are required within ourselves. Self-centered attitudes cause us suffering, because our grasping behavior disregards the natural flow of love and abundance that is the essential nature of the universe.

Struggles often create a sense of isolation and loneliness. The loneliness that we experience is the result of our pre-occupation with the "I" that our egoic mind promotes. Our sense of loneliness leads to anger towards what we perceive as rejection. Our grasping for acceptance is the result of fear and a sense of shame. So isolation, loneliness, anger, hatred and delusions of the mind become the source of our suffering.

We could begin to accept who we are and know that we are whole and capable. When we fill our sense of emptiness with love and kindness, we will feel the connection we crave. Reaching out to others with authentic compassion, we realize that love is all we have ever wanted to give, so from a joyful center we can open our hearts to others.

April 9

Testimony

The work of the eyes is done. Go now and do the heart work
on the images imprisoned within you. – *Rainer Maria Rilke,*
Turning Point, translated by Stephen Mitchell

If we watch television dramas starring lawyers, the shows usually include
courtroom testimonies. Often the guilt or innocence of the accused is
decided through convincing personal accounts of witnesses. The power
of testimony is undeniable; we can give voice to the voiceless, vision to
the blinded, and clarity to the confused by the sheer authority of our
testimony. The moral principles of "not bearing false witness" or "right
speech" in religious communities have been touted for centuries.

Just as we try to avoid experiencing suffering ourselves, we also try to avoid
inflicting suffering on others. We are strengthened in this approach to
self and others when we are aware of our divine connection to All-That-Is.
When the preoccupation with the concept of "I," as an idea in the mind
causes us to focus on self-preservation, we become deluded into thinking
that we are separate from the All. We may think that speaking our truth
jeopardizes our safety, or that seeing the innocence in others highlights
our own failings. All of these thoughts arise in a fearful mind, plagued
with the idea of separation. All-That-Is cannot be divided; the energy that
courses through our existence is one spirit, and we are that.

April 10

To Be or Not to Be

It is the essence of joy to reveal itself, while grief tries to hide, sometimes even to deceive. – *Søren Kierkegaard*. Either/ Or from translation by David F. Swenson (1959)

A stirring inner debate about life or death is the subject of a famous monologue in Shakespeare's *Hamlet*. The question is whether it's better *in the mind* to bear the challenges of life or decide to escape those challenges by dying to them.

Every day we have a choice to be or not to be, not in the way that Hamlet agonized over his life, but in our choice to be who we really are; or try to be an image of who we think we should be. We are love expressed moment by moment in the world. The "slings and arrows of outrageous fortune" are illusions, "a sea of troubles" that will wash away in time. Hamlet painstakingly lists all those illusions that cause us to suffer: oppression, pride, unrequited love, corruption, unmerited credit, unsatisfying work, and delays of the legal system. All of these "slings and arrows" are invitations to believe that life is a threat instead of the opportunity to be fully alive in the present moment. Our being-ness is not a question to be debated. We are spiritual beings expressing love in a conditional universe. We are not human *doings*, but human *beings*.

April 11

Remembering

He was still too young to know that the heart's memory eliminates
the bad and magnifies the good, and that thanks to this
artifice we manage to endure the burden of the past.
– *Gabriel García Márquez*, Love in the Time of Cholera

A French word, *sillage*, refers to the lingering memories we have in life.
Without our holding onto them, those memories would be lost forever, so
we go back to them periodically. We may remember a bright, sunny day
or a rain soaked afternoon, but the thoughts are not the experience itself.
Remembering is a re-creative thought process based on impressions in the
heart and mind that linger. We literally *re-member*, or try to re-assemble
parts of an experience so that we can feel it again.

Remembering pleasant experiences brings both warm feelings and longing,
while remembering unpleasant experiences brings both pain and fear.
The common denominator in both pleasant and unpleasant memories
is that they exist only in our minds; they are impressions that come and
go. It is natural for us to want pleasure and to avoid pain, but each
is a product of our thinking. When we choose to think of pleasurable
impressions, we experience momentary joy; when we choose to hold onto
painful impressions, we experience lingering fear. We can let our thoughts
come and go without judgment and allow joy to rise. Or, we can linger
with joyful thoughts and eventually the fearful memories will be fleeting
impressions.

April 12

Trademark Smile

Sometimes your joy is the source of your smile, but sometimes your smile is the source of your joy. – *Thich Nhat Hanh*, Peace is Every Step

Simply the sound of a mother's voice, the feel of satisfaction from the cessation of hunger, and a dry bottom are reasons enough to make a small baby smile. As babies, we developed a trademark smile; it was ours, arising from within our soul. The basic necessities of food, physical comfort and touch may be enough for the young, but as we grow older our needs become more complex. As we experience unmet needs, the smiles seem harder to muster. We forget that the smiles of our youth were not just a reaction to some pleasure we experienced, but rather a basic satisfaction with our lives. When we smiled we felt good; but we could sense that some people had smiles that signaled discomfort or fear, and others wore beaming smiles of pride, relief or sheer joy. Some people had smiles in their hearts, we could feel them. Others had disappointed hearts; we could feel them too.

As we grew, we lost that sensitivity. Frowns too often replaced our smiles, and clenched teeth showed our frustrations. We forgot that we were connected to the hearts of others. We lost our trademark smiles – the human offering that we can make to others to communicate that all is well. We forgot the special privilege of smiling as a human being; and forgot that among sentient beings, our smiles are a major contribution to joy in the world. We forgot that a smile is lovingkindness.

The evolution of a smile begins with what we are thinking and feeling; a mind that generates fear restricts our smiles. When our thoughts are positive, compassion flourishes in our smiles; and others reap the benefits of our hopefulness and faith. But when we are suffering, focusing on dissatisfaction with the way things are, smiles disappear from our faces and influence the spaces we enter. Our suffering is the result of our grasping and clinging for something or someone, and in that grasping and clinging little is offered to others that will enhance their life experience. When we realize the influence of our trademark smiles on the experience of others and our own sense of joy, we become conscious of the power of our thoughts and feelings. We can find the joy and peace in the present moment and flash our trademark smile to give thanks for life as it is.

April 13

Associations

The beginning of love is the will to let those we love be perfectly themselves, the resolution not to twist them to fit our own image. – *Thomas Merton*, The Way of Chuang Tzu

Once upon a time, a young man started to grow lumps over parts of his body. Many doctors examined him, but none found any medical reason for the lumps. He had been impressionable in his youth, and had wanted to belong to his peer group so much that he had taken on many of their habits. As he grew older, he continued to seek approval as a way to feel loved. One morning, he sat reflecting on his life, and began to forgive himself for forgetting who he was - a compassionate, loving person. He sat for some time feeling lighter and happier than he had felt for a long time. He then went to the mirror to brush his teeth and was amazed to find that all his lumps had disappeared!

We carry baggage with us – some of it is heavily laden with other people's belongings that we have collected and incorporated into our descriptions of ourselves. Some of that baggage has begun to distort who we are. We may have associated the original gathered items with friendships, colleagues, or family members, but as long as their belongings remain with us, we cannot be truly ourselves. We can only be an image of someone else. The behaviors and attitudes that come from our unnecessary and harmful associations originate in the mind, but we can refuse to be influenced by what we habitually think about ourselves or other people. Stale opinions are out of sync with the reality of our lives now, so we can take responsibility for our thoughts, gather them in meditative focus, and let them go. We can decide to cleanse our thoughts of greed, hatred and false ideas about who we are. We can rest peacefully in being the love we are.

April 14

No Victims

The primary cause of happiness is never the situation,
but your thoughts about it. – *Eckhart Tolle*, A New
Earth: Awakening to Your Life's Purpose

One morning a man woke up to a horrible change in his posture. He could
no longer stand up straight without leaning either to his left or right. He
had been thinking a good deal about his past hurts and his worries about
being vulnerable to continuing pain. He had lost his balance, his awareness
of the present; his mind pulled him into either the past or future. These
thoughts had consumed most of his time, and now his thinking was having
a physical impact on him, so he sought some advice. His friends told him
to just be strong and everything would work out. His older brothers and
sisters told him to forget about how he appeared; but his mentor told him
to appreciate who and what he is, because he is more than he appears to be.

Often we are counseled to get over it; we are assured by those who also
experience pain and suffering that our struggles will get better. Although
the counsel is well-meaning, it can ignore the imposition of the false self on
our minds and hearts. We are made small and insignificant by the notion
of victimhood, but we are so much more than what has happened to us. We
are sojourners on life's road, opening ourselves to new adventures every day.

When we appreciate what we are in the present moment, we release all
notions of victimhood, and know that everything is as it should be. Since
everything changes, our feelings of being a victim encourage us to cling
to events that are no longer present. The past keeps open wounds that
want to heal.

The mind creates a victim not only on the basis of what has already happened, but also on the basis of what may happen in the future. We could recognize that we are not what happens to us; if we can name an event or a painful experience, it is not who we are. We are not condemned to repeat what has happened to us, because the universe conspires to love and heal as it continually evolves.

Each moment of our lives is a fleeting breath. When we stay with what we are experiencing now, we are freed from what happened or what will happen. We can get in touch with our extraordinary inner strength. We could release regrets or pain from our past and know who we are now. As survivors of the past, we can instead hold ourselves and others in a compassionate embrace and thrive.

April 15

Abundance

He who is not satisfied with a little, is satisfied with nothing. – *Epicurus,*
The Essential Epicurus (1993) edited by Eugene Michael O'Connor

There was once a woman in a small village who owned a golden stool.
The villagers believed that the stool had magical powers, because the
woman was always happy, while others in the village were unhappy with
their lives. The woman sat in silent meditation often and smiled at flowers
in her garden. She basked in the sun but she also seemed to enjoy rainy
days. She welcomed friends and strangers into her small home, and always
offered them tea. The woman seemed so content that some of the unhappy
villagers wanted her magic. One night, while the woman slept, they took
the golden stool. To their amazement, nothing changed for the woman,
but their golden stool had overnight turned to stone.

The irony of abundance is that when we release the notion of owning
anything, we experience the true abundance of the universe. As we
contribute to the expression of the universe as a life force, we are the
abundance of divine energy. When we see ourselves as mere owners
or receivers of abundance, we have deluded ourselves. We do not have
abundance, we are abundant energy, enjoying our presence on earth in
this time and space. We do not own the entire earth; we are the earth;
we are filled with the energy of ancestors. We do not only breathe in
precious air; we breathe out. The constant inward flow, transformation and
release is a metaphor for the continuance of life – true abundance. Money,
possessions, family and friends are not the truth of abundance; the essential
divine energy that flows through our body and soul – that is abundance.

April 16

Resentment

Let go of resentful stories that prolong suffering. – *Ndidi,* Tea Leaves

A lonely mother received a call from her son, who had been traveling on business. "Hello, Mother" he said, "How are you doing?" She said "I haven't been eating." Her son asked "Why not?" His mother huffed and said, "I was staying close to the phone, just in case you would find the time to call me!"

Resentment is sending a one-way communication to ourselves that we have been hurt. The hope is that the message will somehow be heard by the perpetrator of an offense. Like a message blasted through a megaphone to ourselves, the message irritates us over time. The loudness consumes us and drowns out any sense of peace of mind. Anger that sparks the original message originates in a frightened, self-possessed mind that insists on replaying a sad melody; even though the dance has changed, the old tune plays on. If the damaging anger is not released, the mind repeats the images of the offense; even though the original story cannot be repeated, and feelings are all that remain of the memory. In time, the mind's reproducing capacities diminish, even though the loud protests continue to disturb our peace.

We can look deeply at the story our mind has constructed and release our indignation and blame, but it requires that we see our resentment project as unsuccessful. The rewards of our resentment have been miniscule as we have sat in perpetual vigilance, expecting the past to repeat itself. It never does. The story we create is the fuel for our misery. We can refuse to listen to our loud, fearful minds, acknowledge the pain or hurt, but then refuse to suffer.

April 17

Consciousness

The eye with which I see God is the same with which God
sees me. My eye and God's eye are one eye, and one sight,
and one knowledge and one love. – *Meister Eckhart,* Sermon:
True Hearing, translated by Claud Field (1909)

If we wonder about the nature of the self, the true essence of who we are, we
have begun to also wonder about the nature of death. Can we exist beyond
death? And if this is it, why are we here? The ego wants us to survive, because
its survival depends on ours. We decide that if we know why we are here then
we can fulfill our purpose, and all that we experience in life will have meaning
that we can identify. We are often in a desperate search for the secrets of life so
that we will know how to keep living as long as possible. But we are thwarted
in our efforts, because we cannot find a meaning based on logic. Our logical
mind observes what it thinks is factual, but will continue to ask "why?"

In the absence of any logical objections, our egoic mind assumes that what it
thinks is the truth. When we think something is true, we believe it. If we rely
on our beliefs about the meaning of our lives or the nature of the essential
self, we will become frustrated with the incompleteness of the information.
New information continues to surface challenging the accuracy of our
beliefs; but we may reject new information and declare what we know to be
indisputable facts, because it's safer to do so. Our beliefs become sacrosanct
and our understanding of purpose and meaning in life is explained and
demystified within the confines of our adopted beliefs.

If we question our purpose in life, there are at least 7 billion answers. And
when we create an answer, our essential being is unaffected. The Self will
not be explained, felt or analyzed; it is our divine being-ness, One Spirit.

April 18

World Peace

To work for peace is to uproot war from ourselves and from the hearts of men and women. – *Thich Nhat Hanh*, Living Buddha, Living Christ

There is a requirement for world peace that many would reject; we must give up the idea of "I." Although the idea of world peace brings a warm feeling to our hearts, the supreme sacrifice of downplaying the concept of "I" gets in the way. As long as we express ourselves according to our individual desires, perspectives, and beliefs about ourselves as individual bodies moving through the world, we will continue to experience conflicts.

We humans contribute to the expansion of desire by our essential and nonessential expressions of needs. We have difficulty creating space in our lives for the different needs and desires of "others." The identity of "I" is an idea of the mind that perpetuates the illusion of separation; we believe that there is always an "other" in competition for our possessions. Language seals the separation by assigning different names to similar experiences of the created reality we call our world: my stuff and your stuff. Our words limit us because they place boundaries on what is our direct experience, so we resort to metaphors, parables and stories to encourage understanding. But the ultimate reality is that peace already exists throughout the universe, but our belief in a separate self that is threatened by the contrasting desires of others, keeps us from experiencing peace. When we acknowledge our interconnection with all others, we discover the seeds of conflict within ourselves. Only then are we positioned to release the peace within us to change the world.

April 19

Grounding in Spirit

If a thing loves, it is infinite. – *William Blake*
Annotations to Swedenborg (1788)

Video reports from space shuttle missions often show astronauts floating around the cabin of the spacecraft. Without the gravitational field surrounding the earth, we would all float aimlessly through space. We could not be grounded, attached and solidly fixed to the earth. The concept of being grounded is popular as a metaphor for stability in the midst of stress or struggle. While grounding to the earth may be explained scientifically as the effects of gravity, the grounding in spirit is the effect of knowing-awareness. Our grounding in faith provides direction and focus, but the source of spiritual grounding is found in the awareness of our true self. In the present moment we discover that the ground of spirit is deep and unfathomable, yet we are aware of our belonging to All-That-Is. The infinite nature of our essence is like the breathtaking beauty of space. We are in the present just *being*, with the absence of thoughts and feelings. When we stand in the present moment with Spirit and settle into silent, full awareness, we sink into the grounded-ness of Love.

April 20

Masks

Love takes off the masks that we fear we cannot live without and know we cannot live within. – *James Baldwin,* The Fire Next Time

In the popular musical, *The Phantom of the Opera*, a man wears a mask to cover his disfigurement, but underneath the mask is his true, loving self. For many of us, life's struggles have left dings and bruises that we may try to cover up; some of the effects have plunged deeply into our self-concepts. As a result of the deep wounds, we have become vulnerable and ashamed.

We have created stories about what is beautiful or pleasant to the eye, or what is acceptable to others, but they are convenient, false standards that change as ideas and standards change. As long as we react to standards, we live in continual fear of disapproval. Feeling the pressure to conform, we begin, after some time, to incorporate the mask into who we are as human beings; we begin to believe our own myths and have difficulty determining the truth of who we are. But eventually the mask comes off, since the weight of deception is heavier than we first imagined it could be.

If we could experience the loving beauty within us, the flowering essence that is our precious being, we would slough off the many masks we wear and reveal the essential self that we are. The natural world of plants, animals and minerals wear no masks. They *know* that life is truth and the differences they bring to life are the essence of beauty in the universe. Our natural, untouched essence is universal perfection. We are the shining examples of what the universe is and will always be.

April 21

Firsts and Origins

In our zeal to become the landlord of our own being, we cling to each achievement as a kind of verification of our self–proclaimed reality. – *Dr. James Finley*, Merton's Palace of Nowhere

Being first or original is overrated; the distinction feeds the egos of those of us who crave significance. Our society rewards those who claim to be first, and boosts egos of originators, yet no one of us acts alone, without a supporting cast. We may agree that we are all connected spiritually, but our lives are interconnected in ways that may not seem obvious. Firsts imply a singular, disconnected event or series of events. We discover animals, lands, lakes and waterfalls that already exist. We invent things that are constructed of already existing materials, compounds, herbs and minerals. We isolate a thing and call it ours, even though we cannot own anything.

Our devotion to being first or original is grounded in a story that first is better and anything that is original deserves recognition. Often the firsts or originals are intended to compensate for current perceived inadequacies or inferiorities. There is nothing inferior or inadequate about anyone; such perceptions are delusions that generate conflicts and divisions. We are all perfect, essential beings, precious in our expressions of love and compassion. When we know who we are, we have no need for vacant superiority. There is a first that we can rely on: we know that every moment is a first and every breath could be our last; that awareness is both exciting and humbling.

April 22

Parallel Universe

To remain stable is to refrain from trying to separate yourself
from pain because you cannot. Running away from fear
is fear, fighting pain is pain, trying to be brave is being
scared. – *Alan Watts*, The Wisdom of Insecurity

Critically injured people sometimes enter a comatose state when the body
can no longer sustain consciousness of trauma. Human bodies exist during
that time in a parallel universe: one external reality and one unconscious
state. We also know that often during the unconscious state people can
hear words and sense the presence of others, but cannot respond. They
exist in the world without the painful connection to it.

The losses and traumas of our lives can leave us existing in a parallel
universe, one that is active, and another that is passive. In the active
universe, our daily life continues with responsibilities and routines, while
the passive world is experienced in slow motion as if we are staggering from
a stomach punch. The unified reality we created for ourselves no longer
exists; and we struggle to make sense of how we are feeling. The truth
that emerges is that our created reality is unreliable as a standard bearer
for essential truth; but the passive universe we have created for our self-
protection is unstable as well. We realize that what we create in our lives
are illusions or images of reality. Nothing we have created is solid enough
to lean on or be certain of; but our essential self knows no death or loss,
no tragedy or trauma, and no false images. The divine presence within
us, *Essential Truth*, knows no suffering. If we are still, we can embrace the
consciousness of a transcendent peace, so pervasive that we can live with
the pain of life without suffering.

April 23

Symbols

Words have value; what is of value in words is meaning.
Meaning has something it is pursuing, but the thing that
it is pursuing cannot be put into words and handed down."
— *Zhuangzi*, The Complete Works of Chuang Tzu

The well-known recording artist and musician, Prince, once suspended the use of his name and substituted it for a symbol. He became the symbol. During the time of suspension, he did not only possess the symbol but the symbol became a recognizable representation of Prince without ever becoming the person it stood for.

Symbols are the shorthand for an idea. A symbol of reality is not reality itself. A symbol of peace is not peace itself, and a symbol of love is not love itself. Beliefs can form a system of symbols so convincing that we can begin to accept those symbols as the thing itself – love, truth, righteousness. We suffer under the illusion that the created symbols are equivalent to what they represent; and over time as the system of beliefs congeal into "the *only* love, truth or righteousness" we become convinced that the symbols are the truth. Our signs and symbols begin to speak for us, like logos or personal brands.

Our true selves get buried under the illusions of the symbols. Empty words become symbols for actions, feelings, and ideas. Words are powerful only in their inadequacy to describe the thing they can only represent. Greed and hatred become symbols for fearful thoughts; we grasp to prevent loss, and hate to prevent rejection or perceived harm. Regardless of the symbols we use to represent us or our ideas, we use symbols that obscure who we are. Regardless of the symbolic behaviors or thoughts, the essence of who we are does not change. We could choose the simplicity of being our true self, and give up the limitations of symbols and symbolic actions.

April 24

Homesickness

Truth is not something outside to be discovered, it is something inside to be realized. – *Osho*, Meeting the Challenge of Life's Difficulties

All sickness is homesickness – a desire to come home to the essential self; we become misaligned with our essence and our bodies react. Our natural state is well-being and health, so when we begin to feel dis-ease, we have begun to move out of alignment with our essential self.

The collection of bricks, mortar, wood, grasses and concrete that we typically call home does not constitute our true home. We may feel a sense of comfort awash with energy and the presence of those we love in our physically constructed home, but that is not home. When we become dis-eased and lack a sense of well-being, we may initially miss our physical structure that we call home, because it seems familiar and safe, but there is another home, one that is free of suffering. The home that we crave is not only peaceful; it is here, in the present moment, where all is well. Our place of well-being cannot be found in the past or the future; our wellness is real and therefore can only be found in the present moment with All-That-Is. When we release our clinging to thoughts, still our mind, surrender our desire to control events, and allow our divine energy to be present in our awareness, we have come home. We have a home that exists in the breath of stillness; it is all the love and healing we need.

April 25

Sitting with Feelings

The whole world would have been destroyed if compassion did not put an end to anger. – *Seneca,* Declarations of the Elder Seneca, translation from Michael Winterbottom

A businessman hits back at every opportunity, so that any criticism is deflected immediately as self-protection. After a long day of meetings, he goes to his hotel room and discovers that burn marks have appeared on his hands. Nevertheless, he takes time to send messages to his critics to put them in their place, in spite of the pain of typing the messages.

Like holding a hot coal in our hands, when we resent others or feel the anger of envy, we burn ourselves repeatedly. We enter into an emotional tennis match in an effort to win the game of life, but life is an infinite game, without winners and losers.

If we stop and sit with our feelings, we could feel the corrosive, burning energy of our feelings, and fully comprehend the damage that we are doing to ourselves. We could watch as the feelings arise - the heat and the pain - and question their usefulness. We could just sit with the discomfort, noticing how it influences us. We could notice how we convince ourselves that we are justified in our anger, and believe the thin arguments for our continued anguish. We could sense the moment when the feeling loses its anchor, and shows its true nature.

When we sit quietly and face the fear and tension that vibrate at the base of our feelings, we begin to feel self-compassion for the false ideas of the mind that have taken hold of us. When we stay with the feelings that arise for as long as we can, until the fear transforms into self-forgiveness, we can free ourselves from the grasp of its fingers. As we emerge from that smoldering place, we see our true selves, and reclaim our emotional balance. We regain an awareness of our true self, and find the joy of allowing our feelings to come and go.

April 26

Addictions

Do not look for rest in any pleasure, because you were not created for pleasure; you were created for spiritual joy. – *Thomas Merton*, New Seeds of Contemplation

Two buddies, Pain and Pleasure, decided to take a vacation together. They had a lot in common so they thought they would enjoy themselves. People were not friendly to Pain but Pleasure was a social butterfly; everyone sought her company. *Pain*fully shy, Pain wasn't very outgoing, often hiding his true personality; he could be aggressive at times when he was provoked. Pleasure was a seeker, always looking for a good time, but often becoming disappointed when happiness seemed so fleeting. The more Pain sulked in the room, the more Pleasure sought new excitement; and the more Pleasure went out alone, the lonelier she felt. One day, Pleasure started to avoid Pain, but she was still unhappy. Neither Pain nor Pleasure knows who they really are.

One of the difficulties in managing addictions is the blindness to the needs fulfilled with the behaviors. We may be attached to views of ourselves that do not serve us, and then act to soothe the resulting insecurities. We drink not only to escape the pain but to punish ourselves for perceived failures. We eat to soothe our stress because we feel responsible for what is challenging in our lives. We shop with abandon or hoard objects because we think material objects will love us more than people. We attach ourselves to perceived pleasures in order to *escape* and then realize that we cannot hide from ourselves.

The whole truth is that what we are seeking is the Love we are. Like white on rice, it is stuck to us as our very nature. We look for it but we are what we're looking for. There is no one or no thing outside of us that can add more love to us. We are the love we seek. We are complete as we are; we only need to free ourselves from the limits we place on ourselves by assuming that we are not enough.

April 27

Never Born

Love all things, born and unborn. – *Ndidi,* Tea Leaves

Different interest groups continually make their cases for when life begins. Some say that life begins at conception, and others claim that life begins when a fetus is viable. Scientists explore the evolution of species, and provide information about who we have been, what we are and how we continue to evolve. The questions about life and birth consume the attention of both activists and scientists.

What if we are never born? Origins and beginnings are tough because there is an antecedent to everything. The idea of being born implies a beginning; the disputes about the beginning of life are based in how to describe a beginning, but what if there is only a continuation never a beginning? Where do sperm and eggs come from? Can we locate their beginning? When were *they* born?

Like thoughts, our existence seems to originally appear out of nothing, but there is always something before that *nothing.* If we trace our ancestry back far enough, we as present day humans did not exist. Who existed before us? We could say that life begins with an amoeba or some unknown creature, but what existed before that creature? How far back must we go to establish the beginning of life?

Societies and religious communities have creation stories, but which one is true? No human being was likely present during any of the stories. No amount of research, discovery or opinion will satisfy the question. Each camp of believers can show little evidence, so they rely on their chosen beliefs.

We could regard life as a cycle. We could say that we were never born because energy just is, and we are energy. Suppose that we are born only to the true self, the expression of being that has existed for an eternity and has an infinite life expectancy. We could then acknowledge that our perspectives on the beginning of life are simply a time or event that we arbitrarily designate.

An alternative question is: Can we love life in all its forms, unseen life, young and defenseless, or mature and experienced? Does the length of time in our company make a difference in whether we regard life as important to save or respect? We could become aware of our relationship with life, and the way in which our love and compassion for others expresses in our lives. We could commit to lead our lives with loving kindness for all life, never born, unborn and living, and acknowledge our connection to everything that lives, breathes and exists in consciousness.

April 28

Broken Heart

When painful feelings arise, we breathe them in, opening to our
own suffering and the suffering of everyone else who is feeling
the same way. Then we send relief to us all. – *Pema Chödrön,*
Living Beautifully with Uncertainty and Change

After consecutive days of weeks of relative calm, our peace is disturbed
with a challenge. As we mature, we realize that expecting conditions to
remain calm is foolhardy, but we are often still surprised by the anxiety
that conditions seem to bring.

Occasional distractions or challenges pale in comparison to heartache; no
pain seems to plunge deeper into our soul than conditions of the heart.
We say the heart is broken, as if it fails to function properly. Whether the
brokenness comes suddenly or builds momentum over time, an assaulted
heart burns deeply within us. We understand that it is natural for us to
try to avoid pain, but there is no way to avoid the pain of a broken heart;
rather than avoid it we simply hope to be able to endure the ache for as
long as it remains with us.

Heartbreak is a dramatic event. We can shift our attention from the players
in our heartbreak drama to the heartbreak pain itself. What is true about
our drama? In what ways are we suffering instead of aching? What must we
let go of? What is true and what is a story based in our truth? The answers
to the questions point us in the direction of healing.

We can become aware of the energy we are using to maintain the pain,
and how we are experiencing the present moment, or ignore it in favor of

clinging to the past. We could notice the steady release of pressure from the shock or hurt, and breathe into it.

Or, we could stay with the pain and know that we are not alone in our pain. Life experiences may seem personal but they are universally felt. When we breathe into the pain and with the healing breath find relief, we can know that we are finding relief for all sentient beings who are experiencing similar pain. What we do for ourselves, we do for others. When we emerge from the suffering, we invite others to come with us.

April 29

Craving Significance

I am an expression of the divine, just like a peach is, just like a fish is. I have a right to be this way... – *Alice Walker*, The Color Purple

For a variety of reasons, we may at times become self-conscious or overly interested in what others think of us. We may believe that another person's approval or disapproval will make a difference in our lives. The external focus of our attention is a symptom of our desire to be significant, and as a result of that significance to be loved. We announce our desires for recognition, respect, and high regard with our words and actions. With a false presentation of the self, we hand over our self-respect, self-regard and knowledge of self to others, and ask them to know us. But without knowing ourselves, what we offer others is a representation of who we want to be.

When we crave significance, we don't know ourselves; we don't know who we are. Our trickster egos have once again convinced us that the only way to be loved is to prove we are worthy. This is a futile mental exercise, since we are always loved; we are love expressed in this world. We can turn the spotlight inward and discover all that we are. We are priceless potential existing in a life of abundant loving energy. We can be conscious of the expanse of life, the significance of being here and now, and the perfect Presence of spirit in whose energy we rest.

April 30

A Channel, Not a Vessel

Choose to be a channel of thoughts; let them
flow through you. – *Ndidi,* Tea Leaves

Water becomes stagnant when it is trapped and unable to flow; it is the movement of water that keeps it alive. The river bed is a basin with an open end, a crucible for active life. But even a lake, bounded by land, flows with a limited destination. Our minds have a relentless flow of ideas that can either flow freely through our life experiences, or they can be grasped and become the raw materials for behaviors and actions.

The mind is a *channel* of thought, and although thought is not a thing, when we accept a thought and take action based on the thought we have accepted, it begins to take form. We can call it a thought-form, a created reality. Our relationship with thoughts is intangible; since we cannot touch illusory thoughts, we can only react to them. There's no "time" to respond to the thought since a *thought-life* is fleeting. We may choose to think a thought repeatedly, but it will never stay for long, without our calling it back again and again. If we get stuck in a relationship with a thought, we become its vessel. Like a parasite, it settles in and shifts into an obsession, sometimes a destructive one. It interrupts our awareness of the present moment, and holds us captive. We can choose to be a channel or a vessel. A channel allows thoughts to flow through the mind without judgment. When we are a vessel, we hold onto thoughts as they emerge, grasping the tails and paths of the thoughts intending to create new paths. The thought in the vessel is like a crucible for fears and anxieties. The thought in a channel moves on before it has a chance to become a reason to suffer.

May 1

Authenticity

Fear narrows the little entrance to our heart. It shrinks up our capacity to love. – *Thomas Merton*, Ash Wednesday Essay

Imagine a world without pretense, an authentic world where what you see is indeed what you get. It is a world where everything is real; disguises are tossed aside for truth. For some of us, such a world would be frightening; without the safety of pretense our fearful, unpredictable world would be difficult to navigate. Fear masquerades as a guardian of truth, even though it is a liar. The bare truth exposes the lie: fear is an irrational response to a possibility. If we live with fear too long, the lie becomes the truth for us; the disguise becomes so convincing that removing it is devastating.

In the present moment, all the work of maintaining fear dissolves as the myth it always was, and loving-awareness is visible as who we are and have always been. The life of fear depends upon the absence of love, and that is never a possibility. Love frees us to be who we are, lift the shackles of fear and just be our authentic selves.

May 2

Liftoff

Life is available only in the present
moment. – *Thich Nhat Hanh*, Taming the Tiger Within:
Meditation on Transforming Difficult Emotions

As an airplane speeds down the runway, an exhilarating feeling emerges as we prepare for liftoff. The engines thrust the plane into the air and into the miracle of flight. The plane does not pierce the sky; it is one with it. A stone is thrown into a lake; the stone creates beautiful concentric ripples as it makes its way into the water. The water yields to the entry and celebrates the beauty of the circular movements. The plane and the stone are metaphors for the way life yields to us, and allows us to choose our path. Sometimes the resistance we feel is an internal thrust of powerful energy or a heaviness that sinks us. Without perceived barriers to our joy, we can celebrate the miracle of our lives.

We live in the world of awareness, where every moment is a miracle, and where the act of being alive is our greatest freedom. There are no barriers to being, just union. There are no barriers to loving, just communion. When we know who we are, we are free. When we have freedom from a fearful mind, we feel whole. When we are free, boundaries dissolve, old hurts heal, and the doors to peace stay open. There are no barriers to freedom; we must know the power of our being, find our wings, and prepare for liftoff in the present moment. We can then allow joy to lift us up every day.

May 3

Washing Away Sorrow

No more my heart shall sob or grieve. My days and nights dissolve in God's own Light. – *Sri Chinmoy,* My Flute (1972)

The tears on the face of a sad clown are a fascinating statement about sorrow; the tears are a contrast to the idea of fun and games as pleasant, evoking laughter or joy. Beneath the fun lies a reservoir of sorrow that can be overcome with a huge smile, but sorrow in our lives may be challenging to overcome.

When sorrow comes into our lives it can feel like a huge paperweight on our chest, pressing down heavily and relentlessly. Unless we are aware of our true self, we may forget to breathe under the pressure, and as the pressure builds, so does our need for release. Our tears stay locked up in a corner of our awareness, like an underground tsunami of despair, until we erupt in anger or deep anxiety. As if we are holding our breath, we know that we are holding residual pain that has settled into our consciousness and disturbed our sense of peace. A simple memory or word can trigger the eruption and the pretense of propriety dissolves under the pressure. When the tears flow, they wash away memories we are holding onto: the tears flood us with relief in knowing that life is loving in all its changes. All-That-Is fills us up with peace, and the promise that even when the last breath is taken, the Presence of Love will remain. Joy removes the pressure of regret and the ways we beat up ourselves for mistakes we have made. The sobbing wrenches up the self-assessments buried deep within us and allows them to be expelled. Our trembling as we cry shakes loose the uncontrollable fears of the future. When the last tear has dropped, and the pain has been soothed by our surrender to what is, joy beckons us to return to a state of peace.

May 4

Animal Love

*I have lived with several Zen masters – all of them
cats. – Eckhart Tolle, The Power of Now*

We have positive, negative or neutral responses to animals, whether the animal is domesticated or wild. The human-animal bond was studied years ago as an experiment in improving mental and physical health. More recently, dogs have been used with different populations, such as persons recovering from strokes and heart disease to accelerate recovery. Prisoners have benefitted from opportunities to train service dogs, leading to prisoners' improved social and interpersonal skills. Human-animal bonding has been suspected in the rise of two hormones: oxytocin and vasopressin. Oxytocin is associated with positive social interaction. Vasopressin when released into the brain plays a role in stress reduction and also improvement in social behavior.

When an animal is domesticated, a particular bond occurs, one that can have significant benefits. Domestication is not the only interaction with animals that awakens the mind and spirit. We can hear the songs of birds, the purr of cats, the neighs of horses, the hum of bees or the croak of frogs. We can watch the whales, ride horses or camels, talk to parrots or revel in the majesty of the elephant. The rainforest, savannah or outback is alive with sounds of our animal beings; they are all part of the cosmos. Whether we love them closely or from afar, they can be honored for who they are.

May 5

Fearless

Let us not pray to be sheltered from dangers but to be fearless when facing them. – *Rabindranath Tagore, Collected Poems and Plays of Rabindranath Tagore*

Death is the parent of fear. Without the fear of death, or our idea of death as our ultimate disappearance from the universe, we would gleefully live fully in each moment. With an active fear of death, we exist in a self-protective reality where our mind convinces us that danger and uncertainty are imminent threats to our existence. As a result of our life on the edge of disaster, we fill our lives with plans that we hope will make our future real rather than tentative. We engage in activities to ensure that our lives mean something to others; and we talk about leaving a legacy of our accomplishments. We search for a purpose in being alive and try to pour as much as possible into our future because of our sense of incompleteness in the present. We think all these thoughts, but deny our persistent fears. Defying evidence of our mortality, we pretend that this life will proceed into our designed future, until the truth stuns us with the transition of someone close to us.

If we set aside those worries and fears, we can see clearly that life indeed does not stop, but it will change form. Our only certainty is the truth of the present moment: we are eternal beings with temporary bodies. In this time-space we call now, we are the continuation of life. We are on a relay journey that never started and will never end. The baton is in our hands and each step is a miracle.

May 6

Myth of Superiority

You are an ocean in a drop of dew, all the universes in a
thin sack of blood. What are these pleasures then, these
joys, these worlds, that you keep reaching for, hoping they
will make you more alive? – *Rumi,* A Year with Rumi

If we think we are superior to others, we have constructed an illusion that
is easily discredited; we have voluntarily clouded our awareness of self. Our
cartoon superheroes always have limitations, including "powers" that can
be diminished if their Achilles heel is discovered. As superheroes, they need
a disguise; a useful metaphor for the false identity that the ego encourages
in us. The strength of the superhero is used to destroy "enemies" and save
the good from the tyranny of the bad. The myth of superiority is that by
virtue of extraordinary knowledge, skills or talents, the heroes will make
all things new.

As long as we divide the world into good people and bad people, the
superhero is necessary. The superhero myth will always necessitate a
companion myth: the world is unsafe. There are misguided people in
the world, who are a reflection of the dangerous myth we are continually
creating. We make the superheroes possible because we are demanding
their presence. We are creating the roles of both superhero and villain,
because we have created a need to feel safe, and a need to create chaos to
justify our fears.

The universe is unfolding perfectly. Our fears are illusions just as the
rescuing superheroes are products of our imaginations. There is only one
of us, not us and them, one universal embrace.

May 7

Discovery

One cannot help but be in awe when one contemplates the
mysteries of eternity, of life, of the marvelous structure of reality. –
Albert Einstein, quoted in Life magazine, May 2, 1955

Creative people are developing technological, scientific and social solutions
for the world's problems. Each tries to discover new landscapes or uncover
new mysteries using knowledge and skills they have acquired. As they
communicate the excitement they feel about their discoveries, the light
of purpose and significance shines from within them. Their work has
integrity because it is integrated with the whole of existence; it emerges
from the union of all knowledge, all ideas and solutions. Even though the
invention or insight may be specific in its characteristics, the creation is an
iteration of what has always been known at the cosmic level of existence. In
a world where the illusion is that everything is separate and distinguished
by its uniqueness, innovation is regarded as a breakthrough, arising out of
the ethers of intelligence.

What remains obscured by this story is the nature of the self, the non-
separate, true self that does not invent what is already available. Like
Columbus discovering inhabited lands, or scientists discovering new
planets or galaxies, the existence is not dependent upon the discoverer's
awareness. Our awareness is an opportunity to reveal for ourselves and
others what is already present. The universe exists as one energy, one All-
That-Is; we experience the true self, all of creation, in our awareness. We
already know what we "discover," our work is to remember.

May 8

Heart Choices

It is our choices, Harry, that show what we truly are, far more than our abilities. — *J.K. Rowling*, Harry Potter and the Chamber of Secrets

We are faced with choices every moment when we live in a dualistic world. We dread the consequences of "bad" choices and celebrate the "good" ones. Our assessment of what's good and bad is based on experiences, guidance from others or fear. We consider right and wrong, useful and not useful, appropriate and inappropriate, but still face hard choices, each of which, according to our assessments, could end badly for us. Although separating our experiences into opposing options provides no foolproof method of predicting outcomes, we persist.

As long as we try to make a choice between this and that, we remain in internal conflict. When we stay with what is, the present moment of being, an answer emerges from the heart. When we are appreciative of the way things are, the way things are, changes. If we are making a choice, we are thinking about the future, the next moment, hour, or day when something will happen. In the present moment all is known. When we ponder the choices, choosing none, the answer emerges like cream rising to the top of a jar containing whole milk. Instead of shaking things up or separating the cream from what remains, we experience deeply the sweetness of both.

May 9

Clinging

Thanks to impermanence, everything is possible. – *Thich Nhat Hanh,*
Going Home: Jesus and Buddha as Brothers

Clinging to another is like clinging to water; he will either evaporate
from the sustained heat of our body or flow away from us. The desire
for a relationship with another is not the source of suffering, but the
impossibility of maintaining things as they are over the long-term is
a recipe for disappointment. The temporary state of everything is the
problem, or more accurately, the reality. Whenever we grasp something,
we are investing in an impermanent relationship.

Everything in the universe comes and goes, except our true self. Because
the true self always exists, clinging to it is unnecessary. The true self has no
form, so there is nothing to change; the coming and going of everything
in our reality is the result of its having a form in our mind. Our reality
is created from our thoughts; and we create perspectives about our world
based on what we sense. The world we see is limited by our perception of
reality, so what we see and what others see is different. Clinging expects
others to be what we expect them to be. Since our reality is composed of
our mental images, based on impermanent aspects, what we cling to will
never remain, except in our minds.

When we release our grip on our created reality, suffering subsides. We can
love what is present now, not with clinging but with appreciation.

May 10

Shining Light

Give us the inner listening that is a way in itself and the
oldest thirst there is... You cannot touch me, but your light
fills the ocean where I live. – *Rumi,* A Year with Rumi

In the depths of meditation, the light of our eternal breath moves and
shines brightly. The light is always present, even though we sometimes
hide it "under a bush." Our light is hidden when we focus on what is not
working in our lives, instead of what *is* working. We could follow that light
and become aware of the Source of our being. With each breath, the light
becomes who we are, and the body loses its prominence. Freed from the
focus on the body as evidence that we exist, we are free to love. Freed from
the belief that life is limited, we are free to discover our true self.

We can stay with the glowing light within, or sacrifice our reunion with
the true self and return to a false consciousness. In a world where we lack
connection, we can feel vulnerable; we cling to illusions of safety, even
though we know that the body is temporary. Our clinging to temporary
world images can be frustrating.

When our anger toward ourselves is directed toward others our light is
dimmed. Like a boomerang, the anger comes back to us in full force as
a message of unworthiness and fear. When we forget who we are and
smother our consciousness in illusions of separateness, we also smother
our purpose. When we let go of doubts about our purpose, and realize
that we are here in this life to experience every joyful moment we awaken
the light within us.

May 11

What was That?

When I discover who I am, I'll be free. — *Ralph Ellison*, Invisible Man

When we react inelegantly to what someone has done, we may on reflection wonder what really happened. We can easily develop a dramatic story about being wronged or misjudged, but unless we have buried our anger in an inaccessible place, we have strong feelings about what happened. Our stories become strikingly similar to ones we have drafted before, so over time, a pattern develops. We may begin to wonder why these things keep happening to us. Our "why" questions seem to yield few answers, frustrating us further.

Friends may commiserate with us about how we have been mistreated, and may add their own stories. Although our intent in sharing our troubles with others is to justify our anger, we soon realize that justification does not make us feel better about the hurt we feel. Our stories mask the real issue for us: the failure to ask "What was that?" Our inquiry is two-fold: What was that familiar interaction that I just had, and "What was that I just felt?" Our anger is so powerful that it masks the hurt and disappointment that threatens our sense of well-being. But the "What was That?" also invites us to look deeply at what the anger and possibly fear points to, deep within us. What makes us vulnerable to the hurt and diminishment? The answer always lies within us. It may be unresolved anxiety over past events, diminished self-confidence, or feeling unloved by someone significant in our lives.

Lodged in the pain of the past is a trigger that gets activated when something familiar happens. When we ask, "What was that?" we begin to face the trigger that lurks deeply within our consciousness waiting to have a reason to be resolved. We cannot control other people, and know that we can control ourselves, but we must take the time to ask the questions, and breathe into the answers. We can set aside the worries and fears associated with pain when we ask the questions that help us to face ourselves.

May 12

Simplicity

Nothing is simple in a complex, diverse world. – *Ndidi,* Tea Leaves

We sometimes reminisce about times long ago when things were simpler. Our romantic notions about the past are enhanced by difficulties we may experience with current conditions. Comparisons are ways we convince ourselves that our story is based in truth, and that what we are experiencing now should be better. We crave simplicity because we have no resolution for the story we see unfolding in our lives. We become worried that life will not return to a time when we felt more in control of outcomes, and that our current life story will always be difficult to manage.

We may think that everything would improve if we simply had more money, more education, or more conveniences. In contrast, we may think fewer things - problems or unhappy relationships - would make us happier. Our egoic minds convince us that what we have now is not ideal, so we desire something different. Uncomfortable conditions do not require new desires, but rather clarity about what is actually happening now. But now is often sacrificed as we long for the future, or a different time. Despite our discomfort with changes or struggle, it has the advantage of clarifying conditions; when we see clearly, possible changes can emerge. What we are seeking is the release from fear, with a desire to sense a state of peace. Joy is seeing the true self and knowing that struggle is the result of our own chaotic story, and that peace is always present.

May 13

Blame

When you blame others, you give up your
power to change. – *Anonymous*

Life can be a series of peaks and valleys. We may experience life as a roller coaster ride while others ride along a smooth highway with occasional bumps in the road. Whether we experience a deep valley or a bump, the worry is often whether or not we will recover. The ego sets us up to see the roller coaster of life as real danger as we are carried along with the twists and turns of our story. Whatever happens in our lives is a story produced and directed by our egoic mind. We isolate events or scenes in the story and then make those scenes the entire story, but an accurate story is filled with ups and downs. We may have responsibility for the choices we make as we develop the story along the road, but we miss the joy of the journey if we choose to blame others for our choices.

The bumps in the road cause us to stop or slow down but the bumps are not separate from the road; they are the road. The mountain does not blame the valley nestled below it; and the valley does not long for the height of the mountain; each knows the other is necessary for its own existence. When we are still, we are aware of the full story. The valleys give rise to the peaks; and when we are in the valley we can look up. On top of the mountain, the air may be thin but the view is magnificent; we can enjoy it while it lasts. The twists and turns of our life script make us aware of our resilience and flexibility. We are not only the actors in our life play; we are the play – every scene, every message, every change. We are the playwrights of our story of joy, but blame is a tool of the ego that robs us of joy.

May 14

Mindful

You must learn to be still in the midst of activity
and to be vibrantly alive in repose. – *Indira Gandhi,*
quoted in People magazine, June 30, 1975

For the mind that is still, the world is a place of peace, a place with no worries or fears. In the stillness, awareness is the state of being. The wordless, voiceless state of awareness takes us beyond the mind, feelings, and actions into a place of just knowing. In stillness, the veil of our life story is lifted, and we rest in a state of fearlessness. In the thinking world, we plan, set goals, take actions and have judgments about our lives. In stillness, the feelings and thoughts that emerge are not given form. Without thinking about goals; we settle into being, with no agenda. A still mind has clarity about what the reality of the world is showing us.

When we are mindful, every aspect of our lives has meaning. With heightened awareness of things as they are, rather than as we want them to be, we experience a sense of wholeness. Every movement we make is made with vibrant awareness. When we sit, we just sit; when we walk, we just walk; and when we chant, we just chant. Our prayers are rich with passion and our reverence for life is complete. When we take the time to be still, we realize who we are, and fear leaves us like an unwanted guest.

May 15

Asking for Help

There's a crack in everything…that's how the light
gets in. – *Leonard Cohen*, The Future (1992)

There are times when the challenges of our lives feel too large for us to handle. We realize that where we have sought guidance has been insufficient. We ask family and friends for help, but their own challenges prohibit them from being able to help. We seek help from organizations -religious and secular- and although they may soothe us, the challenges remain. Acknowledging the need for help humbles us sometimes to the point of shame. In our eyes, asking for help makes us vulnerable and imperfect.

But we are not broken or damaged; any crack in our armor of perfection is an opening to truth. The story we have created is an illusion: the challenges, the vulnerability, and the shame. The ego has orchestrated the drama that plays out in our mind and heart with a script filled with false images. The essence of our being is the true self where suffering is a belief in our documentary of what we call the "real" world.

Deep within is the help we desire, the reconnection with the Source of our being. When we touch the glory of our true self, from our natural compassion, we want that awareness and relief for everyone who has ever experienced the pain we have felt. When we close down the destructive play, we do so for all beings who have written the same play in their lives. We have said that one person can make a difference in the world; we now know that our true self-awareness is spiritual liberation from suffering for all sentient beings.

May 16

Framing

Release attachments to events you have framed
in your mind. – *Ndidi,* Tea Leaves

Mental health professionals have often suggested that we reframe anxiety-producing situations to give ourselves a different perspective, possibly leading to new strategies for healing. Seeing through a different "frame" can change what we are experiencing dramatically. The downside of reframing is that it can deflect attention away from the direct experience of the pain of a condition in our lives. As long as we avoid pain, we also avoid the experience of it in its fullness, and give up the possibility of releasing it. If we turn away from pain, we will repeatedly experience its insistence on being acknowledged. Pain is a signal to us that there is something to pay attention to, but if we linger too long with our pain, it becomes a barrier to peace and joy.

The body feels pain but so does the heart. The pain in the heart is of a different origin; emotional pain arises out of unrealized desires propagated by the mind and *framed* according to those desires. The frame is a way to falsely solidify our story as unique to our individual self. Pain is a reality in our lives, but our response to it is an opportunity to assert our inherent power; the pain itself is not our identity, it is a physical or emotional response to changes in the body or the heart.

Our lives are transient stories that change each moment, and when we hold onto any piece of it, we suffer. We may choose to see changes and challenges as messages for us, but if we identify too strongly with the messages, we will struggle to move on when conditions change. We may ask ourselves whether we are looking out of the frames we have constructed around our experiences, or are we looking into our frames to find a morsel of truth. When we get out of the frames we have entered in our hearts and minds, we begin to experience the release from suffering.

May 17

Honoring the World

Constantly regard the universe as one living being, having one substance and one soul; and observe how all things have reference to one perception, the perception of this one living being; and how all things act with one movement. – *Marcus Aurelius*, Meditations

The world of form we are experiencing includes all sentient beings. These humans, animals, marine life, plants and other aspects of our visible and invisible universe create an ecosystem of reality that sustains us. In the continual evolution of the universe, all living things are interconnected with us as life evolves.

When we disturb the natural web of life in the universe, we make adaptations necessary over time. The self-correcting universe is creative energy producing more and more diversity as it expresses in life. When we honor everything in the universe, we recognize the power of one spirit, expressing as everything, everywhere in every way. We recognize that when one part of the world passes on or any part of the universe withers, it resurrects as transformed energy. We know that when we honor the animals that become food, the plants that produce seeds, the flowers that eventually produce honey, and the springs that produce waters, we experience our interconnection. We do not weep for the changes in the world, the changes and transformations are necessary. We honor the sacrifices of every living thing as contributions to the continuance of life.

May 18

Windows and Mirrors

Trying to define yourself is like trying to bite your own
teeth. – *Alan Watts*, The Essential Alan Watts

The brain is a trickster. If we look into a mirror we see an image of ourselves, but we can never actually see the self. Our lives are lived not in direct experience, but in a series of secondary impressions of the experiences. Our mirrors cloud the true experience of life, just as our daily life experiences cloud the experience of the true self. The intervening variable that clouds everything we sense is the egoic mind. If we look into a mirror the mind will soon invite us to focus on some aspect of the image in the mirror; we will not focus on the whole image. The mind may want us to become dissatisfied with parts of the image and focus on flaws. Our head is too small or too large, or the nose is too narrow or too large. Although the critic begins, the mind may expect the mirror to present a more accurate image that is more flattering, and will encourage us to blame the mirror or the lighting. After a period of time, we may grow increasingly uncomfortable looking at ourselves, and then turn away. The mind attempts to control our experiences, pleasant or unpleasant. Instead of looking into a mirror, we could look into a window, a window to the soul.

In the present moment all the worries, fears, and self-judgments fall away as we look through the window of joy and find peace. When we give up trying to define ourselves, find ourselves, or tailor ourselves to the requirements from others, we liberate ourselves. In time, we come to know that all is well.

May 19

Heavy Mental

Fear is always in relation to something; it does not exist
by itself. – *Jiddu Krishnamurti,* Beyond Violence

Although fears are illusions of the mind about a possible future event, their weight is heavy. The pervasive nature of fear is like the rush of water from a ruptured dam; it is sudden, unpredictable and dangerous. Fear is not always sudden; it can have a slowly damaging intensity as it lingers. Slow fear is like being placed in a box that grows smaller and smaller until we feel as if there is no place to turn for safety. The object of fear is loss – loss of life, love, comfort. When we have difficulty letting go of fear, it becomes the source of panic. The ego mind knows all of this.

The egoic mind can serve a purpose in providing choices about how to respond to conditions; we can decide whether to fight a threat or flee from it, but the ego continually overplays its hand, and paints our life experiences with a broad brush of fear. Afraid of its own demise, the ego creates fear as a way to direct our behaviors.

Ideas may enter the mind; but we don't really know the origin of the mind. We may surmise that all ideas exist as energy that flows through us, so when conditions appear, we assess with the mind their likelihood of causing our bodies to feel pain or pleasure. The mind is complex: a fearful mind sees the possibility of danger often, while a joyful mind is conscious of the peace in every life event. A joyful mind is aware and stable, because it experiences things as they are, not as they could be. We are here to experience joy, so when we flow with *what is* in the rushing waters of life, we break out of the box of fear.

May 20

Unfinished Business

This difficult living, heavy and as if all tied up, moving through that which has been left undone, is like the not–quite–finished walk of the swan. – Rainer Maria Rilke, New Poems (1907)

A woman meets a new friend for dinner after several brief meetings for coffee. He seems like the right person for her so she's excited to get to know him better. The dinner conversation seems pleasant at first, but then he starts to complain to the server about the wait for their entrees, and checks his cell phone for messages constantly. He seems to be nervous and a bit distracted. She's disappointed with his inattention, and decides he's just like all the others, especially her promiscuous ex-husband. Later, he called her to apologize, because he realized that he was inattentive and irritable during dinner. Once again, regrets from his previous failed marriages jeopardized a budding relationship.

We all live with unfinished business every day; we forget that it follows us into new relationships, into our jobs or careers, and even into our sense of self. We notice it bubbling up in conversations when we imagine that we have been slighted or diminished in some way. We notice tinges of it in our resentments or grudges. We hear ourselves complaining about how things are in the world, in our cities and neighborhoods, in our homes. It seems so current, so contemporary, those feelings that have their roots in soil with weeds. Our unfinished business continues to grow unabated, sprouting into our lives. When we know the weeds are there, we recognize the instances when they show up. If we face the ghostlike quality of their appearance, appearing out of nowhere, we can let the wounds fully heal, release them from our thoughts and move on. Life gives us the struggles with the past to clarify our present life experience. When unfinished business shows up, we can make peace with it and watch it complete its purpose in our lives. We can then wake up to joy.

May 21

Wheels Turning

A wheel has no beginning and no end; it just turns. – *Ndidi,* Tea Leaves

For thousands of years, human beings have represented the universe as a wheel. The wheels are formed similarly on cave walls, buildings, grasslands and in artwork; the circles or spirals are images of continual changes, each change capturing the evolution of life. Everything that happens in our life story is a cycle of ups and downs, happiness and sadness, fullness and emptiness. The energy that drives the cycle is the power of love. In all of life's conditions, love exists as a constant. Conditions are manifestations of temporary life that comes and goes; we are rooted in dynamic but unchanging Love.

The oak tree contains evidence of the cycle. It not only demonstrates the cycle with the changes of the seasons, and the ongoing transformations of the dying leaves into new leaves in spring; but its growth is recorded in the rings beneath its bark. The rings are more than evidence of its age; the wheels embedded in its trunk reveal the pattern and stability of its ongoing life. Like each new ring of the tree, our life goes on building from the source of our energy, the roots of our being. Embrace the wheel of life as an reliable stamp of stability. Find joy in the beautiful cycle of life.

May 22

Slowing Down

The slow dig of worms aerates the soil for seeds. – *Ndidi,* Tea Leaves

So that we can become fit, we sometimes take a brisk walk or a run in the mornings. We are committed to a healthy life, so we set aside time at the beginning of the day to become invigorated for the rest of the day. Having exhausted our energy at the end of the day, we may collapse from the constant movement. Has the day happened to us, or have we happened to the day? What did we notice during the day that stirred us or filled us up?

Many humans are in a hurry, much like a squirrel dashing across a road to capture an acorn that has just fallen from a tree. The squirrel needs to gather food, and humans need to gather information, data, and resources. The squirrel does not notice an oncoming car as she scampers across the road in anticipation of success. The acorn lying a few feet away is lost on the determined squirrel. We too scamper along missing the gifts along the way toward our goals for success, accumulation or happiness. We try to discover our purpose in a future that does not exist, and measure our worth on a past that is a collection of memories of events and emotions that have passed away. Slowing our movements allow us to gather strength, like the rhythmically flowing movements of a qigong master. Our journey in life is full of peace and free of worries in each moment. When we slow our pace, we narrow the gaps in our awareness and begin to sense the beauty in the details of our lives.

May 23

The Parable

Truth clothed in a metaphor makes it palatable. – *Ndidi,* Tea Leaves

The naked truth about our lives can seem confusing and alarming, because we live in a world of illusions – past and future. Our true nature is clothed in a body that conveniently forms an identity for us. Our collective humanity agrees that the body is a viable form in which to live a life. If the body were enough to identify us fully, we would not wonder what life means or question the purpose of our existence. Our being in the world is a mystery; we not only want to know how to live with others, but also how to live with ourselves.

Our questions do not express fully our dire cravings for answers. Throughout the ages, great teachers, philosophers and prophets have taught us through the power of the parable. Through parables, we began to understand the incomprehensible, to speak of the ineffable nature of our relationship to All-That-Is, and to become aware of the difference between our false and true selves. Parables pierce through the veil of sorrow and fear, strengthen our faith in love, and ensure us that we are never alone in the universe. Parables are pointers and guides; they lead us to truth and assure us that present awareness is possible. As representations of truth, we get a glimpse into the mysterious nature of our lives in parables, and derive peace from the different textures of truth that are free for us to explore.

May 24

Eating Mindfully

Food is spiritual energy with an infinite origin. – *Ndidi,* Tea Leaves

Like ancient objects collected for display in an art museum, each morsel of food has a provenance. Our food has a history and an origin. Before a food item has reached our home, it has been in a store, on a farm or in water. The food has lived and grown and passed through many transformations. We can be grateful to the insects that pollinate and aerate the soil, or the fish that populate the sea. Each has an origin that goes back further than we can imagine. Without a series of changes, the morsel of food we eat would not exist.

When we eat, we can appreciate the grain, trees and animals that have been yielded to evolution so that we could have nourishment. We could honor the hands through which our food has passed on the way to our table. We could feel their kindness and hard work to make this eating event happen for us. When we slow down the rhythm of our eating, we can taste the morsels, hear the voices of the farmers and workers who grow and gather food and honor the love that flows into our experience of eating. We appreciate the markets that provide the varieties of foods and the transporters who make the food available for consumption. Food is evidence of the universal spirit of transformation; the provenance of the food requires changes in the nature of living energy, and awareness of our inherent participation in those changes.

May 25

Conditions

We react when we are functioning on automatic like robots; we respond when we have matured spiritually and have developed true response–ability. – *Swami Gyankirti*, Personal communication

Frustration is an emotion most of us have felt or expressed. The emotion is triggered by events in our reality that cause discomfort. News or *blues* of the day may continually burden us with ideas of gloom and uncertainty; we powerlessly hear of horrific acts of violence or destruction and try to resist falling into the pits of depression and disillusion.

We may experience the loneliness of trying to make ourselves understood when something tragic has happened to us. We may struggle to pay debts, or to organize our lives so that resources and services we need are available. We may want our relationships to change but realize that only we can change. We may become frustrated with our lack of time to do the things we want to do, and continually live with a sense of incompletion.

In our eyes, challenges in our lives are useless distractions from our *life, liberty and pursuit of happiness*. Our external reality is comprised of the stories we create for our own learning. We want to learn what to expect from others, and what to expect from ourselves. We begin to realize that each new understanding can allow us to prepare for the next event. But often our preparation, though helpful, does not ensure that we will be safe from harm, or successful in our efforts. Conditions alert us to danger, real or unreal, but also convince us that nothing is under our control. Our desire for control and attempts to seize control of our lives will always be met with defeat. But the lack of control is a gift; without the control we are free to just be. Without control, we are free to be in the flow of love and joy in the world. We become aware of who we are in our truth.

We learn to give up our habitual reactions to painful experiences as we become familiar with how they affect us. We notice that our reactions do not end the struggles, but can often make matters worse. Instead of reacting out of fear, we can choose to respond. The choices regarding responses to conditions are the true lessons to be learned. We cannot always change the reality of our conditions, but we are always able to respond. A response occurs after a pause; during that pause an internal process weighs the various choices for an appropriate response. Within that pause is an eternity of wisdom that sits quietly in the silence. The choices presented to us are not so much what we can do, but rather who we can be in response. The false self encourages us to defend who we are, but the true self allows life to evolve and change as it always does.

Compassion emerges from awareness of our true self. Our thoughts come and go without becoming attachments; we realize that we don't believe everything we think, and that thoughts need not become actions.

We examine the origin of our feelings, and our words pass through our hearts before they are spoken. When we choose to respond, we show up with loving spirit for ourselves and others.

May 26

Synchronicity

In my world, everything is possible and everything
is relative. – *Paul Coelho,* The Zahir (2005)

Creative problem solving is a technique that some consultants use to address complex problems. Often the solutions create new problems, so those issues have to be addressed as well. The approach reveals the nature of transformative change. Every effect has a cause, sometimes more than one cause; and every cause has many far-reaching effects. When we understand the complexity of life, the idea of synchronicity means that a number of causes and effects arise in our awareness at the same time, resulting in a transformative experience of life filled with surprises.

Joyful living does not mean that we no longer encounter challenging conditions in life, but rather that we understand that every condition that appears has multiple causes and effects. Because we are aware of the complex co-dependency of causes and effects, we do not impulsively jump to conclusions, or launch a strident defense of what we see, hear or experience. Our impartiality toward various challenges, helps us to be fearless in the face of troubles. We realize that worry is like the fear of drowning in a teacup, or like struggling aimlessly in an ocean of joy.

When we are joyful, our lives become magnets for pleasure, even though our souls speak in voices we cannot hear. When we are grateful for the joy sitting underneath the challenges, we notice that conditions change, and *all things work together for good* for us. We may experience the workings of our world as synchronous events where useful parts of a plan coalesce or intersect to create the change in conditions desired. We sometimes call these alignments accidents, but there are no accidents in a self-organizing universe. We do however marvel at the way things work out, or how surprising combinations of events seem to work toward good.

The universe moves effortlessly from chaos to realignment for creative order, and then the cycle continues. Change is the constant experience of life; what seems like synchronicity is the creative process of change and transformation. As we remember who we are, our life's purpose and the nature of reality, we settle in faith and know that the world is a web of love pulsating and moving toward its best self, and we are that world.

May 27

Opinions

If you wish to see the truth then hold no opinion for or against.
The struggle of what one likes and what one dislikes is the
disease of the mind. – *Seng T'san,* Hsin Hsin Ming

In Egyptian mythology, the powerful Sun god Re rose from waters enfolded in a lotus flower to bring us the light of day, and sank into the petals of the lotus again to usher in the night. Myths are often retold over time, responding to new interpretations. Like myths, opinions can change with new data, unless we cling to them.

Our universe is a collection of ideas that we assume to be real. Thoughts are not things, until we behave as if they are. Facts are merely the latest understanding of available data, and as such can change. The universe changes constantly and we change as well, whether or not we are aware of our changes. We know that we can select the ideas that serve us from the steady stream of conscious thoughts. As we accumulate a library of ideas and information, we begin to consider the ideas as truth. Based on the perceptions that arise from our now cherished beliefs, we adjust our behaviors to coincide with the beliefs.

We cannot stop thinking, but we can let thoughts come and go, as they naturally do. In that state of allowing thoughts to arise and disappear, we can experience the joy of having no opinion. Thoughts that have turned into opinions have no substance because they have been built on shifting sands. Rely on the stability of rising above the battle of different opinions and watch lovingly as everything changes.

May 28

Embracing Joy

The soul should stand ajar, ready to welcome the ecstatic experience. – *Emily Dickinson,* The Complete Poems

A school of fish swam in for a council meeting to discuss the budget for the coming year. It seems that the economic conditions had prompted the fish to reduce some amenities in order to survive. The fish leaders knew that their decision would require some belt-tightening and sacrifice, but after much discussion, they decided to eliminate water.

When we are unaware of our value and magnificence, we throw away our enjoyment of life in favor of what we think will make us happy. Distracted by worries, we ignore the moments when joy shines. The majority of our life experience is awash with joy. The sun comes out daily, even if hidden by clouds, or shines creating the light of the moon. We know that light is essential to life and growth, yet the light of the sun may be taken for granted. Animals contribute to the tapestry of our reality, with lessons about how to be; they are as Eckhart Tolle calls them, "guardians of being." Plants and trees are a canvas for the life painting we create every day; we are connected to them in their visual and medicinal healing. Birds sing to one another in community, and soar into the skies demonstrating their love of freedom; we too exist in supportive community with others, and when we remember who we are, our sense of freedom makes our hearts soar. Oceans and rivers fill our environment with life sustaining water; we are drawn to the sound and relentless rhythm of ocean waters, and the quiet journey of lake and river waters. We gaze in wonder at the waterfalls and our eyes widen as geysers spout with forcefulness from within the earth. When we miss any of the treasures of life, continually showing up to light the way to truth, showing us how to just be, allowing us to soar with free spirits, and entertaining us with the sheer wonder of life, we miss the joy of being. Life is awash with the joy of living things; we can begin to look deeply and appreciate joy flowing in every part of our lives.

May 29

Something New

There is a very simple secret to being happy. Just let go of your demand on this moment. – *Adyashanti*, Emptiness Dancing (2006)

A man receives a telephone call from his administrative assistant that his office will have to be remodeled. He asks why this is necessary. She explains, "We got orders from headquarters to rebuild as soon as possible." Still confused, he asks, "Why do we need to rebuild?" She responds, "Because yesterday the building burned to the ground!"

We are sometimes tempted to blame a series of unfortunate or traumatic events in our life for our feelings of sadness or anxiety. We may for a moment feel justified in believing our untrue thoughts about what is happening to us. But what is happening is instrumental in the next phase of our life experience. What we are seeing is the next chapter of an unfolding life. We have no way of knowing what the future holds, but we pretend that we do, and often struggle aimlessly to make things happen in our favor. When events do not unfold as we plan, we worry about our future. Our worries about the future are like wanting a pot of water to boil without a pot and without water: a thought with no substance. When our efforts yield no results, or at least not the results we want, we blame our past behaviors. But seeing the present as repercussions of the past are like wanting the pot of water that has already boiled to boil differently. With those views, we stay stuck in fear, missing the magical adventure of present awareness. But in the present moment, the truth lights the way; we live and breathe with unlimited potential.

May 30

Overwhelmed

Life gives you exactly what you need to awaken.
– *T. Scott McLeod,* All That Is Unspoken

A menacing Samurai warrior threatened to kill a monk who refused to look at him. The meditating monk sat cross-legged in deep silence. After a few moments, the Samurai unsheathed his sword ready to strike and said to the monk, "Old man, don't you know, I could run you through with my sword without blinking an eye?" The monk turned to face the warrior and said, "Don't you know, I could be run through with a sword without blinking an eye?" Knowing who you are is the essence of fearlessness.

Life can seem to be a sea of our own and other people's problems, but what we are experiencing are projections from a fearful mind. When we seem to hit a wall in our attempts to manage priorities, we can step back from the drama, and know that every image within the drama – expectations, conflicts, struggles – are the egoic mind's attempts to protect itself. We can ask ourselves if what we perceive or respond to is actually true. Is the life play that we are directing and producing actually real? If we believe it is real, does it remain an unmovable aspect of our lives, a stable substance that never changes, or do we notice the continuous, unrelenting impermanence of events, feelings, and struggles. Do we notice our tendency to replay the movie of our lives, expecting some new insight for resolution of problems? We can begin to know what is unchanging in our lives – love, truth, joy and peace. Instead of being overwhelmed with irresolvable struggle and anxiety, we become aware of the extraordinary power of freedom from fear. When we know who we really are, there is no fear, and we are eternally free.

May 31

Moon and Magic

In you, as in each human being, there is a dimension of
consciousness far deeper than thought. It is the very essence
of who you are. – *Eckhart Tolle*, Stillness Speaks

The moon does not fight with the sun from which it derives its light. The
wave does not fight with the sea because it is never divorced from the sea;
the sea always rushes to the shores but eventually comes home as if drawn
by its inherent connection to something larger. The tree does not fight
with the earth because it stands anchored within its soil; the tree's roots
owe a debt of gratitude for the stability the earth offers. Because nature's
expressions are true to themselves, following the natural rhythms of their
being, they are not diminished in any way.

The universe is one consciousness, all knowing and present, but not
restricted to the time–space that we so meticulously occupy. Our brains
have structured and selected how we are to be, and how to sense whatever
appears in our world. We are expert architects, brilliantly producing our
realities until we believe they are real and solidly unchanging. An advantage
of being sentient beings is that we can think about what we perceive; the
disadvantage is that what we perceive is not real, but only a perception. A
work of art magically combines color and form to create something on a
canvas, but what we enjoy in its artistic form is still a representation. Our
true selves know the magic of our creations, and allow our dalliances with
beautiful images. Our core being is the magic of the moonlight, the wave
of the sea, the anchored tree, and all else in the universe. Through the
magical lens of one consciousness, we can know the real power and joy of
interconnectedness and the clear beauty in being.

June 1

Outer Realms

We are already safely home in the Presence. – *Ndidi,* Tea Leaves

A turtle wandered throughout a village looking for his home. A friendly rabbit, seeing his frustration, encouraged the turtle to look into a mirror. When the turtle realized that he had been carrying his home on his back for some time, he was embarrassed, and quickly went inside to recover his senses.

If we spend any time at all reflecting on the nature of our existence, we will begin to wonder where we come from, and why we are here on earth. It is easy to think about possibly having been somewhere else, and then wondering where that place might have been. We may become preoccupied with the idea that something bigger, better and more powerful outside of ourselves exists beyond our small existence and that perhaps that is where we come from. Like the alien ET, we feel like visitors, not permanent residents on earth. Our belief systems mollify this anxiety about where we come from, and soothe our tensions about why we are here, but ultimately our spirits want to go home. When we think we have to go somewhere then we wrestle with what we are leaving, and have some regrets about what we leave behind. So, we are lodged in a dilemma of wanting to know where we came from, wanting to return, and not wanting to leave. When we are aware of who we are, we are liberated from the confusion we have created. We are here now in the present moment. We have always only been here, in this moment. We are already home, because we are one spirit, one reality; there is no other place to be.

June 2

Useful Thoughts

We taste freedom when we fill up the mind with
positive thoughts. – *Ndidi,* Tea Leaves

A woman struggled to clear her mind of recurrent thoughts about the argument she and her husband had the month before. Preoccupied with his angry words, she just couldn't let them go. She began to feel an itch that would not go away, and realized that her husband's words had literally gotten under her skin.

Negative thoughts weigh heavily on us. Although we are aware of the emotional toll, sometimes we are unaware of the physical and spiritual effects of our thinking. The mind, body and spirit are integrated in a way that creates an intense relationship, seamless in its influence and effects. Thoughts that are not useful can become behaviors that are destructive and disturbing.

On the other hand, positive thoughts lift the veil of depression and delusions, giving us openings to joy and peace. When we experience peace, we see clearly the mind, body, spirit relationship as life-affirming and loving.

Given the obvious advantages of positive thinking, training the mind to acknowledge positive thoughts is the essence of joyful living. When we decide to release useless thoughts that lead to greed and hatred; grasping and feelings of separateness; or pride and anger, we free our mind of fears and worries. Useful thoughts feed the cells of our body like water quenches thirst; these thoughts nourish the soul. When we recognize those useful thoughts that align with who we are, and incorporate them into our way of being, we experience the soft arms of peace.

June 3

Worship

Love emanating from the true self is an act
of worship. – *Ndidi,* Tea Leaves

A mountain climber slipped and fell at nightfall, plunging several feet until he was able to grab a branch from a tree and hold on until help arrived. He waited for many hours, praying for rescue. As the temperature on the mountain dropped he made a plea to the Almighty, "Please tell me what to do to be saved from death on this mountainside," he begged. He waited for an answer, but none came, so he pleaded again in desperation. As he clung to the branch, a soft voice that seemed to come from inside him said "Let go!" He refused to listen to his own voice and was discovered hanging frozen the next morning a mere five feet from the ground.

Listening to the voice of our true self is an act of worship; it is an opening to awareness of All-That-Is. Our answers are found in our surrender to the true self, and not to the false ideas about who we are and what we are capable of accomplishing. So often we are offering ourselves in prayer *for* something, as if what we need is outside of our essential self. When we come closer to our essential self, we are acknowledging the Presence of All-That-Is; we listen for the voiceless spirit within and come into direct contact with the voice of Spirit. Trust that when we listen and let go of fears, we will always be safe.

June 4

Vanishing Point

We must not only begin, we must continue, even
if the road narrows. – *Ndidi,* Tea Leaves

Imagine a photograph of a path or road where the viewer looks into the distance as the road narrows. In the distance is a vanishing point, a point where the road seems to disappear, but that vanishing point is an illusion, since the road in fact continues.

As we age, we may sometimes see our lives as moving down the narrowing road, to the point of vanishing. If we walk down an actual road, the road is only narrow in the distance, not where we are in the present moment on the road. The narrowed road is in the future, but if we turn around, the road behind us is just as narrow in the distant past.

The full joy of our lives is in the experience of being on the road now, even if there are stumbles along the way. As we continue our joyful experience of life, with loving kindness, compassion and peace, we acknowledge the fullness and breadth of Now. We are where we should be on the road. Nothing is vanishing in reality; everything is changing along the way. As the road opens to us, we can acknowledge what we see, feel and experience along the way and celebrate being at each step. If we take our time, we won't miss a moment, and we will realize what it means to have a truly full life.

June 5

Working with Love

We not only do the work; we are the work. – *Ndidi,* Tea Leaves

Long ago in a village, a woman tried to give away her thoughts, because they had become burdensome. She had sleepless nights, and constant images of inventions plowing through her mind. She arranged a garage sale of sorts to attempt to sell her thoughts cheaply, but no one wanted them. Villagers noticed that when they tried to take the thoughts, they changed into something no one could relate to. The woman realized she had a strange and inseparable connection to what she thought.

Before an invention is discovered or completed, the essential self of the inventor is already expressed in the work; inventors derive satisfaction from releasing something new into the universal stream, but the ideas emerge from within the self. From idea to invention, work is a journey to discovery, an offering of the self.

We are all inventors, crafting responses to life's conditions. We find ways to work it out. Some of us may find work boring, but that is a call to us that we are not having an authentic experience. If we dislike the routine of our work, we crave an aberration, some irregularity that will add complexity. Boredom is a sign that we have disappeared into the ritual of the work, and not the spirit of it. Some of us see work as a way to earn money so that we can do what we love outside of work; inside or outside, we are craving the opportunity to be our true selves. Some of us want the work to change, but instead allow it to change us. We reveal integrity when we find what exists inside the work that has meaning for us.

The essence of the work that aligns with our true self is what gives it meaning. It is not a question of what we do, but who are we being, and what we are creating when we are doing work. A job or position is different from the work itself. A job is a placeholder for expression; the work is the unfolding of the true self. Our work is an offering, an expression of joy.

June 6

Life Gardening

A flower falls even though we love it; and a weed grows
even though we do not love it. – Dogen, Zen koan

We walk through two adjacent fields in life: one field has flowers and the other
has weeds. We are faced continually with choices about which one to water.

Our lives are like a garden, with hurt, unloved plants that become weeds
floundering in shallow soil; but also nurtured blooms with deep roots
enjoying the underground spring of joy. If we try to ignore the weeds, they
will try to take over the garden, hurt the fragrant flowers, and thwart the
bearing of fruits.

In life's garden, we can notice the weeds we have allowed to grow, obscuring
the joy, crowding out the love and compassion. We can face the self-
destruction of the weeds, but forgive their assertiveness and determination
to be acknowledged. If we pull them up, they will come back stronger,
begging to be part of our lives.

In a nonviolent approach, the nurtured flowers in our garden of life can
make space for the weeds, to embrace what is their hurt experience, and
welcome them as fellow residents; but it's not pleasant to see. We can
appreciate their pungent fragrance, their scrawny, wild growth, and listen
to their heart, but we constantly live on the edge of their consuming grasps.
In our garden of life, we can face our hurts, but know that our awakening
does not require that we get entangled in their vines. When we see them
as the manifestations of our fears, and dig into the garden of our lives
for truth and redemption, we embrace the love that makes hurt and pain
shrivel and disappear. We see clearly the many textures of our lives.

June 7

Bracketing

As the sun sets, we know that it will soon be out of
view, but not forgotten. – *Ndidi,* Tea Leaves

A marathon runner becomes aware of a slight muscle cramp midway through the race. He becomes aware of his breathing, and begins to breathe deeply into the discomfort. Soon the attention to his breath distracts him from the intensity of the discomfort and eases the cramp. The pain is a result of dehydration, soon remedied when a supporter gives him a drink along the way.

A bracket contains something set apart but not forgotten. When we want to turn away temporarily from a painful event, we can place a mental bracket around it to acknowledge its presence, without granting it preeminence in our minds. In a state of being overwhelmed, we sometimes place a bracket around tasks or events in order to give ourselves time to organize our approach to managing them.

We are not so proficient in bracketing our emotions; the insistent ego wants us to pay attention to those conditions that try to close our heart and disturb the peace. As we learn to train the mind and tame the ego, we become comfortable bracketing those emotions that distract us from being in the present moment. When we are aware of our true self, the bracketing becomes merely a pause that slows our process, allowing a space to stop and be still. All the events, struggles and hurts we have bracketed disappear in the present moment, because right now there is nothing wrong with us. In the present moment, we become aware that what we intended to save, to bracket for future worry, cannot be found.

June 8

Doubt and Faith

Faith comprises both itself and the doubt of itself. – *Paul Tillich,*
Biblical Religion and the Search for Ultimate Reality

Doubt and faith, at first reading, could be seen as opposites, but they are more than that. Doubt and faith can be seen as inextricably united, since one cannot be true without the other. When we have doubt, faith is always present. We may say that events in our lives test our faith. What we identify as tests are manifestations of doubt. Some may see doubt as a lack of faith, but doubt is a refining process, separating what is hoped for from what is true. Some see faith as a blind belief in what is improbable, but faith is a process of surrender to potential. The combination of truth and potential is the essence of creative energy. If we pray for healing, our expectations are a combination of doubts about the likelihood of a positive outcome, and faith that the outcome will be in perfect order of the universe.

The union of doubt and faith encourages us to enter a space of peace and surrender, where we are prepared to be present for whatever experience we encounter. We choose peace over fear, but realize that we must question our fears to manage them. We allow love to be the center of our awareness, but we acknowledge that fear lurks on the fringes of our thinking. The union of doubt and faith is a metaphor for the power of mind. Our mind wants to make a decision, but the universe thrives as a "both-and" evolution of consciousness. We are not disappointed by our faith or our doubt; faith empowers us and doubt prepares us. The combination honors the creative energy of the universe, and opens our hearts to the truth of our being.

June 9

Ordinary

Nothing in the universe is "ordinary." – *Ndidi,* Tea Leaves

He lived in the familiar trees of an ordinary forest. Living among a whole community of parrots, Orson the parrot did not see himself as special, until a hunter seized him because of his beautiful feathers and willingness to have an engaging conversation.

One of the accepted characteristics of ordinary people is their lack of broad experience; we believe the narrow routine of their lives makes them approachable and safe. But we know that ordinary people are not always as "ordinary" as we think; ordinariness has depth, untested or unrevealed knowledge and uncommon sense. We are comfortable with ordinariness because we assume that ordinary people don't know everything. The "know-it-all" is offensive to us, because of the pretense at superiority.

If we use the biblical story of Adam and Eve in the Garden of Eden, or the Islamic understanding of the tree, we get enlightened about the angst we feel about too much knowledge. In the ancient world, the expression of opposites was a way to communicate the whole. Knowledge of "good and evil" was essentially knowledge of everything. The metaphor is unmistakable in its threat to the superiority of God, Allah or All-That-Is. But there is nothing, no knowledge outside of All-That-Is; and, if consciousness is expressed as human beings and other aspects of our reality, we are the consciousness of All-That-Is. We cannot be ordinary.

June 10

Out of the Closet

Trust that your work will speak for you in a way
that words cannot. – *Ndidi,* Tea Leaves

When we meet others for the first time, often the conversation turns to work. We may identify ourselves according to the work we do or plan to do. In spite of our best efforts, we can never fully express the work, aside from reciting a litany of roles and responsibilities.

We are not only what we do, so at best we can only talk *about* our work. But when we are our work, when we reveal who we are in our work, the work itself needs no explanation. We understand or have experienced the nature of flow when we lose track of time and space, as we become engrossed in the spirit of the present moment. Time becomes irrelevant; what we are doing and who we are being becomes one essence. We apologize to others for our "disappearance" and may feel guilty because of the undeniable pleasure of the experience. In those instances, we have been exactly "on track" with who we are; we have left the false ideas of self and revealed the true self. We are out of the closet where our passion has been buried under the expectations, limitations and fears that have crowded and shrouded our awareness. Our purpose in life is to be without apology, without limits, and without the closet that imposes time and space on our experience of joy. Our authentic work expresses who we are.

June 11

Greatness

Even now one rarely hears of people achieving
great things unless they first stumble in some respect.
– *Meister Eckhart*, Sermons and Treatises, Vol 2

We often do not know our own power and energy, until we must endure
overwhelming challenges. We have heard of mothers lifting cars off
children to save them from being crushed by the weight of the dense
metal. We have heard many heroic stories of nearly inconceivable feats, and
we still doubt our ability to perform, even in crisis. Our egos tell us that
we are limited in our abilities to perform "miraculous" acts. But every day
we live and move is a miracle; not because it is spectacular, but because
it is continuously necessary. We are capable of greater and greater things;
avalanches of love and compassion, peacefulness as deep as massive lakes,
and solar flashes of inconceivable joy. In the consciousness of All-That-Is,
there is no impossibility. When we see conditions in our life that interrupt
our sense of peace, we can embrace the events as egoic images, untrue
scenarios in the infinite game of life. The game does not have losers; there
is nothing to lose. The game does not have winners, because there is no
one to defeat. There is only the relentless depth of Now, bringing us into
close contact with our expansive being. When we are aware of essential,
ultimate reality, all limits dissolve; we then see the effects of our greatness.

June 12

Interdependent

The whole idea of compassion is based on a keen awareness of the interdependence of all these living beings, which are all part of one another, and all involved in one another. – *Thomas Merton,* Statement from his final address, during a conference on East–West monastic dialogue, delivered just two hours before his death (10 December 1968), quoted in *Religious Education*, Vol. 73 (1978)

A brilliant episode of the *Twilight Zone*, tells the story of a man who just wanted to be left alone to read his books, so in the magical world of the episode everyone disappears on earth leaving him happily sitting on the steps of the library reading alone. Then the unspeakable happens: he drops his bifocals on the cement steps and they shatter to pieces.

We are never alone, but we can enjoy periods of solitude. The experience of solitude can be healthy, filled with reflection and silence, but ultimately we have an interdependent relationship with others that is inextricable, and that interdependence is experienced in spiritual connection. After soaking up the pleasures of solitude, we may feel renewed; creativity may be revived and more vivid than before the experience. When we choose solitude we often come closer to an experience of the true self; but when we emerge from periods of solitude, we realize its true value.

We live in a unified field of being and have a spiritual relationship with others that is inalterable. The illusion of separateness and independence may stoke the ego, and convince others of our significance, but the reality of our lives is interdependence and a collective reality. We cannot separate ourselves from what we see, fear and hear in any moment, nor can we separate ourselves from each other. We become accustomed to thinking of ourselves as separate from others; and believe that our spiritual existence is also individual and separate. When we experience ourselves as separate bodies, we also think we are separate from animals or plants and minerals, but in a nondual universe, we are one.

All of these elements are part of our created scenery, our reality. Everything in our energetic environment has a reason for being and a consequence of being. Nothing is inherently separate in our universe. At the physical level of our bodies, there is a complex cause and effect interplay that represents organ functions, brain synapses and sensory processes. We look for the causes of anxieties, diseases and confusions; and measure the effects in order to understand them, but soon realize that the effects are also causes. We cannot extricate ourselves from the continual display of inter-causality; our lives are intertwined, unified energy. When we are conscious of our interdependence with all living things, we monitor our actions and reactions carefully. When we accept that we are intricately related to all living things, we understand that the entire universe is alive in us and that there is one spirit that is present everywhere.

June 13

Rocks and Rivers

Be the water, not the rock. – *Zen saying*

Imagine that we are standing on the banks of a beautifully flowing river. We notice that the shallow riverbed has rocks of different sizes and shapes that lie unconcerned and solidly planted. We then notice that the river waters flow continuously, not aimlessly but deliberately. In the spaces between the rocks, water collects but when the spaces are filled, the overflow continues on its deliberate path. The rocks do not willingly yield to the relentless water and over time become smaller, differently shaped and worn.

The scene on the banks of the river is instructive: we can be the water in life, or the rock. As our life story flows along like water gathering momentum, slowing down, filling spaces and affecting our reality, we can flow with it, in the direction of joy. As a rock, lacking flexibility and denial of the reality of our being, we believe the story that we are stuck. We allow life to pass us by, and life events to roll over us, wearing us down over time. The metaphor of our inability to move, to make choices, is a story; just a story. When we transcend the story we have created, we realize that the water and the rock are aspects of the whole self; we can have compassion for the times when we know we are rocks and celebrate other times when we are water. We can appreciate when we need to stand still and other times when we need to move. When we know who we really are, we face those places where we are rocks and appreciate the times when like rivers we are flowing toward joy. When we are aware of our true self, we know that each experience is life on the journey of love.

June 14

Play

You can't depend on your eyes when your imagination is out of focus. – *Mark Twain*, A Connecticut Yankee in King Arthur's Court

Young children can be comfortable with the imaginative activities of play, sometimes called creative play. Imaginary friends, stuffed animals and live animals are often given powers and attributes that help to continue the games. Books may describe pictures of fantastic characters that make light of fears and anxieties, or teach lessons about love and cruelty. Wholesome characters express humorous views of life lived with loving kindness, but even unwholesome characters dramatize their fears and assure children that the game is designed to end well, although children may unwittingly learn that the play itself is more important than the messages.

Play is a continual exploration of possibilities. Children do not look for an end to play, and are willing to change the cast of characters or the nature of the game, as long as the play continues. But, as we grow older, our play becomes goal-oriented; we want to win the game, and believe that continuation of play leads to boredom. We take this desire for an endgame into our workplaces and relationships; and the results can be painful.

The play itself has not changed, but our memory of the essence of play has begun to be lost to us. If we cannot find the play in our work, the essence of joy eludes us. We forget about the joy in imagination and the innovation, flirtation with divergence and sense of wonder. We forget the lesson about finding joy in what we do by finding the play in it. When we find our playful center, we allow joy to flourish in our lives.

June 15

Self-Consciousness

Self-consciousness is ego-created. —*Ndidi,* Tea Leaves

According to the story, Adam and Eve "covered" themselves after they ate the apple from the tree of knowledge of everything. They became conscious about their "nakedness," their vulnerability in life. To remind them of their vulnerability, the frightened ego asserted its capacity to protect them from harm.

Self-consciousness has ancient roots, but it has contemporary effects; it raises doubts about our worth, our purpose in life and our connection to All-That-Is. We become convinced that we are shameful, and that we need to rely on what others think we should do or be. Our transgressions sometimes make us wonder what we have done to cause such disapproval, when we simply tried to be true to our core being.

Our life conditions can be scary; painful "reality" convinces us that life has a destructive energy that threatens our safety, so our ego suggests that we conform. We feel alone and vulnerable at times, and want to be accepted as worthy individuals, so we agree with the idea that conformity creates safety.

Much of what we experience in life leads us to question ourselves; but we rarely find answers that satisfy us. We believe that we can think or reason our way to a comprehensible answer, but we are continually frustrated.

Our self-consciousness is a denial of spirit, an investment in false stories of who and what we are. In order to experience pure consciousness, we must let go of the false self, the "I."

212

Pure consciousness is the indescribable presence that allows us to create images of our reality without the constraints of fears. We are free to create, but as long as we believe our false stories about ourselves, the ego controls us. There is no "I" to be self-conscious; there is only one spirit that is All-That-Is. What we call self-consciousness is the ego generated doubt and fear in the mind, a steady drumbeat of dread. Joy is the awareness of being one with All-That-Is. We realize that the judgments we have felt are self-judgments, and not the punishments of the universe for being who we are. Pure consciousness is awareness of the true self and with that awareness, we are free to live without fear or worry.

June 16

Ups and Downs

Refuse to grasp onto absolutes; everything changes. – *Ndidi,* Tea Leaves

Every 750 million years or so, the magnetic field of the earth reverses itself, say astrophysicists. No one understands why the gravitational field suddenly goes topsy-turvy. When it happens, north becomes south, and south becomes north on our compasses. We often refer to events, people, positions and other aspects of our world as higher, lower, tall, short, better and worse, up and down. All of our absolutes are relative, based on what our perspectives are now. When we describe our world according to our attributed absolutes, can we be certain that what we are describing is the truth? Are we certain that what we perceive as wrong is always wrong? Is a law or rule always right? With disastrous consequences, our beliefs in absolutes can create rigidity in a fluid world. Like stopping suddenly on a treadmill while it's moving; pain and suffering are likely to follow.

Absolutes limit our choices and close our minds and hearts to different experiences and perceptions. We close our hearts to opportunities for compassion and inclusiveness. With softened absolutes, we resist the tendency to assess conditions using prescribed rules. But when we lock ourselves into a rule and cling to it, we may miss the nuance of changes that essentially "make lemonade out of lemons" in our life. Sometimes when we least expect it, the broken pieces come together in our lives and create a beautiful mosaic of hope and contentment. When that happens, our world turns happily upside down, and in that turning all seems right-sided in our lives.

June 17

Unspoken

Unspoken words that long to pierce the silence are
whispers in the heart. – *Ndidi,* Tea Leaves

The ability of human beings to communicate with other sentient beings,
including animals is a gift of the universe. Bursting with relentless
thoughts, we have much that we could say to express what we think,
feel and sense. The sheer volume of thoughts causes us to be selective
about what we choose to pay attention to. We have structured our world
according to habitual thoughts, our favorites, as a way to have a predictable
experience in an unpredictable universe. As the habitual thoughts become
comfortable ways to minimize our vulnerability, we select terminology and
expressions that match our beliefs, and exclude items that seem to cause
us discomfort.

Some topics become "undiscussables," evidence of the shame or strong beliefs
we carry. Although hidden from our conversations, the undiscussables
are not hidden from our consciousness; the egoic mind makes secrets
the fuel for dissatisfaction, anger and resistance. We may either act out
the discomforts, serving our pain to others; or we may mask our secrets
with rescuing, righteousness, or resentments. These unexpressed thoughts,
feelings and behaviors sacrifice our authenticity and mask who we are.
When we know who we are, we are aware of our invulnerability and
become free of self-judgments. We discover that our imperfect past has
little to say about the present and nothing to report about our future. We
can embrace all of who we are without the crippling fear of judgments.

June 18

Latent Heat

You will not be punished for your anger; you will
be punished by your anger. – *The Buddha*

At the center of the earth is molten lava, blazing heat that sometimes erupts. We know it is there, raging, but we largely ignore it, until it spews from the once-silent volcano for all the world to see. The sun rises every day and casts its brilliant, life-giving rays on our existence, but if we expose ourselves to its powerful rays longer than wise, we will be burned.

The latent heat of anger sits just below the surface of our consciousness, ready to erupt when the tectonic plates shift in response to what we think and feel. Each time our ego reacts to conditions with fear and anxiety, latent heat is absorbed, and lodges in our spirit; it interrupts the flow of loving-kindness and compassion in our lives.

When we vent our anger, we say that we are letting off steam, but the steam is not the issue. Burning fires of resentment, seep out of us from a deep reservoir of fear. If we believe our own thoughts and feelings to be absolutely true, we allow the heat to erupt. If that anger is opportunistic energy, flowing toward an object or person that we have created in our reality, we may become angry with ourselves. For example, we create relationships with people we later regret knowing, and then harbor the resentment of them, long after the relationship ends. Our unpredictable resentment simmers until the right trigger - an imagined slight, a sarcastic statement, or a suggestion of incompetence - justifies our outrage.

Just as the earth shifts, vents and spews lava and ash because the confluence of internal pressures require release, we allow internal pressures orchestrated

216

by the ego to control us. When we recognize that we are ultimately the persons most injured by our anger, we know that we must control our mind, because it has deceived us. In the present moment, we can rest in the frictionless state of being. Our anger will cool when we are "in control of our senses," but also when we become aware of who we really are.

June 19

Inner Sobbing

The tears of the world are a constant quantity. For
each one who begins to weep somewhere else another
stops. – *Samuel Beckett*, Waiting for Godot

Anguish produces entanglements of thoughts, like wet string rolled into a complex ball. The entanglements build up over time, as difficult life events reinforce our despair. If we have an audience, another person who listens to the details of our stories, we may feel some relief from our sense of isolation, but the imprint of the anguish is likely to remain. Sometimes we are encouraged to cry when we experience a loss or a difficult challenge. Tears flow in a burst of anger and frustration, or when something triggers the feelings we are burying. We release our deep hurt when we fully recognize it.

All of these external displays of sadness, frustration and anger pale in comparison to the inner sobbing that pays homage to the wounds within us. Our deep sobbing harbors futility and hopelessness, down in the abyss or the trenches of our consciousness. When we are afraid to release the depths of our feelings, we are underestimating our profound resilience. Like the starfish, at the deepest level of the ocean, we can survive and overcome the dark pressures of our emotional ocean floor, because the sob is the calling of our true self to lift the veil of negative thoughts and feelings of powerlessness. From the heaviness of hopelessness, tears set us free. From the tangled emotions of grief, shame and desperation, we experience a sense of love and surrender.

June 20

Embracing Not Yet

Longing for anything makes having it now
impossible. – *Ndidi,* Tea Leaves

A man ordered a gadget online that could predict the future. There was of course no firm guarantee of when he would receive his product. After several weeks waiting for the delivery, he decided to cancel his order. As he picked up his phone to call customer service and cancel the order, his doorbell rang. The package was delivered.

There is a space between what we expect and what is, that we fill with longing and anxiety. No amount of strong feelings about what has not yet manifested can give us solace when we are in that space. Questions arise that make the realization of our desires more unlikely: What is taking so long? What must I do to make it happen? When will my turn arrive? What's wrong with me?

Although the questions fill the space, they are counterproductive. We discover that "the waiting" happens more often than we like, if we focus on what we don't have. Being thankful for what we already have in the present is a useful attitude to embrace. Our reality in the present moment is the only experience we have and what we desire may be unformed, inexplicable or inappropriate. The universe continually moves in the direction of our vibrations, our personal energy. If we ask, it is given according to our vibrations. What we can lean into is our present awareness, where we can fall in love with "now," and release our grasping for "when or how." When we release our desire for control of life's gifts, we can relax in a space of "not yet" and experience peace.

June 21

The Passion of Protest

I looked at my hands, to see if I was de same person now I was
free. Dere was such a glory over everything, de sun came like gold
trou de trees, and over de fields, and I felt like I was in heaven. –
Harriet Tubman, from Harriet, The Moses of Her People (1886)

For a period of time, a woman drew crowds of people to her presentations
because she shared openly all that she disliked or hated about other people.
At first, her vitriolic statements generated applause and sometimes standing
ovations. After a few weeks of steady popularity, she noticed that the
crowds were getting smaller. On reflection, she realized that she had
alienated everyone, so no one was left to attend her gatherings.

When we protest the way people show up in the world, we resist the
diversity that makes our world what it is. Our universal diversity is
constantly changing, accommodating and adapting to the conditions
that we participate in creating. Going against the natural flow of life is
a violence born of conflicting false selves. When we can be content with
the way things naturally are we make room in our hearts for others to live
their lives in peace.

Nonviolent protest is an offering of peace, rather than judging the value
of other people. Protesters may carry images and placards expressing
solidarity around an issue, but nonviolence expresses a desire for change
in the spirit of community and loving-kindness. Nonviolence speaks to the
heart of humanity, and tests the boundaries of compassion; nonviolence
pushes inward not outward. In the silence of Presence, the outer edges of
humanity as we have created them, are softened and reshaped. Nonviolence
dramatizes the nature of impermanence, and the cycle of change in life; it

unveils the peaceful truth of our being. If we honor life in its constantly changing nature, we know that change is only perceived as violent when we insist on the repetition of what we find comfortable, and resist the changes that appear to us. We become aware that loving what is, is not accepting the status quo, but knowing that the status quo itself is an illusion. Everything changes, whether or not we are aware of the changes. Loving presence brings the light of peace and reconciliation into our awareness, and invites others to enjoy the peace promised within passionate protest.

June 22

Bees

Bees do have a smell, you know, and if they don't they
should, for their feet are dusted with spices from a
million flowers. – *Ray Bradbury*, Dandelion Wine

The sting of a bee is a characteristic of the insect that may overshadow its
critical contribution to life on earth. Bees are a metaphor for the unselfish
work in our lives, our small yet significant contribution to the lives of
everything else on the planet and beyond. We matter. For bees, work is a
way of being, and a way of living. In its humble way, the bee demonstrates
that work is service, and that service is connection.

We know that the frenetic activities of a bee are the result of a deadline
imposed by the queen, but there is an internal drive, a raison d'être that
moves the bee from flower to flower. The work of the bee is authentic and
necessary; it is essential to the bee, because it is who the bee is. The work
is essential to others but also to its sense of self. The bee does not worry
about fulfilling a purpose; it knows its essential nature and immerses itself
in being a bee.

When we are being authentic in our work, we know that the work is who
we are, not just what we do. The bee does not worry about whether other
insects value its contribution; it flits joyfully from flower to flower with the
determination to be a bee. A bee teaches us that work arises from within
us; it is a balance of being and doing, giving and receiving, knowing and
faith. The bee is a reminder that we have the unique ability to change the
world, and that our impact is amplified by our interdependence with others
in our universal community.

June 23

Setting Aside Worries

There is no space for worries in the present moment. – *Ndidi,* Tea Leaves

We are continually sending mixed vibrations about the state of our lives. We hope for the best, but prepare for the worst. We use our imagination to worry about the future or past mistakes, even though there is no way for us to control either. We have practice drills in our minds for dangerous events that never happen and wait for the metaphorical sword of Damocles to drop.

Worries are like prisons that keep us locked in fears about what has either gone away or has not yet occurred. The past that we think determines our present reality is no longer able to affect our authentic self, unless we attach unwarranted power to it. Tomorrow will come and open the gate to joy, but if we refuse to go through the gate, we will eventually collapse from the strain of fear. The next moment will come regardless of what we desire or fear, but our resistance keeps us from joy that is always present.

Worries have an annoying habit of thriving on repetition; it is like walking backwards on a treadmill, thinking again and again that our repetition is getting us somewhere. We are expending energy to develop the muscle of fear, but it only weakens us since we eventually grow tired of going nowhere and not feeling any better.

In the present moment, there is nothing to worry about. Tomorrow is an unwritten chapter in our story, because it does not yet exist. The past does not repeat itself; we only repeat it in our minds. Right now is the strongest part of our life story because it has depth and certainty. Right now, all is well.

June 24

Ending Suffering

Suffering is not a requirement, but a choice. – *Ndidi*, Tea Leaves

The ancient Greeks were adept at using language to describe qualities of an individual. One such attempt was the word *sophrosyne*. According to the Greeks a person was sophrosyne if she had such qualities as self-restraint, moderation and wisdom creating excellence of character and soundness of mind. Each of these qualities can lead us on a path to an end of suffering.

Excessive grasping for more, and clinging to what we think we have, leads to longing for life to be different from what it is. Self-restraint is controlling the sense of having an individual identity that wants something. Who is the "I" that clings? For what purpose do we reach for more? Our moderate views of life conditions and challenges can keep us from settling into camps of true believers who see life as a continuing battle between good and evil. Who creates the ongoing conflict? Who or what is good, and by whose standards? Who wins such a mythical battle of opinions and preferences? Who suffers in winning and in losing? The conflict is in our minds, and the actions that follow stoke fears and create challenging conditions. We can be our own worst "enemy."

Wisdom is the inexplicable awareness of the true self expressed in the world in the eternal now. Our wisdom is not based in knowledge and facts but in the realization of the true self, our inner divinity. When we think and behave according to the dictates of an ego-controlled false self, we set aside self-restraint, moderation and wisdom: we suffer. When we journey within, we release our suffering. Each of us is sophrosyne at the core of our being. Deep within, we know who we are.

June 25

Our Song

Let the beauty of what you love be what you do. – *Rumi* As quoted in Path for Greatness: Spirituality at Work (2000) by Linda J. Ferguson

Male birds sing in the early morning because they are trying to attract mates and establish territories. Often there are lone vocalists, taking responsibility for creating the experience they want. In some tropical areas, birds—male and female—sing duets. Birds sing because they must.

Like birds, we often sing a song because we want to be heard or taken seriously; we call it our calling. We sometimes hesitate to sing our song, because we are not certain whether it will attract the love or peace we seek. We set aside our calling in order to seem more practical and acceptable to others. We think that accommodating another person's needs will satisfy our own. The birds do not hesitate to sing their song. It is not only their work; it is their purpose.

For most people in the world, young and mature, morning signals the time to begin work. The song we sing can have different melodies - some affirming and some discouraging. We can take ourselves to the work of the day, or bring the day to our work. When we take ourselves to work, we have already disconnected ourselves from the work to be done; the work lies outside of our being, so we see it as separate from who we are. Someone else's priorities can lie between who we are and the work we are doing, so we do the work in exchange for a reward, but our "heart" is not in it. When we bring the day to our work, the work is singing to us. We flow with time, not realizing that moments pass by, because in the space of love, time is irrelevant. The song is a love song; the work is our song.

June 26

Well-Being

Struggle is a faithless movement against an ocean
of well–being. – *Ndidi,* Tea Leaves

We are often careful to describe to others the details of the negative conditions we face daily. We call it sharing our day or experience, but we sometimes omit experiences that do not support our main narrative. Some who listen to us confirm the negativity and commiserate with us about how awful the conditions are that we endure. We lay claim to what has caused us pain and identify with what's wrong. Often we explain that we are victims of events and difficult people who make our life untenable at times.

The world of conditions seems real to us, even though the conditions pass and change as quickly as they arise. If we are suffering from ill-health, the pain is either more or less severe as the moments come and go. Yet, we stay with the initial story even though over time those stories become old news about pain that has changed or transformed.

When we observe the healing or physical decline of someone we love, we do not always notice the imperceptible changes from moment to moment. We may claim the old news that blinded us with fear and become surprised with "miraculous" recoveries.

We can know the peace and love of well-being if we claim it as it changes continuously. We could allow the appearance and disappearance of pain to be evidence of the continuous changes in life, and claim the constant flow of well-being that is the true nature of universal spirit. There is an ocean of well-being; when we see conditions as temporary, we are claiming the power of its beneficent flow.

June 27

Living Things

Until one has loved an animal, a part of one's soul remains unawakened. – *Anatole France,* The Gods Will Have Blood

How a child treats animals can be an indicator of how that same child will treat human beings later in life. If a child experiences loving relationships with animals, he is more likely to discover his own core goodness and will be willing to share his goodness with others. If he does harm to animals, he will often do harm to humans, as he encounters difficulty realizing his own worthiness. We are influenced not only by our actions toward animals, but by their responses to us. The interactions are like living templates of relationship.

Animals can be wise teachers; they teach us as children and as adults that love is a powerful connection, and that abuse of power is a recipe for suffering. We can learn the essence of kindness and responsibility from pets and other animals; and also learn that our feelings can be affected by the suffering of other beings. We have much in common with other sentient beings in our universe; and become aware of our desire to be loved and to love when we connect with compassion to animals and other living things. Whether they are untamed or domesticated, animals teach us to live in the present moment, without lamenting the past or obsessing about the future. They also teach us about survival and resilience, patience and joy. Even as their students, we may believe that we have control over them, but we are inextricably connected to all living things, and the connection is a complex relationship of love. As a sign of our clarity about the relationship to animals and other living things, we can substitute our desire for control to appreciation.

We may be fascinated with the "peculiarities" and strange capacities of other living things; and may see them as separate from us; neighbors that should stay in their houses or safely away in zoos or aquariums. Living things - the animals, birds, fish and insects - are not separate from us, but integral facets of our lives. We are all made of the same stardust, the same energy. We all breathe and live and have our being in the essence of spiritual energy. We inter-exist as one spirit in our universal awareness; we are reflections of one another. All the spectacular diversity in our world springs from the same one source. When we respect and love one another, we experience the peace and joy of connection. When we honor life in all its forms, we honor the source of our being.

June 28

We Are the Earth

In your body is the garden of flowers. Take your seat on
the thousand petals of the lotus, and there gaze on the
Infinite Beauty. – *Kabir,* Songs of Kabir (1915)

Soil, seeds and water are not only actual sustenance of life, but also metaphors for the cycle of life. From the fertile soil of universal energy, we have emerged as expressions of life's promise. The seeds of growth were planted long ago beyond a time we can measure. In an infinite universe, time is merely constructed to make sense of something so large that it cannot be measured; we acknowledge being in a time and space that is arbitrarily measured by minutes, hours and days. Water is the renewable energy of the cosmos; it contains the oxygen and hydrogen most species on the earth need to survive.

The coming together of the soil, the seeds and the water is one simple explanation of the existence of life on earth, and yet the mystery of how this combination works is still under scientific investigation. We are the soil, the seeds and the water; this is the truth of our existence. We may isolate aspects of the universe for study, but we share not only DNA with all living things, but also the substance of our physical selves. In the present moment we are aware of the unity of all life and that we can rest in knowing what we are, embracing the continuous transformation of all in a magnificent universe.

June 29

Natural Entertainment

Come home to nature; come home to self. – *Ndidi,* Tea Leaves

More and more sophisticated digital cameras and smartphones try to replicate the glorious colors of the natural world. Images will always be approximations of what we call reality. Our eyes photograph images as well; although images differ remarkably from person to person viewing the same thing. We are what we see, and as such, what we see changes based on who we are.

Nature provides a cornucopia of entertainment as the universe paints and shapes nature into a veritable movie of color and variety. We are central casting in the movie. As stars of the show, nature does not show up unless we appear to witness its beauty. We do not go out into nature; nature is home for us; it is in us. We often report a sense of peace or comfort when we go to a quiet park, or go fishing on a lake. Nature shows us a space within ourselves that we often ignore during our busy days. In a peaceful place we feel alive; we are able to touch the source of our being. Nature wants nothing from us and gives freely to us, just as home releases demands on us and is a familiar place. Nature performs for us without craving applause. Our presence is gift enough. We may think that we leave nature behind when we return to a bustling city or our crowded life, but nature remains with us, soothing us, nurturing us, calling us to peace.

June 30

Abandonment

Unconditional love holds us in an eternal embrace. – *Ndidi,* Tea Leaves

We cannot have a full life without at some time feeling abandoned physically, emotionally or spiritually. We grow up developing attachments to caretakers and others and sometimes experience unmet expectations. When our expectations are unmet we feel a sense of betrayal or loneliness. If we experience being forgotten, discounted or ignored, the result is an experience of abandonment.

Our survival may feel threatened when boundaries are violated. We want to forget about what has happened to us, but the feelings persist. The anguish can be so overpowering that we decide to abandon ourselves.

The pain of abandonment can be what happens in our lives. The suffering that follows is orchestrated by an ego that creates a false self that lies to us; it tells us to be ashamed, hide feelings, be careful of making mistakes, and to forget about our dreams. Conditions show up to convince us that the worst can happen and that we must diminish ourselves in order to feel safe.

We want to be loved more than anything, and having experienced pain from unloving behaviors, we doubt that love is possible. Layers and layers of untrue stories about our lives can convince us that we are something we are not. We are not what happened to us. We have never been abandoned by the universal energy that is our true self. The Ultimate Reality, All-That-Is shines within us, through us and as us. Conditions for our pain have emerged in the past, but in the present moment the awareness is peace and unconditional love. We can burst out of the web of falsehoods and free our soul. We are always cherished and loved.

July 1

Getting Life Straight

Embrace the meanderings of life and work. – *Ndidi,* Tea Leaves

Nothing in the natural world is a straight line, even if elements appear to be straight. The gentle curves of nature are not aligned, not plumb or stabilized like walls of a building. We sometimes try to straighten our lives; we organize our work spaces and rid our homes of excess objects and clutter. We may believe that straight is good, but life presents itself as curved and wandering.

We may imagine our life's work, and then life's events and conditions seem to interrupt our straight line of thought to our goals. We may suffer from deferred dreams and unrealized careers, but the wandering river of life keeps flowing. As the river flows, it changes, influenced by what the path presents, yielding to each new obstacle, and then it flows around that obstacle or over it. The river has no goal except to flow, to move and to be a river. When it ultimately flows into the sea, it does not stop moving, as if a goal has been reached. Instead it moves more quickly, as it transforms into a wave. Work is being who we are now, flowing freely with each new ripple, rolling over rough patches, and embracing each new moment.

July 2

The Trap

Like grasping sand with open fingers, we cannot hold on to
anything without eventually losing it. – *Ndidi,* Tea Leaves

Avoidance of pain can sometimes bring more pain because what we focus
on tends to seek ways to continually be present for us. But clinging to
pleasure can also bring pain and loss. The trap of life is that when we
pursue something, it eludes our grasp, and when we allow things to be as
they are, what we desire moves toward us.

When our vision is turned outward for happiness, we can get lost in
disappointment. Clinging to the false self, the "I" that we think is our
true self, has a similar result. No amount of "looking out for oneself" or
taking care of oneself alone can result in happiness. The temporary feelings
associated with happiness are a response to something we cannot control
now or in the future. Nothing that arises and disappears like happiness or
pain offers any stable sense of self; the shape-shifting nature of life events
is unpredictable, and leaves us wondering what happened.

In a changing world, we can appreciate the moments of happiness and be
grateful for the clarity that comes from pain. The egoic mind blocks our
appreciation with stories of failure, frustration and fragility. The trap set
for us by the frightened mind is for us to believe that what we experience
as emotions are evidence of our existence; we say that "to live is to suffer."
When we know who we are, we are aware of the freedom of the true self;
we know that fear is a trap and unconditional love is the substance of all
things.

July 3

Unappreciated at Work

Work with the intention to lend yourself to others; you cannot withhold who you are. – *Ndidi*, Finding Joy–Finding Yourself

When work is considered an opportunity to be appreciated, significance rather than service becomes our main focus. Appreciation becomes a gain in significance over others and loss becomes a symbol for a sense of powerlessness. But our work is more than an opportunity; it is an expression of who we are.

As long as we are dependent on others to feel our inherent power, we can become dependent on an audience that we cannot control. The audience is the false self, reminding us to believe stories that are untrue. The lack of truth is based on the notion that we are separate beings; we believe the false ideas that some individuals are better and more intelligent, skillful, talented or experienced than others. Like Russian roulette, we hope that the trigger will not release a bullet of incompetence or failure, because we believe that disapproval or criticism could be deadly.

Work is not a deadly game of winners and losers; it is the expression of love and creativity. We are compelled to create through the essence of what we do for others. Whether we offer a service or a product in our work, we are expressing our true self in a world that is entranced with the false ideas of competition and greed. Our true self is always there, in the midst of the activity, being the true substance of creative energy. Being our work is awareness of the true self. We don't have work to do or success to have, we are the work; so we can let go of the need for appreciation and approval, and be open to the transcendent state of joy. In the present moment, all is well and we are whole.

July 4

Vision

When you work you are a flute through whose heart the whispering of the hours turns to music. – *Kahlil Gibran*, The Prophet

Work is an act of love and a spiritual journey. No one can dampen the enthusiasm of work that is joyful and intentional, yet we sometimes fall short of our immovable goals and give up the vision. Disappointments along the journey can be frustrating but the vision we hold shines light on even the darkest days. Most will agree that persistent work is necessary to be successful, although there are many ways to measure success. Good performance may achieve specified goals but there is more to life and spirit than reaching goals.

Personal integrity relies on strong intention and a clear vision, yet we sometimes say "yes" to work that does not stir our souls, and say "no" to work that is our spiritual identity. When we adjust those mismatched behaviors, saying "yes" when we feel inconceivable joy, and "no," when the work does not feed our soul, we begin to work with integrity. Work that is entered into with joy is an act of service to our collective consciousness.

July 5

Overcoming Failure

Misfortune comes from having a body. Without a body, how
could there be misfortune? – *Lao Tzu*, Tao Te Ching

What does it mean to fail? Failures are storms we notice because we have
expected the air to remain calm. The mind has promised us that rain only
falls on a neighbor's roof, or that our hard work will yield benefits. Our
egos have convinced us that we deserve something in return for our efforts
and that we will be recognized for our brilliance or earnest desires to help.
Our shattered expectations deal a powerful blow to the ego and our sense
of significance. The storm seems to arise quickly and terrifies us. We run
for shelter, nurse our wounds and try to recover. Instead of being there
for us, the ego encourages self-blame and shame. Failure is an immediate
reaction to unexpected challenges, not a personal indictment. When we
see the failure as a description of who we are, we have begun to believe
the delusions of the ego; and have been convinced that we are the failure.

We could see failure as potent feedback about the temporary nature of life;
then the feedback might shake but never obliterate our awareness of who
we really are. Without the story of failure laughing at us and encouraging
us to hide our vulnerability, we can experience the clear, calm shining that
is our true self. Being vulnerable will not destroy us, only the denial of our
true self will cause us suffering. During the appearance of all conditions
in our lives, our true self remains the constant essence of our existence.
Embrace vulnerability as a story of our life that reveals the humanity of
the bodies we all live in, but let go of self-blame for being a creator of new
learning.

July 6

The Power of Work

You work that you may keep pace with the earth and the
soul of the earth. – *Kahlil Gibran*, The Prophet

An acorn lodged in fertile soil will eventually become an oak tree. Is the
oak tree within the acorn all along the journey to becoming a mature tree?
We are well aware of the ecology of transformation; we know that the
essence of the tree is the acorn now transformed. We may be thankful for
the acorns but when the tree emerges we forget the power of the acorn to
love and be loved by the earth.

Work is like an acorn that bears within it the majesty of the tree. In a
nurturing environment it transforms and grows. When the acorn of our
work is love its energy pervades the soil of the collective consciousness
and slowly emerges from the dark energy of creation to fill our spirit with
majesty. Work is the powerful expression of our essence, not in the doing
of work but in the being-ness of it. Work is the opportunity for love to
be manifest. Love is always present in us; work gives us the opening to
release it.

July 7

Follow the Evidence

Direct experience of the self is voiceless and
formless. – *Ndidi,* Tea Leaves

With the dawn of the personal computer age, the internet and social media, we do not have a shortage of information and data available to us. The digital experience convinces us that we are having an interactive experience, but we are having a dance with images of reality. The internet is a metaphor for the collective mind that is us. We interact in social media, but we do not fully comprehend the vastness of it until we make a contribution that many people like or dislike. Like the crowd-sourced Wikipedia, whatever we input into the vast matrix that is the internet is what we get when we choose to retrieve information. What we are seeking is what we have constructed. What we see or hear is a representation of reality that seeks our agreement.

The phenomenon of digital technology interfaces is not the complete life experience that we can enjoy. If we move away from the machines, we gather a new kind of evidence, a new life experience. When we turn our attention inward, we realize the tyranny of words and information as we try to quiet our minds. We become aware of the limitations of words as a way to communicate and seek ways to truly express our beliefs, but at the level of conscious awareness, we know that we don't know. In communion with the power of One, we experience the universal intelligence as it is; and see possibilities and creative energy rather than limitations and blockages. When we touch the spirit of Universal Mind, we realize that we are here to experience life directly and fully.

July 8

Making Changes

We are not limited to what we can do. – *Ndidi,* Tea Leaves

A woman of age decided to return to practicing tai chi after many years of absence from the practice. She was surprised that she remembered the complete movement and kept pace with the rather accomplished class. She pushed herself to finish the class, even though she felt some discomfort. After the class was complete, she walked unsteadily to her car and drove home aching from overextension of her knees. But with a determination to relax into her practice, gradually, she discovered the movement within her.

Sometimes we take a break from healthy practices that once supported our journey, and wonder what prompted us to move away from what worked for us. We admit that life can sometimes distract us from what supports us. But sometimes we return to what worked in the past, and find that we return with new eyes and new needs. Glimpses of former teaching may arise, now and then, but most of the time we may feel like beginners. Learning as a returning novice requires a kind of humility that is both frustrating and rewarding. The humility obviously emerges when we continually make mistakes, or just feel silly.

The reward of this humility comes from letting go of fear and how we look to others. Performance is a show for others, literally! When we let go of our need for perfection, we experience self-compassion; we learn to fail with no regrets. We also learn constructive interdependence, so we no longer need to know everything, but have confidence in what we can contribute to the whole experience of life and learning. When we are present in the moment, who we are being takes precedence over what we are doing. When we learn self-compassion we free up a space in our heart for awareness of the true self. We become more than what we can do, and rest in the comfort of being who we really are in the process of change.

July 9

No Proof

There is no connection so powerful as
listening fully. – *Ndidi,* Tea Leaves

We know the incredible frustration of trying to prove something to someone who is not open to our point of view. It's easy to make that person wrong, if we're not careful with our thoughts and opinions. Even though it seems as if we are trying to prove a point, we are identifying our self with the point we are trying to make, and have fears that we could be exposed as wrong.

When we listen fully to another point of view, and risk being vulnerable, we can then tell our own story and reveal the truth of our being. Who we are transcends points of view, positions, or beliefs. Our struggle to be right is grounded in a story we have created about life.

We have nothing to prove. Our true self is never threatened by issues of rightness or wrongness; it transcends the struggles into a space of pure love. Awareness of the limitless true self is always enough, always love, and always truth.

July 10

Sin is a Big Mistake

Not even "sin" is permanent; love is. – *Ndidi,* Tea Leaves

Some may say that the origins of sin are greed, hatred and delusions of the mind. Regardless of the origins, the goal is always ultimately to be loved. When we understand deeply the temporary nature of all things, our mind defers to the true self, knowing that greed and hatred are futile exercises. We become aware that the mind deludes us into thinking that grasping, clinging and clawing for something will achieve happiness for us.

We seek what is seeking us, and our misguided actions or opinions will not bring us closer to what is already within us, around us and expressing as us. On the contrary, hatred, greed and delusions keep us from the awareness of our true self; and that is the ultimate "sin." We already are what we are looking for, longing for, missing, but what we seek is so close, there is no way to it, no path to be taken. Love is the only "reality."

If we look at others as sinners, and righteously claim to love the sinner in spite of the sin, that is a delusion. Our judgment has conditions that place a barrier on the other; imposing barriers makes love impossible to share. Love does not create boundaries; our sense of being right does. We may momentarily accept another person, but our acceptance is conditional, based on a promise that the person will change behaviors and be more like us. Love is not us vs. them; Love is One Spirit.

We are often accustomed to seeing what a person does and who a person is as the same thing. We may choose to punish a person for a sin but we cannot separate the body from the sin, so we punish both. Each of us makes mistakes based on insatiable desires; we have beliefs that we are different from others, and what they do are threats to our well-being, but our fears cloud the mind. We fail to question our delusions about what it means to be human or worthwhile, and decide to separate ourselves from what we believe is wrong.

But we are not what we do; the true self is not action; it is our essential being. The essence of who we are gives meaning to divine forgiveness and love. If we hold the insight of the true self as beyond all doing and having, and as the pure awareness of being, we will release ourselves from the prejudice of accusations and desires for revenge; we will know our connection with all in the universe and let go of the reverberating effects of the suffering we create for ourselves and others.

July 11

Literalism

Even the "letter" of the law changes as conditions
change. – *Ndidi,* Tea Leaves

Literalism challenges the infinite mind with the promise of indisputable facts. Like any pronouncement in a world of diverse perspectives, the promise is always broken. Our words place immediate limits on communication; when words are spoken, meaning is unleashed for multiple interpretations. The various interpretations of words, literature, scriptures and prophetic texts are sometimes enslaved by literalism. Metaphors, similes, parables and fables are beaten into literal submission in the service of locating the truth, but the infinite mind receives finite words like round pegs into square holes. Some people struggle to find meanings in words, with many people trying to communicate through their own clouded lens.

Since we have an individually-focused experience in a collective consciousness, our interpretations of reality become complex. We lament the loss of agreement, but as long as we cling to our belief in the words themselves instead of the consciousness that lies within the words, we will violently disagree. Words conjure images of something based on views or feelings, but words are mere substitutes for the direct experience. From those vaguely comprehensible images, we assert our significance and create "otherness."

We could honor our community of souls with realization of our unique life experiences, and celebrate the points where our web of experience touches others. From a space of connection, we can discover the destructive nature of our desire for sameness; and grow comfortable with the diversity of thoughts that foster changes in the world.

July 12

Dancing Dervishes

If you look at a dancer in silence, his or her body will be the music. If you turn the music on, that body will become an extension of what you're hearing. – *Judith Jamison,* Dancing Spirit: An Autobiography

The annual journey of the salmon upstream, the flight of the geese, and the spawning of the silver fish are reminders of the continual dance of the universe. When we join the dance, that mysteriously enlivening dance of the universe, we come to life in a new way; we find joy.

Sufis are well-known for their twirling dances that fling them into euphoric trances. Within that space of detachment from routine activities, the dancing dervishes connect with the divinity within themselves. We too can connect intentionally as we are mindful of the continuous movement of the universe. When we are still, the universe moves and when we are in motion, the universe continues its steady movement of creation.

When we align ourselves with the movement of the universe, we acknowledge the impermanence of everything and the potential for ecstasy. We become aware that the rhythm of all things is in perfect harmony with change.

When we notice the arising and disappearing of phenomena – the cessation of singing of the birds after mesmerizing melodies; the disappearance of the geese as they squawk their way to new heights; the distant journey of the salmon to safely lay eggs; or the ebb and flow of pain that disturbs our peacefulness - we know the enchanting rhythm of the universe. We can join the inevitable ebb and flow of life without fear but with a sense of adventure. When we open ourselves to the flow, something beautiful emerges from deep within us.

The Golden Bowl

The true self is neither lost nor found. — *Ndidi,* Tea Leaves

A woman goes for a walk in the nearby woods on a sunny day. Suddenly a large, brightly shining bowl appears nestled among three bushes. The bowl is strangely attractive in its glistening glory. Before she approaches the bowl, a flood of questions come to her mind: Where did the bowl come from? Why is it here? Is the bowl real or a figment of my imagination? What's inside the bowl? When she finally looks inside the bowl, nothing is there? She walks away puzzled but when she turns around to look again, it has vanished.

The emptiness inside the golden bowl is a metaphor for the essence of the true self; we encase the true self with a bowl called the body. The bowl seems real but the contents cannot be grasped or even named. The true self is always present even if we cannot always perceive it or clearly define it. We see glimpses of our true self, not with our mind but with our heart. The mind interferes with our knowing the true self; questions and doubts flood the mind. We may become frustrated with the elusive emptiness of the true self, until we realize that the emptiness is evidence of its boundlessness. The Presence of All-That-Is is not out there; we are in the midst of it. The true self does not leave, even if the body does, because there is no place where the true self is not present.

July 14

Changes

Whatever your life situation is, how would you feel if you completely accepted it as it is –right Now? – *Eckhart Tolle*, Stillness Speaks

If we believe that everything is as it should be, a change does not correct anything. A change is an opening for the evolutionary universe to express itself differently. We change our opinions, perceptions, and positions, because our eyes and ears are opened to hear and see more.

When a person gets better after an injury, it is not a correction; it is as it should be. The body is always whole in the mind of spirit; when we say we are healing we are actually coming into alignment with our inherent wholeness. Our attempts to control our healing can sometimes interfere with our natural return to wholeness; the ideas of the egoic mind are the greatest culprits in such interferences. We think we know what is best, but what is best is what is happening now, because our experience now is contributing to what is and what will be.

We bounce from opinion to opinion, "correcting" our views as we get more and more information, but change is the evidence of impermanence, the way of the universe. Nothing is corrected, because nothing is wrong. Change opens new windows, allows the fresh ideas to come into our awareness, and allows us to get swept up in the winds of joy. There is only well-being in the universe, but if we choose to see changing conditions as aberrations, distractions or errors, we will miss the enchantment of evolution.

July 15

Quiet Power

Universal power is present everywhere, quietly
moving. – *Ndidi,* Tea Leaves

If we walk along the beach as the ocean splashes against the shore, we can witness the quiet power of the waves that announce their presence continuously. If we allow ourselves to be continually surprised by the budding beauty and blossoming of the trees and flowers in spring, we can know the quiet power that moves and changes. If canyons and craters, mountains and meadows stop us in our tracks with their majesty, we are in the presence of quiet power. If the industrious ants march triumphantly into a home as if they owned it, quiet power is in motion. If a whale lifts its blubbery body into an arc of beauty leaping high above the waters of the sea, quiet power asserts its naturalness.

We too have the power of quiet flowing in and out with each rhythmic breath. The entire universe breathes with the same power; every animal, bird, fish and plant embraces the life force of the universe. Life in its naturalness emerges without force or grasping, without fear and trepidation; but fears often claim us and channel our thoughts into survival and supremacy. We become louder as we proclaim our significance; we forget to honor the life force that flows through us and as us. We announce our presence with force, when our true strength is soft and subtle. When we remember our power, quiet power, we become secure in knowing that we are One Love. There is nothing in the universe more powerful, yet gentler than Love.

July 16

Reputation

Trust is cherished by the giver and receiver. – *Ndidi,* Tea Leaves

The loss of trust from others can shatter a person's reputation like a crystal bowl dashed against a stone wall. The shards of glass are dangerous if touched, difficult to reassemble, and scattered. We say that the destruction of a good reputation can lead to shame and humiliation, or depression and a sense of powerlessness. Constructed by people who view themselves as separate individual souls, a reputation is a tool for further separation. In the spotlight, people can be more closely examined for their flaws and favorable aspects; reputation is a view that makes people into objects, distinct and different from others. The egoic mind likes the differentiation; it basks in the rise of the reputation and slinks away from blame for the destruction of it. But, even in shame, the ego is hard at work, rebuilding the reputation with false stories of blame and unworthiness.

We are not what other people think of us. We cannot control conditions, but we *can* control our response. We can train our mind to allow thoughts of our demise to come and go, without clinging to any one of them long enough to become depressed or shamed. The true self remains when all the layers of accusations pile on like heavy metal; the broken pieces of our lives never have to weigh on us. As we reassemble our lives, after a destroyed reputation, we can honor the newness of the crystal bowl, reassembled in form, but never having lost its essence.

July 17

Wholeness

The length of suffering depends on the sufferer. – *Ndidi,* Tea Leaves

Being homeless can be painful, a challenge to our sense of worth, but it is not who we are. Experiencing physical, sexual or emotional abuse can be painful, confusing and trust-shattering, but abuse does not define us. Feeling misunderstood or rejected because of racial identity, sexual orientation, or socioeconomic class can be painful, isolating and lonely, but categories or attributed identities are not who we are.

Often our responses to conditions and identities bring more pain: anger, revenge, and self-denial. Whenever this cycle of pain begins to spiral into daily life, we could remember to have compassion for our self and all others who are experiencing the pain that wracks our self-confidence. We could make peace with the innocence within us. If we immerse ourselves in the liberation of the present moment, we can know that we can be free of suffering. Life does not end because something painful stops us in our tracks or pounds our chest with feelings of inadequacy. Pain gives us clarity about what we want in our reality; without the discomfort of pain we could not know our own strength or what deserves our gratitude. We know that life is ever-changing, and when we flow with change, our universal potential re-balances the misalignment that causes pain. With an opened heart and clear vision, we grow in awareness that the true self is wholeness and love.

July 18

Love and Hate

Love cannot co–exist with hate. – *Ndidi,* Tea Leaves

Some have noted that there's a "thin line between love and hate." In the present moment there is only consciousness of love. The false self sees the two ideas as separate and mutually exclusive, but that is a deceptive story. Both exist in our consciousness. We may love the taste of salt, for example, but if too much salt is added to a dish, it becomes distasteful. A new loving relationship may be warm and exciting, but if one person clings to the other, over time the relationship weakens. We sometimes say that we have too much of a good thing.

Two people, who don't know that they are already connected as spiritual beings, will seek closeness that is already a reality. When we understand that love is all there is, and that we cannot get any closer than oneness in spirit, we give up the clinging and possessiveness and relax into the love that we already are.

When we choose to hate another person or group, we are clinging to our delusion of separation but also to the idea that we deserve love more than another person or group. Love is not something you get; it is something you are. It is not just a feeling, because feelings come and go; it is an awareness of being. Love is the rock, while hate rests in the quicksand of the mind. When we love as if we have an unquenched thirst we know that love is our identity, and in loving we come home to our true self.

July 19

Breathing Awareness

The next breath is a gift of awareness. – *Ndidi,* Tea Leaves

The universe is alive with sound. When we meditate we listen to our own breath, and within that breath is the breath of spirit. We breathe automatically without thinking, but how we breathe changes based on our unknowing response to conditions. We breathe shallowly under stress, and when we are relaxed we breathe more slowly. When we breathe in through the nose and out through the mouth, we get a different feeling for example from breathing in through the mouth and out through the mouth. Life changes constantly, but one constant is the continuous breath, synonymous with life.

Meditation uses the vehicle of our breathing to quiet the mind. It heightens our awareness of the sounds in stillness, but after a few moments without moving, the sounds lose their prominence and the emergence of the divine within us becomes our awareness. There is nothing to know or understand, because awareness is beyond comprehension. In meditative stillness, if we ask a question with the mind, the answer comes without words. If we seek relief from suffering, relief is present as if it were always here, now. When we want to know who we really are we just have to breathe.

July 20

The World as It Is

Just as the wave cannot exist for itself, but is ever a part of
the heaving surface of the ocean, so must I never live my
life for itself, but always in the experience which is going on
around me. – *Albert Schweitzer,* Civilization and Ethics

Nature is a teacher who wants to make friends with us. The universe dances with joy, and the natural world knows the melodies. If we notice and listen, we realize that we have always been a part of the dance. The natural steps have heart and flexibility like the bending palm trees in the wind, or the rivers flowing with determination to continue the journey. The doors of nature are always open to visitors, but when we are in communion with the natural world we feel at home. The sense that there is no hurry, urgency or regret in the natural world attracts us to it. Abundance of color, form and texture in the flowers and fauna remind us of the abundance that is ours in the universe. We witness the cycle of life and transformation in the ebb and flow, growth and withering of plants and animals. Nature displays the incomprehensible power of the divine, and the interdependency of living things. We know that when we honor the natural world we honor the life of the universe.

Sailing on a quiet lake, we feel the gentle undulating movements of the water; we are calmed by the womb-like nuances of motion. Under a canopy of trees, deep into the forest, giant trees do not judge our decisions or humiliate us with accusations; they love us in silence. Flowers with shocking colors nearly make us lose our breath as we take in their beauty. The wind kisses us on the cheeks as it wantonly moves through a town; and a cool breeze caresses us as sun rays beam down with welcomed warmth. We are nature's witnesses in the world, but also actors in its drama. We sometimes seek its entertainment as a last resort, but we have always been inseparable.

July 21

Too Much Self

We can dissolve the boundary between us; it serves
no useful purpose. – *Ndidi,* Tea Leaves

Mina is a collector. She accumulates trophy images that she stores in a room called her *"self."* The room looks like a storeroom with layers and layers of experiences piled high in the room. Sometimes she cracks open the door to the room and gently removes an experience to share with someone else. There is no compassion in the room, so she looks for compassion outside of herself; she realizes that something is always missing. She believes that it is out there somewhere, but she cannot find it. In time she grows weary of caring; and believes that she has no time for compassion that cannot be located.

We sometimes connect with others by sharing our pain, and hope that we will find joy. But, one day we enter our room called "self" and all the accumulated experiences fall onto our head; the weight is unbearable, so we cry out in agony. As we lie buried in our experiences, we feel stuck. We look at the experiences and notice that so much has changed since the first sharp pain of events occurred. We wonder why we are keeping such a heavy load of pain in a room, our heart room. We suddenly see how small the room is, and how much we have grown. We scramble to our feet, open the door wide and liberate ourselves from too much "self." Without the false self we can see things as they are, let them go when they go, and live in communion with others as one spirit.

July 22

Vibrations

By paying attention to the way you feel, you can fulfill your reason for being here, and you can continue your intended expansion in the joyful way that you intended. – *Esther and Jerry Hicks*, Ask and It is Given

A drummer takes her position sitting comfortably with a Djembe drum and begins to strike the surface with slow, rhythmic movements, increasing in energy and frequency. The experience of the drummer cannot be described in words, nor can it be captured through observation; but when the drumming begins to cause involuntary movements in those who hear and feel the vibrations, the direct experience emerges.

We live in a universe that vibrates; we get energized based on feelings from vibrations. We usually pay attention to feelings we enjoy and our vibration will intensify; or we can allow feelings we don't enjoy to scatter the intensity and focus. Feelings we enjoy may be love, peace and compassion, and feelings we do not enjoy can be fear, anxiety, sadness and envy.

When we are in rhythm with the flow of the universe, and allow feelings we enjoy to be in that flow of well-being, we experience joy. We cultivate enjoyment vibrations by intentionally observing what is life-affirming in our reality. We also increase our positive vibrations by expressing gratitude for what is. We look for the innocence in other sentient beings; find the joy in sadness; recognize the falsehood of fears; and, express compassionate joy when other people are happy. Our life experiences are a manifestation of our vibrations. When we deliberately cultivate positive, intense vibrations that emerge from our core self, we are liberated from suffering and frustration.

July 23

Consequences

Some people create their own storms, then get
upset when it rains. – *Anonymous*

In the *I Ching*, a Chinese classic that underscores the dynamic nature
and ceaseless transformations of all things in the universe, the subject
of consequences is explored. Before we can understand the nature of
consequences, we can look at the current conditions. The *I Ching* attempts
to answer the question: What happened? We could ask the question, what
is the cause of the conditions and what are their effects? We could ask,
"What matters in these conditions?"

We assign importance to the conditions we experience; they do not
have significance in themselves. Consequences are neither rewards nor
punishments; they are responses to actions we have taken. We decide
whether the responses are useful to bring joy, or whether they are not
useful as distractions of the mind. We learn that greed, hatred or immature
thinking are not useful and lead to suffering. We learn that abundance and
well-being occur in feelings of compassion and loving kindness toward all
sentient beings; we discover that we must lose in order to gain, experience
challenging conditions in life in order to appreciate periods of peace. We
may try to refrain from judgments, but we can be easily drawn to self-
judgments by a mind that has self-doubts. The effects of any action are
embedded in the action, just as every problem contains many solutions.
Everything is interconnected with everything else; so an action not only
has a reaction but a reaction has an effect that affects others.

When we appreciate all that is, we do not give special emphasis to
consequences. We see each occurrence of cause and effect with equal

emphasis, since one is known only because of the existence of the other. As changes occur and effects of actions become clear to us, we can observe the changes, breathe in deeply, and then willingly release the surprise, regret or hurt of conditions in our lives, with our out-breath.

July 24

Subtle Wisdom

To finish the moment, to find the journey's end in every
step of the road, to live the greatest number of good hours,
is wisdom. – *Ralph Waldo Emerson*, Experience

Institutions of higher education are veritable fountains of knowledge, steeped in research and the ongoing collection of data. Often concepts developed as a result of years of investigation are reluctantly changed when new information surfaces. In a knowledge-based society, what we know seems to matter.

Wisdom often confidently ascribed to people with maturity and experience may be considered, when knowledge alone seems inadequate. But wisdom involves careful examination and questions about truth. The universe is the pinnacle of wisdom, the steadily moving force that lingers when temporary effects disappear. Truth is wise, not only from information, but from the conscious sense of being. When our religious leaders and prophets share their wisdom, they do so from a place of conscious awareness and spiritual peace. They have been conduits for the wisdom of truth to emerge, but if that wisdom is seen as stuck in the personhood of the teacher, the flow of wisdom is stymied. Subtle wisdom knows no boundaries; it is forever true and unable to be fully articulated. As the Upanishads tell us, "God is consciousness. God is absolute experience. God is ever new joy." When we are fearful, even partial knowledge based on incomplete information may cause us to limit our expression of love and compassion. People who are without homes or adequate resources may frighten some of us; or people who are culturally, racially or physically different from us may bring out our implicit bias. But the wisdom of the universe is compassionate; one spirit is all there is to consider, so the artificial separations that sentient beings make are not in universal awareness.

Subtle wisdom is intelligent; it is the mind of the universe that creates and loves its creation. When we are aware of the subtle wisdom that courses through us, around us and within us, we have no space for fear. We can be confident that the universal wisdom, subtle wisdom is always present, unchanging stability that exists beyond knowledge.

July 25

Wading in the Water

Struggle deceives us; healing and liberation are
implicit in our existence. – *Ndidi,* Tea Leaves

A story is told that enslaved Africans in the United States were led to safety by the emancipator Harriet Tubman. Ms. Tubman and others used words of the then popular song, Wade *in the Water,* to warn enslaved Africans to leave the woods and roads and to get into the water to thwart the tracking of dogs that bounty hunters used. The water was a protector, a distraction from pain, injury and suffering; the water was a peacemaker. For enslaved Africans, water could be their savior.

In the Old and New testaments of the Holy Bible there are verses that reference "troubling the waters" as a way to be made whole. Water symbolism is powerful as an archetype of wholeness and change; and moving waters symbolize continuous change. Healing waters figuratively lie within us, but actually the entire human body is approximately 60% water. The brain and muscles are 75% water; blood is 92% water; and bones in the body are 22% water. Without a continual supply of replenishing water, the body would die within a week.

Life sometimes troubles the waters, but not in a good way. We struggle to still the waters, to find solutions to whatever is going off track, but sometimes the water itself is the saving grace, the protection and the safety. When we know our true self, physically and spiritually, we wade into the conditions, like a duck floating into a pond; we face the fears that get us stuck. We decide to follow confidently the paths that lead us to peace, because we realize that fears will not solve anything, and faith will. We feel freedom in the Presence of All-That-Is, and peace washes over us like a life-giving stream. We immerse ourselves in the source of our being and trust our inner guide that will lead us through the valley and through the woods to safety.

July 26

Vending Machine

If your daily life seems poor, do not blame it; blame yourself that
you are not poet enough to call forth its riches; for the Creator,
there is no poverty. – *Rainer Maria Rilke,* Letters to a Young Poet

Creating a desire for more in life is the modus operandi of the egoic mind.
We have a tentative relationship with our desires; we are never certain that
what we desire will be manifested, but we add many things to our wish list.
We hope that getting another material object, achieving success in careers,
enjoying a loving, intimate relationship, or having excellent, disease-free
health will make us happy. Many belief systems provide a blueprint for
getting what we desire, but the process always involves conditions that
must be met in order to be assured of a positive result. Some see the
universe as a kind of cosmic vending machine, where we simply follow
certain rules and a cosmic divinity will provide what we want.

In a dynamic universe every thought has potential, inherent power that can
become form -- manifested desires, so whatever we ask for, and whatever
challenges we face have the potential to become our reality. Appreciation
for what appears now, and who we are now provides the vibrational energy
to bring us into alignment with what we think is not yet manifested. What
we want is already given in the now. The egoic mind wants us to believe
that manifestations in our reality are the result of some prescribed actions
or behaviors, but unconditional love is already ours. The egoic mind
convinces us that we must pay a price for love, but the universe is love
generously displayed for all to experience, now. When we ask it is given
because it is already a reality, we must align with it in order to enjoy what
is already in our midst.

July 27

Experiences

...when we taste a plum or smell rotting leaves, these simple, direct experiences are our contact with basic wakefulness, with basic goodness, with sacred world. – *Pema Chödrön, Living Beautifully with Uncertainty and Change*

A weather forecaster barely finishes her report about an upcoming storm when meteorologists have new information and calculations that the storm may not have the intensity originally predicted. Initial reports of a disaster change hourly as new data come to a news desk. We watch in dismay as everything changes, because we identify strongly with what we see and hear, even though we may not have direct experience of it. We have a social contract that convinces us that what we see is real, solid and reliable.

But when we allow our fearful mind to control what we experience, we become its servant; we see no choice in how to respond to thoughts that control us. Even though there are no predetermined impacts of our thoughts, we become convinced that there are limited possibilities. The conditions in our lives limit us if we believe there is no way out of them.

Conditions appear and others convince us that fearful images are the truth. Many of us believe that what happens in our lives is the price we pay for living, a kind of payment for being the progeny of "sin." Society penalizes us for thinking outside the box, outside the conventional structure of shame.

We can refuse to identify with conditions that are inherently temporary, and free ourselves from the false representation of our lives. Our true self rises above and beyond conditions. We can choose to tame our thoughts, see the power of the present moment, and find the liberation from fear.

July 28

Humility

Humility is the surest sign of strength. – *Thomas Merton,*
Thoughts in Solitude

There is nothing more resilient than humility; its strength and endurance
are found in the refusal to be directed by the ego. We may think of the
humble person as self-effacing, diminished or discounted. We may think
the attitude of humility is reserved for "people of the cloth," the poor or
downtrodden among us. Practicing humility is stripping away false ideas
of the self as separate from everything else in the universe. Those who are
truly humble speak to improve the silence, transcend the divisiveness of
conflicts, and reject opportunities to judge others. The humble person
derives joy from giving to others, but gives without expectation of a return.
The humble person knows the trap of protecting one's dignity as a trick of
the grasping ego; she is willing to be authentic with others even if it means
becoming vulnerable.

Humility is like water that runs smoothly over rocks, fills the crevices
between them, freely transforms into gentle rain, and is willing to fall
gently to the earth to flow again to uncharted territories. When we are
humble we see ourselves in others; we hear more because we listen, but do
not react to everything we hear; and, we cherish the opportunity to honor
life as it appears rather than how we want it to be.

July 29

If Only

We're taught to try to live without regret…learn to live not
without regret, but with it. – *Kathryn Schulz*, TED talk, 2011

In the moment of decision, even decisions made hastily seem right at the
time. In hindsight, we judge ourselves thinking that perhaps we had not
gathered enough data and information to make a viable decision, or we
followed a hunch or our feelings in making the decision. If the choice turns
out to be an inappropriate one, we begin a process of "if only" arguments.
We try to rewrite a painful outcome by revisiting the conditions that in our
mind created the unfortunate choice. We may beat ourselves up because
we relied on feelings or failed to see what was hidden from us. We wonder
why we dated or married someone; why we bought a car or an extra pair
of shoes; or why we decided not to get a particular training or education.
With every choice is a regret, but also an opportunity. If we worry about
the choice that was made in the past, we are likely to fill up with regrets.
If we fill up with regrets, we cannot appreciate the feedback we acquired
from the choice we made. When we make friends with our life as it is
now, including choices we have made, we are liberated. With freedom
from regrets and shame, we are able to pour our attention into the present
moment where what is appearing in the now can capture our attention. Be
thankful for your experiences and consider them part of your life's journey.
Rehashing a choice we made keeps us stuck in the past, attempting to
change something that almost worked for us, while the world moves on.

July 30

Adaptation

...one of the sources of resilience is the ability to measure
and perceive early warning signs so as to adapt.
– *Andrew Zolli*, Resilience: Why Things Bounce Back

On the icy tundra of the arctic, the white polar bear survives as it blends into the surroundings, but if the ice melts and brown earth emerges in its place, the majestic creatures will over time become brown to blend into the environment.

Darwin did not suggest that the strongest or fittest of a species survives, but the most adaptable. In a changing universe, our willingness and ability to adapt is essential. If we want to change how we experience our lives, we can start with adapting to what is happening, to appreciate what is happening now. If we lean into the beauty of now, we flow with the changing universe; our agility allows us to escape the attachment to the way things were in the past or the status quo. We learn that changing our mind can be a way to tame the mind, to keep our thoughts from controlling the nature of our experience of life. When we adapt, we release our resistance to the way things are now, because we realize that nothing remains the same. When we align with life we are conscious of a changing universe; we become aware that change is a recipe for peace.

July 31

Solid

A sand dune only appears solid from a distance. – *Ndidi*, Tea Leaves

If we build a house, we must be certain to start with a solid foundation in order to have a sustainable structure, but even with the best construction, overtime the house will shift and move slightly. What seems solid as a rock is not really immovable. We assemble materials to build but we cannot prevent the inevitable changes that will occur. A house like water moves and changes.

Unlike the house that we create with tools and skills, we cannot create water. The manufacture of water is difficult because of the explosive quality of hydrogen in contact with oxygen. Even more difficult to create is energy; it cannot be created nor destroyed, just transformed. Like water, energy moves; it flows.

On the other hand, a rock does not flow, although it can be changed; it seems unmovable and solid, although it too is energy. For many years, the rock has been a metaphor for the unchanging essence of the universe, a familiar and believable representation. In a world of changes, the idea of a rock is a comfort in times of struggle and chaos. We think we need something to cling to, stand on, or believe that will not change. The challenges in life we face are the effects of our unwillingness to face change, and our belief that the rock will save us. We could rest in knowing that the rock could refer to the true self within us, the unchanging ultimate reality that is present each moment of our lives. It is the immovable, unbreakable essence of the self that is a constant Presence - the rock of being.

August 1

Images

The face of divinity is reflected in all living things. – *Ndidi,* Tea Leaves

Because we have struggled throughout human existence to understand who we are in an unpredictable world, we have created divine beings in our image, for solace. Our desire for a tangible, personal communication with a presence that controls all things has led us to construct a familiar image. We may be comfortable with what we have created, and may feel a special relationship with our divine representation of this power, but we have doubts. When challenging conditions show up in our lives, we sometimes question the intentions of the divine image we have grown close to. We have followed all the required rules and maintained certain standards of behavior, so the appearance of painful events leaves us confused and angry. We hold onto the beliefs that those who share our views are protected in a special way by the divine power we have created. But then we hear that others have created their own divine image, and they also seem to have little control over conditions. We become puzzled by the irregularity of appearances in the lives of different people; positive events occur in the lives of those we consider unworthy, and negative events seem to occur in the lives of those we consider worthy and faithful to beliefs. Devotion to our divine images does not ensure that we are chosen, favored or protected from the conditions that appear to us. While we continually look outside ourselves for validation that we are saved from harm and destruction, we turn away from the divinity that lies within us. Some say that we are created in the image of the divine, but we come to realize that we have instead created the divine in our own image. When we own our divine essence, we gain clarity of mind and heart. The universe is alive with divinity; we are all connected ---every living thing.

August 2

Guilt

Facts are many, but the truth is one. – *Rabindranath Tagore,*
Sadhana: The Realisation of Life (1916)

Guilt is not a viable emotion, but is a protective shield we wear as armor when we do not wish to face the shame of actions or relationships. Guilt is a keeper of secrets, a shelter when mistakes and misguided actions make us vulnerable. We are not what we have done in the past, even if we are willing to take responsibility for our actions or thoughts.

Guilty actions are the result of grasping, hatred or delusions of the mind. We could relieve our suffering if we release our intention to control something or someone. Grasping creates harmful attachments to objects or feelings that lead to suffering and misguided behaviors.

Hatred is a poisonous attitude that is fueled by our belief that we are separate from one another, and that one life is better than another. Our controlling mind deludes us, persuading us to believe stories of our lives that are untrue.

Guilt prevents us from being aware of our magnificence. In the present moment, joy clears away sadness and allows love and peace to emerge. With the removal of the cloud of guilt, we see our misguided actions as sharpeners of our awareness, and gates to expanded consciousness. Guilt is another layer of the false self that blurs awareness of what and who we are.

August 3

Rights

Our rights cannot make others wrong. – *Ndidi,* Tea Leaves

What are the rights that we all have? If we say that we all have the right to live, then many rights are taken away every moment of our existence. If we say we all have the right to love, then many attempts to love or be loved can be interrupted by prohibitive beliefs. If we say that we all have the right to be happy, or at least to pursue happiness, who judges the way each of us pursues it? We may say we all have a right to our beliefs, but do we support all actions based on those beliefs? When it comes to rights, we sometimes make people wrong with our judgments.

Joy arises when we act with compassion and love. When our actions elicit the innocence of others, we can see our own worth and allow joy to arise. When our actions come from a place of love not persuasion or resentment, we allow joy to permeate our being. When we realize our interdependence with every living thing in the universe, we realize that our existence is supported in every way by the entire universe.

Rights are a way to establish the worth of someone or a thing that is already honored in the universal spirit of love. Do animals have rights? Do the trees and flowers have rights? Do the sun and moon have rights? As thinking beings, we could end the questions and the opinions. When we try to prevent people from getting something that is inherently theirs, we inflate our "I-ness." The ubiquitous, egoic "I" segments our world into friends and enemies, wrong-people and right-people; safe beings and unsafe beings. Our endless categories are delusions of the mind, ways to elevate the self in our mind. Rights are not wrong; they are affirmations of our being. When we dissolve our judgments about others, we release our need to exclude others according to rules that we have created.

August 4

Energy Conserved

Universal energy is indestructible. – *Ndidi,* Tea Leaves

Energy can change form, but where did that energy originate? Let's trace back a chain of events. A bicycle is rolling down the hill, transferring potential energy into kinetic (movement) energy. The bicycle got its potential energy (energy due to position related to gravity) by the rider using metabolic energy to move the pedals. The pedals use mechanical energy to move the chain, which moves the wheels. The rider's metabolic energy came from chemical energy that was stored in the molecules of the food she ate. That chemical energy entered the animal whose meat she ate by the animal digesting a plant and breaking the bonds in its molecules. The plant made the molecules by using light energy from the Sun. The Sun's light energy came from electrons in its atoms lowering energy states, and releasing energy. The energy in the atoms came from the nuclear reactions in the heart of the Sun. What started the nuclear reactions? Physicists think the Big Bang was the beginning of the earth and our galaxy, but we are likely part of a multitude of universes –a multiverse.

The short answer is that the energy we encounter and use every day has always been with us since the "beginning" of the universe and always will be with us. Energy changes forms but does not disappear; that is called the law of conservation of energy. We are changing and transforming daily; the evidence is in the mirror, our memories and perceptions. As energy transforms, a constant, silent, true self remains. Our essential self is universally conserved energy.

August 5

As If

You don't describe what you see; you see what you describe. – *Michael Bernard Beckwith,* Overcoming Challenges, YouTube, April 2012

Affirmations can be powerful tools for transformation if we believe them. The mind can either thwart our affirmations or support them as a possible future, but the future is always suspect. Experience tells us not to trust the future, because it has yet to occur, so we wait conditionally for a future that we can live with. How then could we affirm positive thoughts about some time that is tentative?

All is possible in the present moment, not in our actions but in our thoughts. Our affirmations are confirmations; now is the time-space that creates our well-being. Affirmations activate joyful vibrations and simulate the state of being desired, as if we are experiencing what we desire now.

The "As-if" principle assures us that we can create our reality if we act as if it is happening now. In the present moment, the only "time" we ever have, there is no future time. Everything exists in the now; we can feel it in the core of our being.

Proponents of affirmations invite us to think of what we want, tell ourselves that we have it, raise our vibration to one of love and appreciation, and imagine that what we want is ours. The truth of our lives is that we are encouraged to desire something we already have or to be someone we already are, because everything already exists in the present moment. We may believe that our skills in behaving as-if will determine whether or not we get what we want, but there is nothing different for us to do or be. Our vibrations are not dependent on a choice of words or actions, but on loving energy of appreciation and gratitude.

Our affirmations are statements of dreams that we can see and feel. The dreams are not in us; we are in the dreams. When we are being who we are, nothing is impossible, nothing is outside our awareness, but when we focus on doing and having, our attention is on what we lack.

All of our affirmations are attempts to experience the love we seek. Love is present now, so we could rest in awareness that desires are not only affirmed but already present.

August 6

Reverence

Idleness is never a lack of something to do, but rather a
lack of something to love. – *Ndidi,* Tea Leaves

A woman sits at a table arranging flowers. She is part of a team of flower arrangers who produce the same arrangement of artificial flowers every day for eight hours. A documentary film maker asked her how she is able to continue the work that is so repetitive without becoming bored with the routine. She answers to the surprise of the interviewer, "Each moment is different, so each arrangement is new."

Our work may seem routine or unimaginative, but within each moment is an opportunity to discover newness and reverence for the gift of now. As time moves to the next moment, we are faced with our experience that has nuances of change from the moment before, barely recognized in our continual fascination with what's next. Each fleeting moment arrives with new joy; if we ignore or discount the gift that is the present, we have a shallow experience of deep work. If we miss the nuances of change in our work, we see our daily work as unremarkable. If we lose ourselves in the past or the future, we miss the opportunity to experience the joy in our work now. The treasures of work are found in our state of being, and less in the act of doing. Be fully present for each moment of work, because each moment is an opportunity to be fully who we are.

August 7

Mercy

Mercifulness is kindness born in love. – *Ndidi,* Tea Leaves

Each person or animal we encounter is a unique opportunity to experience the graciousness of mercy. If we fully express our true nature, we will touch the deep essence of who we are. Our mercy creates a space for other beings to live and to thrive; and for our own hearts to be filled with joy. Some may say that mercy is the gift of the divine; we are perhaps told that we are receivers of mercy rather than givers, but we are always in the universal flow of love.

The scampering rabbit who avoids destruction from our automobile because we slow down on a narrow street, appreciates our mercy. The children playing mindlessly on the same narrow street, who escape injury, benefit from our mercy. If a person we trusted implicitly shatters that trust with dishonesty and greed, we can be merciful in our response. If we throw the small fish back into the lake it calls home; advocate for a teenager who has broken a rule; or forgive a parent who failed to know us when we were young, we touch the essence of mercy.

When we look deeply at the sweetness of the true self, no animosity is present, because we are without fear. Mercy is possible when fear has dissolved, when concerns about our individual significance and power are rendered irrelevant, and when joy and love arise from our soul.

August 8

Unrelenting Devotion

There is no greater joy than love without
expectations. – *Ndidi,* Tea Leaves

We may express our solemn promise to abide by certain laws and expectations, according to our belief systems. We may be willing to sacrifice ourselves to keep vows that we have taken to be faithful. We may express our devotion to Jesus the Christ, God, the Great Spirit, Allah, Krishna or the Beloved, and feel the comfort in the sacred connection that we experience. We may also feel the tremendous relief from despair that comes from the connection, and the certainty of our deliverance from ultimate destruction or death. The comfort we feel is a reflection of the love that we are. When we savor the comfort and focus of devotion, we experience a small hint of the essence of One Spirit. In those moments, we are connecting more deeply with ourselves. We may feel most secure in connection with others, or most loving when we observe kindness in the world; but our connection to unrelenting universal love is never in jeopardy.

When we feel secure in the faithfulness of Presence, we become fearless. The Presence is always, everywhere present in us, throughout our temporal bodies and in our conditions and appearances. When we sense that constant Presence, we feel assured of our place in the universe of well-being. When we turn our focus inward, we discover that we are heirs to unrelenting devotion.

August 9

Ambition

Greed is the lack of confidence is one's own ability to
create. – *Vanna Bonta,* Degrees: Thought Capsules

After nearly everyone had introduced themselves at the workshop, a man
decided to tell the group of educators that he was a salesman. When he
noticed the grimaces on the faces of the other participants he shared, "I
have never actually sold anything to anyone; I just fulfilled their desire
for happiness."

Most of us are not satisfied with the status quo when it means that we make
little progress in our careers or work. We may want to make a difference in
the lives of others while we engage in more challenging work, or we may
want to change the world in some way. Our ambition can be driven by a
desire to contribute to the happiness of others.

If we are not careful, our altruism can turn a corner into greed, and risk
destroying our original intent. Like a moth flying into a flame, the desire
for more can be attractive and deadly. The attraction is fueled by an egoic
mind that believes that happiness lies in achievements that lead to wealth,
status or recognition. If we cannot appreciate what we are experiencing
now at work, we are unlikely to experience happiness in the future. When
we work in a state of resentment, fear or anger, we are developing the soil
for seeds of ongoing despair. Our energy is directed towards escaping
from pain and suffering, instead of remembering the joy and peace of the
present moment. When we are aligned with love and compassion we are in
sync with our spiritual center, then we work with integrity, fulfilling our
purpose while responding lovingly to the desires of others for happiness.

August 10

The Crucible

The work space is also home to our essential nature. – *Ndidi,* Tea Leaves

A work space is a crucible where decisions are made that transform the worker and the work. We may be asked to follow a specific process, or complete a set of tasks; we may direct an operation or create art and music. We are using creative energy in a specific time and space that will leave a legacy.

In everything that we do and say, we are expressing our sacred energy and being. Forces come together in a crucible of intentions to influence our well-being. Decisions are made with the hope that the future will produce influences that bring happiness, peace and joy. But with an uncertain future, we allow love to guide us, and surrender control of outcomes. We live in a world of faith, where we give up worries, and follow our hearts.

Whether we work as a producer of goods and services; practice the healing or medical arts; grow vegetables on a farm; or sell crafts as a street vendor, the space where we exist is a sacred crucible, when we integrate who we are with what we do.

August 11

Discouraged

We are often discouraged by one chapter in the
book of our life. – *Ndidi*, Tea Leaves

After spending years getting an education while she cared for her three children, a still young woman sank into despair when she learned that her youngest child had an illness that could bankrupt the family. She felt as if happiness had slipped from her fingers like grains of sand. She wondered whether it was worth her time and energy to become educated, if she could never be successful.

A father is laid off from his job of 22 years and dreads facing a partner and 4 children at home. He is humiliated by what he considers his failure to be a whole person, and believes that he is nothing without work.

After serving in two wars, a young soldier returns home to a local job market that cannot use her skills. She wonders about her earlier choices to enter the military and postpone her training as a teacher.

The frustrations of life conditions can easily send us reeling from what we perceive as the unfairness of life. We struggle to find out what we can do to change our conditions and want desperately to rise out of the rubble and breathe again. Deep within our hearts lies a strength that vanquishes our discouragement. The strength is an unchanging conscious awareness of no limitations and no boundaries. When we "know" that strength, our heart opens to a new reality. Experiences are part of a story in the past, but they are not the entire book of our lives. We find the courage to face our current challenges when we realize that conditions come and go and are a temporary tale. When we stop and become fully present in the moment, allowing the next steps to come to us, we can appreciate a difficult chapter in our book as simply part of the overall story.

August 12

Striving

If you realize that you have enough, you are
truly rich. – *Lao Tzu,* Tao Te Ching

Striving is like being drawn and quartered. The process seems focused
at first but then we realize that we are being pulled in many different
directions. There is great wisdom in temporary non-action- the focus on
just being, rather than doing- when the striving becomes stressful. Stillness
and non-action help us to know that the search for perfection in the future
is futile because perfection exists right now. Stretching ourselves into a
future that does not exist, while running away from mistakes in the past,
pulls us in two directions; the result is physical and emotional pain.

Our egos encourage us to strive without ever explaining what the prize will
be. If we believe that there is something we must do, have or be known
for in order to be happy, we have begun to believe that life is dependent
on what we do rather than who we are. In the state of awareness of the
glorious nature of life, we are like magnets for abundance. Happiness is a
state of being, not doing or having. Striving is an endless process of chasing
happiness, when we can *be happy* now.

August 13

Limitless

Grasping means we have forgotten what we
already have. – *Ndidi,* Tea Leaves

A bird tries to get into a second story window by pecking insistently with its beak. Each attempt is met with resistance: first resistance from the double-paned window; and secondly from the homeowner inside who claps her hands loudly to encourage the bird to fly away. The bird returns over and over again, pounding on the window, trying to get in; he has forgotten that the space he already has is greater and more expansive than the space inside the house.

Sometimes we unknowingly accept limits when unlimited abundance is always here for us. We see possibilities outside of ourselves, beyond what we have now, without recognizing the potential abundance in front of us or within us. In our zeal to be somewhere else, or to be someone else, we forget that what we need exists for us always in the present moment. What we seek may be inspiration, a feeling of authentic love from another person, a recognition of deep abiding peace, or a moment free of pain. When we experience the expanse of now, our hearts are opened for all the things we desire, and we know that we can fly with joy.

August 14

Morality

No expiration date exists for unconditional love. – *Ndidi,* Tea Leaves

How do we humans determine what is moral? Often we intertwine what is legal with what is moral. We consider what is consistent or inconsistent with our belief system to determine what is acceptable. Morality seems to be circumstantial; war, capital punishment, murder and suicide, and honor killings have moral arguments lodged in their defense. Whatever seems to be acceptable to a culture, society or religion in a particular space of time and location can be construed as moral.

The variations of morality are as plentiful as the ideas in the mind; the judgment is based on who is permitted to judge. We may defer moral questions to our chosen divine authority, based on writings or oral transmissions of truth. Our moral judgments are based on what we perceive as right or wrong at a particular time; sometimes that time was thousands of years ago, or when different truth-tellers were in power. Morality principles for any society can have an expiration date as conditions and priorities change. Child labor is no longer acceptable; women are no longer chattel; and slavery, once a privilege of the wealthy and powerful is no longer respectable or legal. Conditions change and with them the concept of morality.

What does not change is the true self that has no judgments, no opinions, and is pure, unconditional love. Awareness of the true self is a fundamental shift from judgments and moralizing to the sense of connection and love. The shift is imperceptible since the true self has always been the unwavering, unconditional truth of our being.

August 15

Light of Truth

The light of truth has never left us: look inside. – *Ndidi,* Tea Leaves

A man is found crawling on the ground near a street lamp, apparently looking for something. Carl approaches the man and asks, "What are you looking for?" The man answers flatly, "My keys." Where did you last see them?" Carl asked helpfully. "In my car," answered the man. Carl, perplexed, asked the man why he is looking under the lamp. The man answers, "Because the light is better here."

When we have lost our way, confused and frustrated with the conditions in life, it can be tempting to look outside of ourselves for answers. We may search in books, religious communities, associations, work or relationships, but we are often disappointed. We cannot know enough, work enough, or accommodate others enough to feel whole. Others are shining a light on our lives every day with projections of how they think life should be lived. We are tempted to listen to them until we begin to feel incomplete or uncomfortable in our own skin. After some time, we may begin to remember who we really are and release the fear of being lost in the impressions of who we are.

Answers have never been found outside of us. Truth is not material, temporary or transactional; the lamp has always been inside.

August 16

Secrets

There is no greater agony than bearing an untold story inside you. – *Maya Angelou*, I Know Why the Caged Bird Sings

Secrets can make us sick – physically, emotionally and psychologically. The seeds of secrets grow over time. Festering stories grow in importance the longer they are suppressed. Secrets show up as aches and pains, distrust or feelings of insecurity. Like heavy metal balls, deceptions obstruct our airways. Secrets, buried in a deep hole of pain, are covered by shame and feelings of unworthiness. Our secrets ask others to believe a false image of who we are; and co-conspirators encourage us to be what we are not.

The most powerful secrets are the ones we hide from ourselves. When we try to ignore our power and strength to create our reality, or when we believe that we are not worthy or loved, we delude ourselves. When we deny the core divinity of our being, we lie to ourselves.

Our mistakes have been feedback to us, but our self-imposed judgments have been useless to us. We cling to our secrets, not because revealing them would destroy us, but because we believe we could not withstand the judgments from others. Vulnerability is the price we pay for liberation. When we remove the power of secrets to rob us of happiness, we stop the destructive growth of shame.

August 17

Inspiration

A goal is an end; life has milestones but there
is no end. – *Ndidi,* Tea Leaves

Work that is integrated as who we are has no goals or expected results; the work itself is the complete experience. The artist paints because she must, not because there is an end to reach; each brush stroke is a movement of spirit. The dancer dances because without him the dance is not possible. The builder can either construct a mansion or a cabin; the ultimate spiritual energy she uses to create is the same.

When the work is love made real and alive it is no longer the mundane definition of work; it is evidence of our alignment with our true self. Work is our ultimate truth expressed. There is no goal that is sufficient to fully grasp or articulate its power; a goal falsely designates an end when nothing will end. The inspiration and power we use for work is infinite, and the journey continues even when we think we are finished. Life is filled with markers of life lived fully, but there is no goal except those we choose to assign to ourselves. When we acknowledge the journey of life as an endless experience of discoveries, we settle into the beauty of existence, and anticipate each daily adventure.

August 18

Natural Renewal

Nature is a metaphor for renewal. – *Ndidi,* Tea Leaves

We often notice the changing of the seasons, the budding, blooming and blight of the flowers. The cycle of growth is familiar, so we anticipate the repetition of the process. We complain about the changes in temperatures: too rainy, hot, cold, cloudy, humid, but in our own way we try to adjust to the changes. We dress differently to accommodate changes in the weather, and rebound from catastrophic natural events; but we feel powerless to control events that are unpredictable. We may talk about nature's wrath or Mother Nature, and miss the essence of renewal and reawakening that the natural environment within us and around us continually teaches us. When we *become* nature, recognizing our intrinsic connection to everything in the universe, we become aware of the patterns of existence. We begin to recognize the unfolding re-balancing that constantly occurs. As we begin to pay attention to changes in life, we could know that life is continually re-balancing and re-aligning to ensure that all is well now. Just as the natural world renews itself, so do we. The changes are nuanced at times, but always present.

August 19

Working from Home

The heart is open for business…for an eternity. – *Ndidi,* Tea Leaves

Many years ago major employers discovered financial benefits from allowing employees to work at home. The benefits of the idea grew so much that with the greater sophistication of technology over the last 30 years, working at home has become almost commonplace in parts of the world. The familiar, comfortable surroundings of home have increased productivity and opened up possibilities for small businesses and individuals. But there is another way in which we can work from home; we can work with the passion that comes from expressing what we love through our work. When we are working from the heart we are also working from home. We have an inherent contract with ourselves to express our love in all we do. Work is our opportunity to keep the promise.

August 20

Ants

Our true work expresses who we were meant to be. – *Ndidi,* Tea Leaves

Ants are relentless in their survival as a species; they have inhabited the earth for more than 100 million years and exist all over the earth. Lauded as a symbol of a hard working species, ants are social, communicative and protective of their colonies. Although there are many different species, ants have garnered a reputation for their resilience and organization. The ant has a role, sometimes a sacrificial one, since the game of life for the ant is an infinite game of doing whatever is its responsibility, to continue the existence of the colony.

The work of the ant is being an ant: worker, drone or queen. The ant has no flow charts or strategic plans but its purpose is preserved and continued by just being what it is. We could be as authentic as an ant, and give ourselves to our work. The work is not out there to do; the work that is our true nature languishes inside us waiting to be remembered and expressed.

August 21

Coming Apart

An unfolding life is not coming apart; it is
becoming itself. – *Ndidi,* Tea Leaves

A traditional ceremonial prayer scarf in Tibetan Buddhist culture is called the khata. The scarf is offered as a gesture of greetings and well-wishes, and is given with feelings of respect, gratitude and affection. Sometimes the ends become slightly frayed when they are worn for some time.

As we continue to live and breathe in this life, conditions may try to convince us that everything in our lives is coming apart, fraying at the ends and becoming unstable. But like the scarf that becomes more and more precious with age, so do we and our capacity to see the inherent stability of the true self.

There is a steadiness in life that exists regardless of what seems to be coming apart in our reality. The Presence that our awareness knows does not repair the frays or reverse the progression, but witnesses the unfolding beauty of each moment. We can witness the evolution of our lives as it comes apart so that new beauty can emerge.

August 22

Money

Money is an idea in the mind. – *Ndidi,* Tea Leaves

We can agree that money is a medium of exchange that has *attributed* value but actually little intrinsic worth in today's world. Years ago, livestock, gold, sacks of grain and other food items were used as currency. Our paper money, alloyed coins and digital transactions have replaced those valuable items of past years. Barter, or non-monetary exchanges, required basic trust since the exchange was regarded as trading items of equivalent value. Whether we engage in barter or monetary exchange, the idea of value lives in the minds of the exchange participants.

Money is energy like everything else in the universe. The flow of money is then regarded as vibrational. Vibrations are like the reverberating energy of two cymbals slammed together. In order to make the dramatic sound of the cymbals, they must come into contact with each other. Universal abundance is like a single, continuously present cymbal that responds to our willingness to make contact. A symbol from the past is not likely to help, and a cymbal we expect in the future has little use right now. Our attitude of joy and gratitude for our life right now are the cymbals we need to make the celebratory sound of abundance.

We feel good when we have money available, but in order to allow the flow of money in our lives we must feel happy first. We must appreciate the present, find joy in each moment, and vibrate to raise our spirit to a level that attracts abundance. All the abundance we will ever need is available to us right now. We must train the mind to accept the truth that there is nothing lacking.

August 23

Honoring Life

Our greatest contribution is to allow life to
continue. – *Ndidi,* Tea Leaves

After spending the day protesting the poor treatment of animals, a young man returns home, takes off his leather shoes, begins to eat a burger and fries, and then angrily pursues an annoying fly that has invaded his house.

There are times when our best intentions do not match our behaviors. We know that life is a cycle of birth, living, and transformation, and that every living thing experiences that cycle. Animals throughout the world sacrifice themselves daily for the continuation of life in the species; or give an opportunity of life to their young. Salmon swim upstream to spawn the next generation of salmon, and penguins endure brutal cold to protect their young with the warmth of their bodies. The departure of living things happens and we participate in their demise, but we can honor their sacrifices. We can remember that everything in the universe is here for us and we are here to appreciate the abundance of life. There is an interdependence that creates our reality. Living things leave so that we can stay; they transform so that we can continue. Living things are our brothers and sisters – relatives in different forms. When we honor every living thing, we give thanks for the opportunity our interdependence offers; and we can ensure that life continues.

August 24

The Life of Flowers

Look for joy in the faces of garden flowers; just being
flowers is enough for them. – *Ndidi,* Tea Leaves

When a flower is chosen lovingly from a field or garden, its death is
imminent; our appreciation captures the flower and removes it from the
soil that nurtures its growth. When we plant seeds and admire their
unfolding beauty, flowers flourish in our rich, watered soil. Joy is like a
flower; it is nurtured in the soul, watered by truth and flourishes in love.
Joy is not captured and placed on display; it is experienced in the present
moment, with no need to grasp for it. Joy cannot be described but its
beauty is felt as voiceless peace. Joy may arrive as a splash of colors that
endures all seasons of apparent despair; it has a fragrance that warms the
heart, softens the furrowed brow, and slows the heart to a subtle rhythm.
Like flowers bursting in a garden, basking in the sun, joy expresses the
true self that is the essence of love.

August 25

Service

There are those who give with joy, and joy is their reward...They give as in yonder valley myrtle breathes its fragrance into space. – *Kahlil Gibran*, The Prophet

Conditions in the world create continual inequalities and inconsistencies. Our responses to those conditions can take many forms; one form is service to others. When we see ourselves as separate and disconnected from other human beings, we begin to see the conditions surrounding other people as their own creation and responsibility. We are not our brother's keeper, we *are* our brothers and sisters. We breathe the same air, and are composed of the same stardust. All that we do and believe is based in our desire for love and approval. We express this desire in a number of different ways, but the root cause of our behaviors is always the same. Conflicting ideas in the minds of humans and animals create the conditions. We are all able to respond with loving care. When we realize that as human beings, our work is to love from the core of our being, and to offer lovingkindness to all beings, we grow in awareness of our purpose. Service is the third economy, one that lies outside of a market economy of materialism and finance. As we run toward our own pleasures in this life and run away from pain and suffering, we can remember that we are all branches of the same tree that weathers the storms of life. Service is our recognition that we all want relief from suffering. We all seek the redemptive grace of care.

August 26

Enough Time

The trouble is we think we have time. – *The Buddha*

Woody Allen once said that "life is what happens when we're busy making plans." The battle, more like a war with time has been one launched in our own mind. The concept of time is constructed in the mind in a failed attempt to control our life experiences. Controlling time is much like boxing the air; the sense of control is elusive as we expend energy without making contact.

Believing that the passage of time is necessary for the manifestation of our desires is like fighting a losing battle with a mental sandcastle. When we become still and pay attention to what is happening, we notice the seeds of our desires budding. Seeds do not plan to be fully blossomed in some distant future; within the seed is the blossom. Our desires are not in the future; they exist now, in the present moment.

When we let go, we vibrationally come into alignment with what is. The sandcastle only exists because we painstakingly build it. Like most sandcastles, it washes away, as our imaginary grip on time renders us defeated, weary and stressed. We overcome challenges when we surrender illusions of control of them.

Now is all that we ever experience of life and love. All else is a constructed reality that continually offers frustrating, crazy making, twists and knots that cloud our awareness of who we really are. We are timeless spiritual beings, expressing who we are as we love. We acknowledge who we are *being*, with love, compassion, kindness and breathing in the present moment of life. Be still. We can lay down our defensive armor of limited time. All is possible *now*. All is well *now*. All is as it should be *now*. All is love; so we can let go of fear.

296

August 27

The Tunnel

The light at the end of the tunnel is not the
illusion, the tunnel is. – Anonymous

Around the world underground tunnels provide ways to traverse waterways and move through otherwise impassable lands or mountains. Mining companies throughout the world can use tunnels to access minerals and metals from the earth. Oil and gas travel through tunnels on the way to markets. With each tunnel there is an entrance and an exit; but something exists outside of each of those openings. Each opening is both an ending and a beginning. Often we focus our attention on the light at the end, and dream of reaching that light; but if we cling to that desire, we miss the twists and turns that make up our journey.

When we focus on a distant reality we miss the joy of the present, and when we reach that destination, we find ourselves craving a new journey, having forfeited the one we just ended. We need not worry, the light itself is not an illusion; the rays that the light emits to guide us are the gifts of life. Those rays bend and bounce off the sides of the tunnel; without the walls and curves, the light would blind us. We travel slowly toward the brilliance and in that slow pace we prepare ourselves for the treasures of the guiding light. The conditions we face in life can be challenging, but the light is there for us, encouraging us to keep moving.

August 28

Zebras

Freedom is experienced in connection. – *Ndidi,* Tea Leaves

Individual zebras reportedly have different stripe patterns, but in spite of their individuality in appearance, they are known to be social animals. Family members look out for each other and groom each other creating strong social bonds. The subtleties of difference in stripes do not interfere with their affinity for each other. As wild horses essentially, zebras love to run freely in herds or 'harems' as they are called.

Like zebras, we crave freedom, the unencumbered movement through our life's journey. We too are social beings and derive pleasure and security from our relationships. Our different stripes are evident as well, but we sometimes use those differences to separate us rather than bring us closer to one another. Like zebras, we may protect our herd called our families and friends; and create boundaries against strangers. We have basic instincts to survive, but sometimes the egoic mind exaggerates the dangers, drawing a tight boundary around our individual experience of life. Although we show up as different expressions of the divine, we all are part of the same living herd. When we appreciate our spiritual interdependence we see our being-ness in All-That-Is as our ultimate connection to every living thing.

August 29

Call of the Drum

The drums were still beating, persistent and unchanging. Their sound was no longer a separate thing from the living village. It was like the pulsation of its heart. – *Chinua Achebe*, Things Fall Apart

Every living thing is like a musical note that is essential to the symphony. Without the blend of each of the notes, the symphony would be incomplete. We are fully present for life when we are aware of the notes we play and how important they are to the drum symphony. The African drum calls us to celebrate life, to dance with both the crescendos and the silence between beating events in our lives. Instead of waiting for the next shoe to drop, we can appreciate that there is a shoe – evidence of life as it is. We don't know what will happen in the next moment, but we can answer the call of the drum of life, the call of appreciation for life now.

The Native American drum reminds us of the interconnectedness of human and animal life; we hear the sounds of the animals of the forest and the prairie, and dance to the relentless beat as if it reflects our own hearts, because it does. We realize that even though the beats of life seem repetitive - daily work life, rituals, and expectations - each moment is different and can be a source of joy and celebration. The jazz drum compels us to experience the passion of being, as the power of the resonant sounds stir us deeply and convince us that we can do anything we believe in. Whether we recognize the heartbeat of the earth, the healing rhythm of the universe or the beats of the drum, we are called to be alive with the music, connected to the energy of sound and responsive to the resonance of being fully present. The call of the drum is to release our love into the universe, honoring life as it is. When we open our hearts we sense our internal rhythm and know that every one of us is called to move joyously through life.

August 30

Unity

When we try to pick out anything by itself, we find it hitched to everything else in the universe. – *John Muir*, in documentary film, John Muir in the New World

Some glues are made to bind only temporarily, like the adhesive on post-it notes; with only minimal pulling, the bond will break. Unlike that weak attachment, the bonding that always endures is love. Since love is the energy of the universe, that which binds us to everything else in perfect harmony, we cannot ever be separated from anything else. Irreversibly linked to everything else, our choices and behaviors have a reverberating effect on the universe. Our linkage creates the evolutionary nature of the universe; as we change, the universe changes. Unity is more than a pleasant concept; it is the fuel of the universe. If we recognize this interdependence, this unity of all things, and we recognize the love within us, we cannot ever hurt another with callous disregard for the spirit of life. We honor life in all its forms and cherish the bonds.

August 31

Generosity

In a generous heart, the endless flow of love and compassion
has no fear of drought. – *Ndidi,* Tea Leaves

In a universe that expresses abundance in its creations and diversity, we humans can align ourselves with the generosity of spirit. Our contemplative spirit sometimes compels us to engage in activist practices such as vigils for social justice and bearing witness to negative conditions. We may become overwhelmed by the pervasiveness of pain and suffering, and work or volunteer to relieve that suffering. As we work to improve lives, we begin to realize that the impact of our work has a profound affect on our own sense of purpose. We begin to feel as if we are deriving perhaps more joy from our work than those we are helping.

An alternative feeling as we serve is to become frustrated with progress as the suffering persists. Our frustration is a signal to us that we are becoming attached to what is not as we sacrifice the appreciation of what is. At the core of our contemplation is the recognition of peace within, an inexplicable peace that we want to share. We realize through reflection and resting in the conscious awareness of All-That-Is, we can be the mirrors for others who are afraid to look at themselves. Our work is to reveal our true self in the service to others; in opening our heart to others, we expose them to themselves. We want them to discover the abundant love at their core, so our generosity is not in the material things we share, but in the gentle tap on the door of the spirit of others. May the work we do be the person we are.

September 1

Improvisations

Even our plans in the end were just improvisations. – *Ndidi,* Tea Leaves

Mockingbirds are born with a song, melodious and pleasant to the ear, but they are not content with their own song. The innovative birds borrow melodies from birds in their surrounding environment, and within a very short period create a new song from the notes they have apprehended. Like mockingbirds, we can appreciate the joy around us and create a new song and story of our lives.

When we know that we don't really make mistakes, but instead get lots of feedback, we are free to create innovative parts of our life stories. If we miss a note or create a melody that is too shrill or too sad, we can always create a new song. If we create a song that is filled with shame or regrets, we can derive healing from sharing the lessons we've learned. If we create a song of struggle and loss, we can acknowledge that the song is incomplete; and if the chorus does not include triumph and gain, it is dishonest, because everything changes. We sing many songs and recover from unrealized dreams, but when we reflect on our lives, we realize that it is all improvisation.

September 2

The Creative Self

Moments in our lives don't create us; we create
moments in our lives. – *Ndidi,* Tea Leaves

Joy is the experience of being wholly connected as the universe in the present moment. We are spiritual beings existing as an intelligent universe of thought. We are "in the matrix" so to speak; there is an intelligent presence within that responds vibrationally to our thoughts, and creates a reality we call our life. As creators of our lives we construct reality in our mind, by controlling how we perceive life as it evolves. And even if we choose to entertain thoughts that cause us discomfort, we can also choose to question the veracity of those thoughts. Actual events in our life are what the mind senses—sees, touches, tastes, hears, smells; but the *experiential response* to what we sense is entirely our own creation. When we know what we are capable of creatively, we make careful choices, and allow our inherent passion to emerge in how we live. When we realize our freedom, we create joyful moments in our lives.

September 3

Out of Nothing

Joy rises out of the space between this and that,
positive and negative. – *Ndidi,* Tea Leaves

Positrons and electrons repel each other and prevent their mutual
annihilation. If they were to interact, the result would be disastrous for
us, creating an explosion of light and a state of neutrality, nothingness.
Everything in the universe would fall apart without those repelling
elements of matter.

Often we think things are falling apart in our lives and become frightened
or melancholy, but the fallen pieces of our lives are simply creating space
for something new. When we enter a zone of creativity, we are in a space
of neutrality or nothingness in the mind, where out of nothing something
emerges. We may refer to an inspiration as a light bulb idea; we may seek
to be enlightened or speak of following the light. In the zone of creativity,
we experience the light, the source of love. Neither positive nor negative
energy, it is the majesty of creativity; just stillness, formlessness. We may
think that creation is the joining of matter, solid objects that can be
touched or sensed, but where does a poem come from? What creates the
notes of a song, or the brush strokes on a canvas? We may live in a world
we perceive as real from our senses, but joy emerges out of no-thing, and
for that we can give thanks.

September 4

Healthy Joy

Joy exists in the healthy relationship with self. – *Ndidi*, Tea Leaves

Many books have been written about healthy lifestyles, particularly focused on diet and exercise, but health encompasses so much more. We may attempt to manage stress, volunteer at a local shelter, or spend time enjoying the abundance of nature. We may be diligent in addressing our health needs and attempting to care for our physical well-being, but healthy joy requires more.

Relationships are the ribbons of commonality that tie aspects of our health together. What is our relationship with food? How does our relationship with food influence our relationship with ourselves? Do we eat alone or with others? Our relationship with food can tell a story of triumph or trouble. We are indeed what we eat.

Since ancient times we have experienced a sense of community and commitment by sharing a meal. We can get affirmation of the love in our lives from the simple gathering around food for laughter and conversations. Festivals, rites of passage, barbecues and bridal showers are formal opportunities to eat as a community.

Diets encouraged by cultural norms or practices can be a way to establish our relationship to an identity group. But we sometimes have unhealthy relationships with food, so the food itself often becomes the depository of our fears, anxieties and discomfort.

We have relationships with stress that influence our coping strategies. We often struggle to avoid tensions, and yet we think constantly about the conditions that cause stress. We may have a love-hate relationship with exercise or movement, seeing it as a chore or responsibility, but also a pleasant sense of accomplishment. Even though we may carve out a few days to "go into nature" we may return as stressed as we left, and resentful of the short time for peace and relaxation.

We seek well-being in numerous relationships within a reality we have created; but if we look deeply into those relationships, and into ourselves, we will come into an awareness of our true self, and experience healthy joy.

September 5

Tao of Loving Spirit

Silence is the path to Love. – *Ndidi,* Tea Leaves

At the very heart of love is an inexplicable presence; it exists beyond all intellectual explanations or descriptions, and yet our consciousness is aware of its all-encompassing truth. Love simply is. We may clothe it in our earthly experiences – a rapturous poem, an explosively enlivening jazz composition, an exquisite work of art, a baby's smile, a babbling brook. Love shows up everywhere. The only requirement for us to experience love is to have conscious awareness of it, even when we are unable to define it.

One of the ways we can experience this presence is to pay attention to small wonders. The subtleties of love are ever-present in our lives. We sometimes look for dramatic changes in our life experiences like sudden wealth, remission during terminal illness, or a perfect intimate relationship. A sunset's glory, available every evening, may be taken for granted. We may miss the loving gesture of a stranger if we forget that no one is really a stranger in this world. We may miss critical lessons in life that could release us from repetitive suffering and disappointments, because we don't see others in our lives as teachers and mirrors. We may miss our life in all its details because we have spent each moment thinking about the next moment. Love is the source of life; it is who we are. Be silent often and know this presence – more powerful than words. There is no way to this love, except in the silence of the present moment.

September 6

Frustration

Noticing and counting the beautiful reasons unexpected things happen for us ends the mystery. If you miss the real reasons that coincide with kind nature, then count on depression to let you know you missed them. – Byron Katie, I Need Your Love – Is That True?

When we finally realize our identity, we can lift ourselves from feelings of powerless to consciousness of our universal presence, but the journey of awakening has just begun. When we fail to get what we want we experience frustration. As we try to be fully in the now, the past breathes its foul breath into our mind and begs us to ask again for relief. Unfinished business can cause us to try once more to repair what we see as broken in our past. But when we reach a place of frustration, the beauty of our transformation is at a key turning point. Frustration is essential to creativity, and as creative beings, we emerge from frustration like lotus flowers from muddy ponds. With new eyes, voice and heart, our frustration becomes the fuel for change.

Change is not achieved by force but by the power of peace in the moment. The present moment calls us to let it be. If we heed the still, small voice that invites us to just be in the moment, a clear direction for change becomes evident. Our creative energies reveal their innovative and evolutionary power; problems are not just changed, they are transformed.

When we surrender to present moment awareness, speaking to us in a wordless expression of love, we can expose the futility of frustration, and replace it with peace. Instead of looking for an answer or peace in the future, we have faith that all is well in the power of the present moment.

Lingering Pain

The soul becomes dyed with the colors of its
thoughts. – *Marcus Aurelius,* Meditations

Feelings of loss are painful. We say that our heart is broken, no longer able to function properly in wholeness. A deep sense of sadness consumes us and we feel heavy with the weight of it. After our anger and pain begin to subside, we engage in an endless internal dialogue about our worthiness or how we could have avoided such a disastrous end. If our broken heart stays fissured and bare to the world, we are likely to repeat our response to the painful event over and over again. The circumstances change but the bruised heart remembers. We can break this cycle of despair and heartbreak by facing the pain, rather than avoiding it. We can make friends with what hurts us; it is our story. What does it mean to make friends with emotions, with a broken heart? We can locate the pain in our bodies and nurture it, soothe it. We can ask ourselves if all the stories we are attributing to others are really true. We can acknowledge our contribution to the ending without self-condemnation. And when we have settled into a connection with our selves we can create a different story, we can incorporate the lessons we have learned, and gain closure. A wonderful contradiction is that as a painful chapter in our lives gets re-written and closed, we are able to open our hearts to joy once more.

September 8

Intuition

The direct experience of reality is creative intuition. – *Ndidi,* Tea Leaves

Conventional wisdom would assert that knowledge is acquired information, facts, skills and experiences, but knowledge does not account for exceptional abilities that many people demonstrate. Our intuitive abilities can account for direct experiences of truth without the apparent use of logical reasoning. Some of us are comfortable with knowledge but less attentive to our own intuition. Our rational mind cannot make room for unexplained phenomena; because we want proof in order to feel in control of our world. The difficulty with relying on facts only is that facts change with new information. Intuition, derived from the Latin word *intueri* meaning to consider is a connection to spiritual insight and conscious awareness of the true self. Intuition is a reminder that we are always connected to the source of our being. When we acknowledge the creative energy of intuition, we become aware that beyond the boundaries of our bodies, what we intuit is the active, passionate creativity of the soul.

September 9

Right and Wrong

The Truth is neither this nor that. *—Ndidi,* Tea Leaves

A popular trickster tale from Yoruba people in Nigeria, West Africa is the story of an argument between twins. The trickster Eshu-Elegba asks the brothers to stand facing one another. Elegba puts on a jester's hat that is black on one side and red on the other. He walks between the two brothers and asks each to tell him the color of the hat. Each responds with a different color. Elegba then walks in the opposite direction. The brothers then know their different views are based on where they stand.

Right and wrong are variable concepts based on where you stand; if we stand in another's shoes, we see another perspective. Our most cherished ideas about what is wrong can be challenged by conditions. Is it wrong to kill another human being, animals or other sentient beings? Some of us would answer "yes" enthusiastically, even though we may eat an animal or crush an insect as we walk on the sidewalks. We may kill other human beings in war and execute prisoners of that war, or vehemently support capital punishment while rejecting abortions as murder. We forget who we are and follow the temporary guidance of the false self. We may forget that the rightness or wrongness depends on where we are standing at the moment. If we cannot see the innocence in all that we are prone to judge, we will choose fear over love and judgment over openness. We will forget who we are and worship at the alter of the false self. We could begin to weigh the beliefs that are the foundations of our various "stands" and know that the Truth provides multiple answers.

A wonderful Hindu concept found in the Upanishads is *neti, neti* – not this, not this. To remove ourselves from the dilemma of right and wrong, we can simply say, "neti, neti." In the present moment, judgments and rationalizations are suspended, because our opinions and righteousness are based on past experiences or future fears. We want consistency in our lives and that is counterproductive in a changing universe. In the present moment our likes and dislikes are muted, rendered irrelevant, and a deep sense of peace is known.

Journaling

When a bird gets free, it does not go back for remnants left
on the bottom of the cage. – *Rumi,* A Year with Rumi

Keeping a journal is an opportunity to see the power of thought forms,
i.e. words that influence our emotions. When we write about something,
we have moved away from the direct experience of that object of our
attention, the event itself, but we have created an image or stirred an
emotion. Journaling may be a powerful release of emotions that are worthy
of donating to the pages of a journal; and the freedom from censure of
painful or pleasant thoughts and memories can be attractive as a way to
begin healing. But if we choose to revisit what we have released, we may be
tempted to re-imagine our feelings, casting us back to the past, a moment
in time that no longer exists. What we feel now, in the present moment
exists fully and deeply.

As a contrast to our present experience of life, released pain can be
instructive, but the true power of the journaling experience is in the
release. Reviewing past behaviors or thoughts keeps us from experiencing
the present moment where our passion to create blooms. Some may say that
recording painful or disturbing experiences as well as happier ones helps
us to face the changing nature of life's experiences; we can also track our
progress on the path. Whenever we hold on to an event that happened in
the past and revisit the pain, we suffer. Experiences are already imprinted
in our minds; the joy of creation is imprinted in the soul, our true self. The
mind reminds us; the soul is here now calling to us to be present.

September 11

Visualization

Peace lies within us waiting to be appreciated. – *Ndidi,* Tea Leaves

Although most of us think in both words and pictures, about 60-65% of people think in images. Visual thinking is prominent among musicians, artists, engineers and architects, or others for whom images play an important role in their lives. Visual thinking is encouraged during guided imagery experiences when people are asked to visualize a place or experience that brings a sense of calm or relaxation. During a visualization, we may be guided to imagine being on a sunny beach soaking up the warm sun, and listening to the gentle rush of the ocean's waves against the shore. We may imagine ourselves floating with no pressures or limitations, letting go of stress and settling into a state of deep peace. The speaker or guide is the voice of the experience. Inner seeing and sensory awareness combine to defy time and space and place us into the scene that we are co-creating with the speaker. Although the visualization is not in the past or the future, and is not based in tangible reality, we feel it and know it as our experience now. We have a passion to create images of the peace within us, but when the visualization is complete, the experience is a new imprint of peace, a model of rest that we can hold as we move onward to the next moment.

September 12

Writing

… tell us what the world has been to you in the dark places and in the light. Don't tell us what to believe, what to fear. Show us belief's wide skirt and the stitch that unravels fear's caul. – *Toni Morrison*, The Nobel Lecture In Literature, 1993

A person walks into a bookstore and asks to see a copy of life. The store owner asks, "Which one would you like?" After glancing through a stack of copies of lives, the man decides he is better off creating his own.

One of the ways to become motivated to write creatively is to use a prompt. The prompting questions or experiences can cause an eruption of creativity where none seemed to exist; but the best way to write is to begin. One of the better prompts for writing is reading. Often the popular writers are those who love to read. Libraries contain so many treasures hiding in plain sight on their shelves; and the quiet atmosphere understates the activity on the millions of pages that are bound as books. Whether we are reading for confirmation of a thought or expansion of our awareness, the creative energy of a book stimulates the senses. A book is not the only source of creative inspiration; magazines, newspapers and blogs can expose an idea, like cracking open an oyster to reveal a pearl.

Spiritual and religious texts encourage us and increase our faith, but they also explore our doubts. Our studies of prophetic experiences help us to identify who we are. Poetry can be like movies in print, or soft and warm like cups of tea. We peek into the life of a writer when we read inspired creations; images are formed, thoughts are expanded, and the heart is opened to possibilities. When we choose to be open to experience we are prompted to create and to respond to life as it is now. We are continually writing our own compelling story in life as we breathe in the joy of our experiences and face our "dark places."

September 13

Labyrinth

Tell your heart that the fear of suffering is worse than the suffering
itself. And that no heart has ever suffered when it goes in search of
its dreams, because every second of the search is a second's encounter
with God and with eternity. – *Paulo Coelho*, The Alchemist

Sometimes life meanders along a path that we have not ordered, taking
twists and turns that seem to lead nowhere. At the beginning of our
experience of consciousness, we entered a labyrinth; our intention was to
enjoy the experience, to see where the path could lead. As long as we notice
all the twists and turns as integral to the path, we understand that each
is necessary. At first, we assume that the conditions we observe will be
permanent baggage we must carry along the way, but we soon realize that
nothing is permanent. We have guides that we attract along the way; they
remind us that the real path is within. We test this theory and discover
that the path within is expansive, and we cannot express clearly what we
know in this expansive universe, but we sense that there is nothing lacking.
We rest in faith that every moment along the path reveals the treasures
of the universe, so we let go of our desire to know what lies around the
next turn. We make constant decisions to continue until we reach the end
of the labyrinth, even though we do not ever know when or where it will
end. When we finally reach the end, we realize that we have arrived where
we started, but the journey has given us new perspectives. The sense of
completion stirs in us, and we are aware that all is well. We rest in the
commanding presence of the true self we have discovered, and for the first
time know for certain that the Self has always been and always will be our
spiritual identity.

September 14

Deep Listening

Love tiptoes into quiet moments and kisses you on the
forehead to wake you up. – *Ndidi,* Tea Leaves

During the experience of meditation, the mind can be active, jumping
from ideas to plans. We think constantly, even though we're not certain
where our thoughts originate. If we spend time with our thoughts, we
may not derive full benefit from the stillness of meditation. In the present
moment of meditative space, we can enjoy the sounds that we either take
for granted or ignore routinely. We may hear the roar of an air conditioner
or heater, the tick tock of a clock, the engines of an airplane flying high
overhead, or the bark of a dog outside. We may notice our own breath or
the tapping splatter of raindrops on a sidewalk outside. The sounds are
evidence of our expanded existence. We are reminded of our inability to
separate ourselves from our environment; in our quiet sitting, we realize
that love is appearing in many forms tantalizing our senses and confirming
the fact that we matter. We begin to welcome the interdependency that
exists among us and all sentient beings. As we settle into our being-ness,
we recognize that the boundaries we thought existed between ourselves
and other living things have softened. We become aware that the true self
is the center of our existence; and sounds within our world are part of a
life canvas. When we acknowledge all that is here for us - the sounds, the
presence of others, the beauty in our world - we are compelled to tell a
new story. When we listen deeply for the love pulsating in life, the rhythm
of our world, we get the full painting of the artist instead of just a sketch,
and sense our own magnificence.

September 15

Altruism

Sharing love is revealing your true self. – *Ndidi,* Tea Leaves

Corn had become scarce on a farm where chickens depended on its nutrients for their health and well-being, so the farmer began giving all of his corn to his chickens, amid some resistance from his family who loved corn as well. He reasoned that his family had plenty of fruits and vegetables to eat and would not mind the sacrifice for awhile. His family loved chicken, so they agreed to sacrifice the corn so that the chickens could be healthy enough to eat. After several months, the farmer finally decided to kill a plump, healthy chicken for the family dinner, but the farmer's family pushed the chicken away, because they had become accustomed to seeing the plump chickens playing in the yard; and had decided to become vegetarians.

What we experience changes our perspectives, but also our hearts. Because we are able to think thoughts and reflect on our behaviors, we can monitor instances when our selfishness interferes with our natural state of joyfulness. When we close our hands, we close our hearts; we deny the always present love in the world. Our generosity and compassion not only change the experience of others; it changes our own experience of life. Altruism is our opportunity to share the love in service and make choices in life that express who we really are. An act of compassion is not a loss; it is a privilege. Often when we give, we realize how much we already have.

September 16

Holy, Holy

If what you are looking for is already present, your journey
ends as soon as it begins. – *Ndidi,* Tea Leaves

The omnipresent spirit of the universe cannot be localized. There is no
place that All-That-Is does not exist, by definition. We naturally revere this
power because we allow ourselves to be awed with the manifestation of its
unrelenting presence. We are at a loss for words in attempting to describe
what we feel, what we experience in every moment. We search for a way
to express what we know to be true, but words are insufficient. We search
for a way to be closer to this power, but we are already in its presence every
moment of our lives, so there is *no way to it.* We want to know the truth
of our existence – who we are and our purpose in life, but we are free to
establish that purpose since we are love's expression. We travel with the
light of the world, the joy that is always present for us, even though we
may ignore it. We feel it when we open our hearts to others, love them
fully and completely, without judgment. We sense the presence when we
are still, when love fills us up and tears flow, leaving us cleansed and pure.
We tell ourselves that we are alone sometimes, but we know that to be
untrue because our breath reminds us of the presence of All-That-Is. We
say that the Presence is holy, set apart from all else in the universe, but it is
everywhere present, resting within us, so we become aware that we are its
expression in this time-space. In the now we realize our true self; and in
our transcending the sensory reality of our lives, we experience awareness
of our essential nature.

September 17

Compassion

If you want others to be happy, practice compassion. If you
want to be happy, practice compassion. – *Dalai Lama XIV*

With intense creative energy, we love others. Our passion, the sorrow we
feel for their suffering, compels us to be the love we came to this universe
to express. Compassion is the strong desire to alleviate the suffering of
others. Regarded in most religious traditions as one of the higher virtues,
compassion is the essence of co-suffering. But the act of co-suffering is
not an end in itself. Compassion is an opportunity to transform suffering
into liberation.

Compassion has a direct line to happiness – our own happiness and
therefore the happiness of all beings. The feelings of compassion begin
as a flower of joy within our own heart and burst forth in all its glory
when our own pain and suffering are reflected in others. Every time we
express compassion a previously hidden source of our own suffering arises
in us. In fact, when we recognize our own pain vividly, at some point we
are most equipped to understand another person's similar pain. We may
be convinced of the uniqueness of our individual lives, but the depth of
pain and suffering is a collective experience. When we are compassionate
with another person, we invite that person to let go of the feeling of
isolation that often accompanies suffering. We invite them to grasp hope
and transformation, and to let go of fear. We help them to know themselves
as whole and capable. Compassion is profound intimacy that shares the
internal strength of the core self. In the present moment, we know that
strength, and we allow it to be liberated in our hearts.

September 18

Qigong Energy

Move with life; love with kindness. – *Ndidi,* Tea Leaves

Without special sports equipment or clothing, a Qigong teacher directs students to follow the positions and soft, flowing movements. The energy flows unblocked through the body and pulsates in the extremities. The heat of the chi has always been present surrounding the body and energizing the spirit. Qigong can be a metaphor for love, the always present energy that flows within us, warming us as it flows to others.

We don't need any special equipment or clothing to express lovingkindness; it is our natural way of being. When we know who we really are, we are aware that love is our way of being. Some may say that we cannot give away something that we don't already have; but loving spirit is our inherent nature. We may have difficulty expressing our true self as love, because we are unaware of the love that we are.

Some may say that the exercise of love is too strenuous, too difficult to sustain, and too risky after feeling hurt. The love that we describe is most likely strong attraction or even lust, if we feel vulnerable or exposed. Our suffering is evidence of our clinging or grasping, not the unblocked flow of unconditional love. As a state of being rather than a behavior, unconditional love is not transactional and has no expectations or conditions. Greeks described it as agape, love of everyone. Like cheerful beams, agape love moves effortlessly through our existence, emanating from our core self. Some may say it does not exist in some sad, "sinful" souls, but the heat of lovingkindness sits deep within us, every one of us, and can be activated as we move toward one another in peace and deep awareness of the true self.

September 19

Dialogue of Love

Love is an awareness of truth. – *Ndidi,* Tea Leaves

Where divine love is an ocean, intimate love is a babbling brook. We may spend countless days of our lives attempting to attract the brook, when we are submerged in the waters of the ocean. What we crave controls our mind, but when we acknowledge what is true in our lives, suffering releases its damaging clutch. When we are aware, when we remember that we are love, our sense of peace relaxes our need to cling. We can stand as whole persons and enter into dialogues with others. From those dialogues come a spirit of communion. When we remember who we are, we naturally speak the language of love: empathy, non-judgment, compassion, sharing, honesty, appreciation and humility. The magic of love is that the offering of ourselves is without the expectation of a return; we love because we must, not because we hope to gain something. We are already whole. Nothing is lacking. When we are being love, the dialogues are easy.

September 20

Lacking Nothing

When you find yourself in a hole, look up. – *Ndidi,* Tea Leaves

When even the bare essentials of food, shelter and safety are elusive, we still have potential. Every day that we breathe, potential is present. When we are at our most vulnerable points in life, we have thoughts and fears of being destroyed because we need something or someone. The challenge during those times in our lives is to keep going, to be confident that everything changes. We do not know whether everything will be resolved in the future, but we can be certain that whatever we are experiencing now will be different. The conditions that we see are not the totality of our experience, because everything, even this moment, is temporary. The dramatic appearance of challenging conditions can easily convince us that the worst is yet to come rather than the best will come in time. We may think it is unrealistic to think that anything will change for the better, when our fears convince us that things only get worse. Things get worse when we cling to an idea that encourages us to worry, but worry is a negatively creative activity of the mind. As co-creators of our reality, we give energy to our reality by what we choose to pay attention to. Positive thoughts about the present are dress rehearsals for the future; negative thoughts or refusals to be thankful, create a different future.

September 21

Extremes

Avoid extremes; they're like running up to the edge of
a cliff with no place to go. – *Ndidi,* Tea Leaves

Stretching and the movement of chi energy are hallmarks of the yoga experience, but over-stretching can be uncomfortable. A yoga mat, straps, blocks and blankets are notable supports for the enlivening movements and deep relaxation. Stiff muscles are loosened as the gradual stretching and different postures soothe tight places that want to be free. Yoga is beauty in motion.

We can learn the lessons of moderation from yoga, not limitations but the gradual expanse that comes from moderation. There is nothing that we need to add in order to improve our stretch or balance in yoga, except practice and belief in our potential. The stretching beyond what is comfortable is an invitation to suffer, just as stretching ourselves in work or play is an example of grasping that can lead to discomfort and self-alienation. Yoga teaches us that what we are is enough, and that what we are capable of is already within us; we simply need to gradually release our excellence.

September 22

Soft and Strong

The strength of the palm tree is its flexibility. – *Ndidi,* Tea Leaves

Most of us know that paper is manufactured from trees. Hardwood and softwood trees are used to make a variety of papers. The hardwoods produce short fibers with weak, finely textured paper, but the softwood produces tough, durable paper. The strong becomes weak, and the weak becomes strong.

During the course of our lives, challenges can either weaken us or make us stronger depending on how we respond to them. If we allow ourselves to be molded by love and compassion, noticing the soft message in harshness, or the hard lesson in softness, we can know the constant theme of survival in our lives. If we react to the conditions in our lives as if they are permanent irritants, we are allowing our ego to make us hard when we have a softness within. Our errant ego may try to convince us that we are soft, inadequate or lacking in life experience, grace or acumen, but we are more than any of those requirements. We are always what we need to be at any moment, if we realize who we are. We are the promise of love, the experience of life, and the possibility of peace. The joy in us is all we will ever need.

September 23

Self-Realization

The only urgency in life is to remember who we are. – *Ndidi,* Tea Leaves

A generous man, living near a beach was so committed to helping others that he went to a homeless shelter to offer shoes to the poor. He was eager to donate his own shoes, until he realized that he was barefoot.

If we commit to being in service to others, our self-realization is necessary. We can encourage others to face their fears and love who they are, but we cannot be fully present in their lives if we are not present for ourselves. Our best gift to others is to be fully who we are, not a representation of who we think we should be.

We can ask ourselves who we are and listen in silence for the answer, but we must be patient, since the answer is voiceless. In order to know ourselves deeply, we have to be willing to give up our current notions of truth. We will have to doubt that we know anything and feel comfortable with not knowing. When we go deep within to the essence of our being, we can have fewer questions and allow our stillness to be a revelation. Awakening to the truth of who we are is awakening to the eternal. We face the moments of our lives as the precious passages that they are, and slowly but deeply give birth to our essential nature. Many who are invested in our awakening will offer us guidance, but only we ourselves can uncover the mystery of our identity, our true self. Others will be attracted to our authenticity and true self-awareness, and in that awareness, we will offer the greatest service to others.

September 24

Bruised

The bruised ego wants to hold onto its story. – *Ndidi,* Tea Leaves

There is a bruise that over the years turns into a wound that will not heal. At first, it is a shock to the system, a kind of disbelief that creeps into our consciousness, and takes up residence. But it does not sit quietly; it festers and morphs into anger, resentment, and rage. Others may not notice its steady spread into the reality of our lives, and the tremendous impact it has on our sense of well-being. The spread is insidious, touching relationships, our sense of safety and worthiness. Most importantly, it does not want to experience a repeat incidence of the pain, while it steadily cultivates the thing it fears.

Emotional bruising is lethal, not only in the experience, but also in the protracted pain and suffering it produces. Being left behind, feeling unprotected and exposed to possible harm, and being rejected without explanation leaves an imprint of shame and insecurity that many come to accept as the reality of their lives.

In spite of the power of emotional bruising in our lives, it is an experience that prolongs our suffering if we hear the story in our head as the whole truth. Bruising is an event that carries with it intense pain in recurrent memories. Over time, remembering the event triggers the emotions, so the power of the story is maintained.

The story will develop spin-offs and sequels that will continue unabated until we realize that we are not the story of our experiences. We may begin to realize that we have grown enamored of the story and the responses we garner because of the story. We may think that the understanding of friends or sympathy may help to heal the wound, but the spinoffs continue. We may attract people into our life that will act out the story for us over and over again; or we may protect ourselves from the possibility of abandonment by never getting close to anyone. Our story may cause us to abandon ourselves - dreams, plans, opportunities - as a kind of punishment for being bruised. The long-running story preempts any current experience of joy and peace, like a frequent commercial on a favorite horror TV show.

Our true self offers a different story. The Presence cannot ever hurt us because its nature is unconditional Love. In a self-organizing universe, everything happens as it should, even though it does not seem "right" at the time. Everything comes and goes, at its own pace, except the true self. Everything changes continuously, just as one moment floats quickly into the next moment in time. Love surrounds us and fills us with courage, if we notice it.

We have the capacity to change our story to a love story. Like the true self it too will not end, but our feelings during each episode will help us to remember and appreciate who we are. The script in our new story reminds us that we will always have what we need, and that we have always been loved.

September 25

Sadness

They are the prisoners of their personal history... They accumulate experiences, memories, things, other people's ideas, and it is more than they can possibly cope with. And that is why they forget their dreams.
– *Paulo Coelho*, The Zahir

Sadness is like wearing a heavy coat in warm weather; it's uncomfortable but we refuse to expose our pain to others. We say that we are not sad, even though our throat is hoarse with crying inwardly. We say we are not sad even though our arms ache from the weight of carrying the burden of unfinished business. We say we are not sad, even though our ears burn from the messages we constantly whisper to ourselves about our unworthiness. Our eyes, bloodshot with tears, tell a different story. Our denial is a thinly veiled protection of the diminished ego that we still nurture. The ego has convinced us that happiness is a lie hoisted upon gullible believers. Because of the mask we wear, others see us as cold and aloof, or obsessed with ourselves; our sense of their rejection makes us sadder. We want to believe that there is another way to live.

Happiness is the only friend who is disappointed with us; it wants us to get rid of the mask of ok-ness and be vulnerable. It wants us to be grateful for the contrast of sadness that assures us of its opposite. Without the concept of sadness, we could not fully appreciate the joy in our lives. But sometimes we linger much too long in the grip of sadness. Happiness wants us to face the unrealized dream, not so that we can finish it like a task to be completed, but so that we can be ok with it, and know that we can move beyond the pain. We can realize that we will always have more life to explore, but what we have missed so far doesn't have to deplete us.

Happiness wants us to find the joy at the center of our being, and stop looking for it outside of ourselves. Happiness wants us to know that we may have lost our smile temporarily, but we have not lost ourselves.

September 26

Destruction

Creation and destruction are the two ends of the same moment.
And everything between the creation and the next destruction is
the journey of life. – *Amish Tripathi,* The Oath of the Vayuputras

The Ashanti people of Ghana are known for their lost wax casting method which produces intricate objects of gold and other metals by creating a wax mold, filling it with gold, and then heating the object. A brilliant technique that was an example of the creativity of a group of problem solvers, the lost wax casting method is a metaphor for the quality in destruction.

In order to release our core nature into consciousness and become aware of our true self, we must unlearn the falsehoods that cloud our perception. Like the wax, events in our lives are temporary since each event ends; it is destroyed in order to make room in our consciousness for new beginnings. Destruction is a necessity, so when we let go of events as they begin their transformation, our suffering is released as well. We can fashion our lives around endings and focus on loss, or we can arrange our lives around beginnings and focus on the births of ideas and newness. Either way, death follows birth and rebirth follows death. The cycle continues. The mold may melt away but another form is quickly revealed. Move with the cycle, celebrating the destruction since it reveals the treasures of life. We are continual witnesses and contributors to the creative cycle in the way we live, love and breathe life into beautiful beginnings.

September 27

Vulnerability

We cultivate love when we allow our most vulnerable and powerful selves to be deeply seen and known, and when we honor the spiritual connection that grows from that offering with trust, respect, kindness and affection. – *Brené Brown*, The Gifts of Imperfection: Let Go of Who You Think You're Supposed to Be and Embrace Who You Are

Out of the crack in a sidewalk, a beautiful violet blooms, unfazed by the rough surroundings that could restrict or threaten its growth. Its survival is temporary, but so is every other flower that blooms. The opportunity to assert its beauty is reason enough to show its face to the sun. The violet is being who and what it is.

Adopted by her grandparents, now an Olympic gold medalist, Simone Biles is a beacon for those who think they are limited by their beginnings. With grace and inner strength, Ms. Biles announces her presence in the world, making herself vulnerable to criticism and analysis, but also open to love and appreciation. She knows who she is and whose she is.

As a symbol of faith, we trust that stories of vulnerability are reminders that the journey of life is creative, regardless of the resources available. As a symbol of enlightened transformation, the energy of vulnerability encourages us to embrace each moment of creation with our joyful face and with reverence for the present moment.

We can be at peace with where we were previously in our life story; have faith that the future will emerge as is should be; and continue to bloom in the present moment. When we are preoccupied with what has happened in our lives, where we came from, or the nature of our past mistakes, we are forgetting the richness of the soil from which we have grown, and turning away from all that we are now. Celebrate who we are and bloom each day with new fragrances of peace, love and joy. A creative life is as much about showing up courageously as it is about showing what we are able to create.

September 28

Always Possible

Perceived boundaries dissolve when the universe
opens new windows. – *Ndidi,* Tea Leaves

Creative energy moves without a plan; what seems to be predictable can sometimes surprise us. Such is the case with quantum tunneling, a convenient metaphor for improbability. In quantum tunneling if an electron, normally repelled by an electromagnetic field manages to appear on the other side of a barrier that should repel it, physicists say there has been quantum tunneling – an unlikely occurrence has occurred.

Conditions in our lives sometimes seem impossible to manage. Like the physics phenomenon of particles breaking impenetrable barriers, our challenges can seem daunting or almost impossible to negotiate. We wonder how something so outrageous could happen in our lives, particularly when we are surprised, shocked or embarrassed. We are usually thwarted by an insistent ego that convinces us that what we think are impossible challenges are also our fault. The mind that controls us is successful in interfering with our creative energy. If we have tamed the mind it will be an asset in allowing our inspiration and resilience to see through the veneer of impossibility in our conditions. We can tunnel through the haze of hazards and see things from a different perspective. What was impossible is now changeable. What seemed permanent and fixed is now temporary. Nothing remains as it is. The shifting sands of our lives create exciting times for us, with new shores and surprises to be explored each moment.

September 29

Omnipresent Love

Anxiety is love's greatest killer. It makes others feel as you might when a
drowning man holds on to you. You want to save him,
but you know he will strangle you with his panic.
– *Anaïs Nin,* quoted in French Writers of the Past (2000)

Fear is a useless struggle against a future that does not yet exist. Our images
of impending disaster often lead us to panic, which is the frantic siren of a
threatened, false self. The ego is the director of the frightening drama that
is based on past fears and mistakes used as props, and the fever of intense
emotion as the main action.

We panic because we have forgotten who we are and what we are capable
of being. We convince ourselves that the world is unpredictable and
frightening, and that we are unprotected from its cruelty. These delusions
diminish our sense of self and compromise the integrity of our existence.
We are not pawns on a chessboard; in fact, there is no chessboard. Any
game in life that has winners and losers is decipherable. If we decide to
enter such a game, we know the rules; it is a finite game.

But the infinite game of life is a joyous ride that allows us to create our reality
as we journey through it. Our only goal is to play with lovingkindness and
compassion, so that we can enjoy our life as it unfolds. The truth of our
existence is that love is always present and joy is its companion. If we look
for love within, it will show itself brilliantly. If we believe in our ultimate
reality, love will show us peace.

September 30

Always Enough

You yourself, as much as anybody in the entire universe
deserve your love and affection. – *Sharon Salzberg*, quoted
in magazine article, "Woman of Power" (1989)

The sense of not having enough is uncomfortable, because we equate not
having what we need as personal failure. But often needs are creations
in the mind orchestrated by the false self. We want something more, or
different in our lives, and believe that we can find it outside of the true
self. We convince ourselves that who we are is not enough, and that our
constructed reality is hiding gifts from us. We are denying ourselves, our
true identity; it is a self-betrayal. There is nothing lacking in an abundant
universe; but we live in a vibrational universe, so when we are in alignment
with the abundance of the universe, the ultimate reality will bring us into
awareness of all that we need. When we become "truly self-assured," we
discover that what lies within us lacks nothing and is everything. We peek
into that space within, the vast space of universal abundance, and become
immersed in the grace of gratitude. In that space, we feel the peace of
knowing that we already have what we need to experience peace.

In a state of peace, we realize the falsehood of *more,* since there is no *more*
when there is *everything* available to us. The *fallacy* of wanting what we
already have is a testimony to the consistent lobbying of the false self.
Through greater awareness we connect with the true self, our core being
that cannot lack anything. We realize that *being enough* makes the idea of
more or less irrelevant. In a life of abundance, we will always have enough
love, enough peace and enough joy.

October 1

Crazy-making

Fear manipulates the mind in favor of untrue
versions of the self. – *Ndidi,* Tea Leaves

A popular film of the 1950's was called *Gaslight*. A character in the movie orchestrates a plan to drive his spouse crazy by convincing her that what she observes is not true, even though he is creating the events that she observes. Crazy-making happens in relationships; it also happens in our relationship with the self.

A fearful mind can be a crazy-maker. We may be encouraged to doubt our perceptions based on past experiences; or be brainwashed into thinking that nothing ever changes, even though we see evidence of change every day. The seeds of doubt set us up to fail when challenges appear in our lives. But if we practice solving the problems in our lives, we can render them less daunting. We are less frustrated by a problem we think is solvable. But we feel vulnerable when we have no control over events and then become malleable as a target of untrue thoughts and feelings of insecurity.

Life can be experienced as precarious or adventurous; we can be continually afraid of what will happen next, or ready for any new adventure. The projections and urgencies of the mind come from a sense of its importance. The egoic mind is suspicious of peace, preferring to see life as a precarious struggle to survive. Without the pessimistic ego making us "crazy" we can enjoy the adventure of life.

As a gatekeeper of our reality, the tamed mind has a specific role; it allows us to be reflective and to think about what feels nurturing to our essential being. When we remove ourselves from the crazy-making mind and become still, the reality of our existence will become clear. In the present moment, a sound mind knows its place. In a world of deceptive images in the mind, stillness settles us into the crystal clear waters of peace. We have nothing to fear.

October 2

Imbalance

Love balances the body and mind. – *Ndidi,* Tea Leaves

In an atmosphere of soothing fragrances and whispering sounds of the natural environment, an acupuncturist or masseuse attempts to unblock the points in the body where energy no longer flows freely. When energy flows freely through the various channels of the body, we feel a sense of well-being.

As conditions appear in our lives, our response to them can interrupt the positive, unobstructed flow of energy. We may observe a disaster such as an earthquake or a tsunami and even though we are not physically in danger, the notion of the precarious nature of life enters our mind. We may actually experience physical or emotional trauma, and hold tension in the body after witnessing a horrifying event. Our anger and frustration may constrict the flow in the liver, or overthinking a challenging situation may cause energy to tense in the head causing a headache. Our life experiences are continually creating a blueprint of unhappiness and fear, if we allow the reactions to trauma and complex conditions to create imbalances. When we are servants to a senseless mind, we overlay that blueprint onto a situation and become engrossed in its twisted-ness. Like a moth to a flame, we are drawn to the story of enemies, opponents and conflicts. As we descend deeper into the web, we no longer notice our own contribution to the frightening story. Instead of being aware of the one spirit of the universe, we run into the cave of the false self. We begin to solidify the notion of "I" and the counterpart "other." Our attention is then directed toward others who have not lived up to our expectations, and those who support our view from the cave. The indignant "I" closes our hearts to love and peace, and leaves us unsteady and insecure.

When the heart is closed, imbalance emerges; it is the heart that gives us balance and turns our energy inward. With an open heart, we no longer focus on our separation from others, and the promised protections of our false self. When we are aware that everything we ever needed to be safe, secure and free of suffering already exists as our essential nature, we can relax into inner peace and regain our balanced view. As we emerge from the cave, the light of our true self helps us to regain our balance and frees us from suffering.

October 3

Enlightened

We are already enlightened; we realize it when we
step out of the darkness. – *Ndidi,* Tea Leaves

Buddhist monks sit in silence for years seeking the moment when enlightenment will occur; they seek release from their karmic existence, the repeated life experience of endless suffering. Hindus meditate, do yoga, and chant mantras to be free from desire, suffering, and the cycle of rebirth. Many contemplatives and mystics pray inwardly to commune with the voiceless divine, and some traditional Christians pray outwardly to Jesus the Christ in supplication and with faith that their devotion will bring salvation and eternal life. As one of the pillars of Islam, Muslims pray five times each day in reverence to Allah, the Arabic word for God.

Within each of the powerful devotions and consecrations lies the light of ultimate truth. There are many paths to a similar end, the entry into a space of love. The prophets and messengers who guide us have seen the light within us, and within themselves. In their compassion for humanity they have offered the paths and encouraged our participation on the journey of discovery. When we realize that the light at the end of the tunnel is real we become one with it. When we are aware of the divinity within us, we free ourselves from the conditions and challenges of the world. In the light, the pure light of All-That-Is, no darkness is found.

October 4

Interpretations

When we make rules for other people, the origin of
those rules is disputed. – *Ndidi,* Tea Leaves

The late Billie Holliday, a well-known jazz singer of the last century, was known for her ability to describe the intensity of feelings in her songs. One song is a directive to a promiscuous lover called, "Don't Explain." In spite of our tendency to question anything we don't understand, some behaviors of others simply need no explanation; the same is true for the foundational truth of spiritual texts.

Sacred texts that have been written, recited then written, or orally transferred have created openings for others to interpret the meaning. We want to clearly understand the meaning of spiritual teachings so that we may apply the prescriptions for ultimate peace in our lives. Instead of providing clarity, the inspired teachings have led to various interpretations, explanations and enhancements designed to unveil the truth, with each iteration causing questions about what is absolute truth. Since many eyes have looked inside the meaning of the texts, conflicting notions about the truth have emerged.

When we believe that we are right, we may give up the need to be kind; we see different perspectives as threatening our own views, and seek like-minded thinkers to ensure the supremacy of our truth.

Conflicts have erupted from various scriptural interpretations and turned into violence and exclusion. Yet, every major religion in the world has internal diversity of thought and ritual. In spite of the diversity, camps, sects or communities of believers have been formed to guard the truth from the contamination of nonbelievers, or even divergent members of their own sect or denomination. The layers of explanation and interpretation have buried the truth of the inspirations under the extraordinary power of ego-driven minds. Although the diversity of beliefs within any of the major religious communities meets the needs of different people, interpretations also change over time, adding another layer of complexity.

When we peel away the layers of qualifiers and rules of behavior; or get rid of the notion of insiders and outsiders, we can see clearly that the core truth is unconditional love and deep abiding peace. As the 14th Dalai Lama says, "People take different roads to fulfillment and happiness. Just because they're not on your road does not mean they are lost." We must find our own way to step out of the darkness; the light of Love, the great unifier, is always present to show us the way.

October 5

Passionate Creation

For love is the ultimate meaning of everything around us. It is not a mere sentiment; it is truth. It is the joy that is at the root of all creation. – Rabindranath Tagore, Sadhana: The Realisation of Life (1916)

After months of delays, a woman decides to leave her hometown and venture off to a city several hundreds of miles away to pursue her passion to become a crisis counselor. She arranges for a taxi to take her to the airport and loads her luggage into the trunk when the taxi arrives. On the way to the airport the taxi runs out of gas on a bridge. The taxi driver apologizes and calls for assistance. After some time, the gasoline arrives and they continue to slowly cross the bridge. The sluggish traffic becomes so heavy it stops, and she soon discovers that there is an accident ahead that has closed two lanes. Feeling frustrated with the delays, she begins to sob, but through bleary eyes, she notices a man walking toward the railing of the bridge. His head is hung low and he too seems to be sobbing. Without thinking she gets out of the car, approaches the man and discovers that he is her uncle.

There are no real accidents. Where we create joy is less important than who we are being in the moment. Our passion to be an incarnation of joy is so strong that it must be expressed regardless of conditions that appear. Passionate creation is relentless in its need to express compassion, caring and lovingkindness. As an offering to us, we discover it in the moments between desire and action. It is the pause where nothing moves except the strong emotion within us. With that unquenchable thirst to be the love we are, our creative gifts call us to serve, and in that service we find joy.

October 6

Bliss

Follow your bliss...I think what we're seeking is an experience
of being alive, so that our life experiences on the purely physical
plane will have resonance within our own innermost being
and reality... – *Joseph Campbell,* The Power of Myth

We continually miss the bliss that is always available in our lives because
we insist on remaining in a continual state of denial of what we know we
are. Not fully accepting ourselves, we look outward to the world for clues.
That world has been created as concrete and solid, so that we can make
sense of it, but its substance changes. We stick with the concrete to avoid the
awareness of who and what we are, because we are afraid of our own power.

If we take a step toward joy, and embrace our bliss, we are wary of the occasional
questions from others about whether we are authentic in our "optimism." A
small voice from the ego coaxes us into a life of sameness and conformity, so we
decide to meet the needs of others' expectations of us, and give up awareness of
bliss in our own lives, in favor of the safety of sameness in the crowd. But we
cannot ignore our flowing heart longing to be poured into the world. We may
actually feel embarrassed that we lose our self in the bliss of a baby's smile or
the glow of a sunset. We may convince ourselves that what we feel, the presence
of the divine within us, is simply an unexplained emotion.

Bliss is a perfect state of being, but if we regard perfection as unattainable,
we will become a perpetual seeker. If we get a glimpse of joy, we can savor
it. Bliss is a state of being that defies description. When we search for bliss,
we are searching for ourselves, our true selves, and since we *are* the true self,
we will not find it in others. When we set aside opinions and expectations
of others; bliss pervades our being.

October 7

Finding "Me"

Meditation opens up our core being. – *Ndidi,* Tea Leaves

Several years ago a documentary took us on a journey through the human body and provided an inside look at the organs and blood vessels that work together like a mature symphony to keep us alive. Throughout the documentary a spot called "me" could not be found; that inner space is undetectable. It does not show up on X-rays or MRIs. If we attempt to find it we will be frustrated, yet we suspect that we exist as "me."

Thanks to the Genome Project, we can isolate genes and determine our genetic makeup. We share genetic DNA with other sentient beings, but once again isolating a "me" could be difficult. The puzzling non-appearance of "me" is further complicated by our unique expression of humanity, even though we share DNA. We are profoundly convinced that we are separate human beings, and that the world around us is just that, around us. We have feelings that we can name and share, but we don't know where they come from either. Surely, if we have feelings, there must be a "me." We have thoughts, continuous thoughts, reportedly even while we sleep or dream. How can we have thoughts, if there is no "me" to have them?

We have traveled to outer space with complex rockets and probes, but the short space distance inside is difficult to navigate. At the microscopic view, we are a collection of cells, and at the quantum view we are primarily space, but in all the space that we are a "me" cannot be found.

Yet, during the experience of meditation, the inner space is known, not as a space with boundaries and demarcations, but as an expansive, deep and formless self. Just as outer space is proving to be endless with many galaxies or multiverses, the opening to the inner space is also infinite and without boundaries. Although we think of ourselves as separate from everything else, during meditation we sense the connection to everything else in the universe. We let go of the idea of the "me" and touch our infinite self within.

October 8

Loved

Lend yourself to others, but give yourself to yourself.
– *Michel de Montaigne,* The Complete Essays

We may wonder what it means to be loved. Many have tried to describe the experience; some have provided tips on how to acquire love. Others have given advice about how to keep love when we have finally found it. When we feel love toward another person, the feeling raises the level of vibration in us, and the magnetic field that surrounds us "attracts" another person. We say that people are "attractive" or have a "magnetic personality." We may know the feeling of love as the desire to bond or have children, but being loved is more difficult to describe. Being loved is being recognized for who we really are; loved at the core of our being, and not just at the surface.

Beyond the initial attraction is an indescribable, unexplained joy in being in the presence of another person. We recognize our own being in the other; and our relationship with the other person feels like a close relationship with ourselves, because in fact it is. We are inextricably linked to one another in spirit, even though we express ourselves as individuals. What we do for our beloved we also do for ourselves.

No clinging is necessary, only appreciation and lovingkindness. If we want to be loved, we must be loving. If we want to feel appreciated, we must practice appreciation. If we want to feel cherished, we must practice cherishing. And, if we want to feel love, we must allow it to flow freely from our essential nature. Loving is a way of being; being love itself is who we are.

October 9

Greed

Greed never satisfies its aim— to prevent others from realizing their own significance. – *Ndidi*, Tea Leaves

Brad wins $500 dollars in the state lottery and gambles it away in a day trying to win a million dollars. Shirley collects unusual cups so she bids online for a new one, even though she is not certain where she will store it. Murray owns 300 pairs of shoes but he wears only two pairs. Giorgio dates several people at once so that he never has to be alone with himself. Ben enjoys all-you-can-eat buffets even though he is pre-diabetic. Marion cannot help herself; she must share everything she knows about other people to anyone who will listen. No one trusts Marion.

When we are consumed with greed its wrath can take many forms of behavior. One commonality is that greed always involves grasping; the consumption of material things, relationships or significance drives greedy behaviors. We believe that acquiring more objects or cash will complete us and therefore bring us happiness. We may believe that more friends or intimate relationships will bring us freedom from loneliness. We may believe that eating more, thinking more or speaking more will bring us satisfaction and freedom from pain and suffering.

The pain we feel is the response from a bruised ego that believes the untrue story that we are not loved beyond our imagination, or that we are not enough for this world or society. When we discover that we do not need anything outside of our true self to be happy, we are liberated from grasping. We realize that we don't need happiness to be loved, but we do need to love in order to be happy.

Greed is a cynical view of life and of ourselves. All that we need comes to us, if we let go of needing anything. Love is always present in our lives; we must loosen our grip so that we can experience it.

Greed is passionate energy gone wild. What may begin as excessive passion to create wealth, works of art, music, friendships or success, becomes a frenzy of grasping for more and more. We have heard the stories of impassioned composers, crazed artists, deceptive investment brokers, or frenetic entrepreneurs. Greed knows no contentment. Like a desperate junkie, the person suffering with greed craves the next acquisition or competitive edge as if it were the next high.

The person possessed with greed is addicted to what comes next. When the next hit comes, its effect is less and less satisfying, until the desire is transmuted into anger, frustration and cynicism. We can interrupt this pattern and face our feelings of inadequacy; we can clear away our delusions of lack and insufficiency. Our constant additions diminish us; we are controlled by what we want to apprehend.

Our greed is the internalized sense of lacking something. Somewhere in our painful past we think we lost the one thing that would make us happy. The past has no power except the attention we give to it. We can begin to let go of our emotionally wounded ego and face the pain that we have transferred to the present. In the present moment pain is no competition for the power of peace and joy that wash over us. In the present moment we come face to face with our magnificence, our divine inheritance.

We have always been enough, although we had doubts. We have always been loved, even though we thought our things made us more attractive and worthy. We have always known that we could not continue the game. Deep within, we know who we are. When we get still, relax and let go, we remember.

October 10

Collective Awareness

Conscious awareness is evidence of our humanity. – *Ndidi,* Tea Leaves

In the midst of disasters, the human spirit rises as if it has been lying in hibernation waiting to be awakened from slumber. The collective awareness of the end of this life we are living, suddenly arouses a deep love for one another. Earthquakes, tsunamis, floods and droughts bring us together in strangely beautiful ways. The sleeping dragon of love gets drowsy again once the immediate danger has passed, and we humans may slink back into our dark hole of self-preservation.

In order to keep our sense of humanity awake and alive, we could remember the feelings we have when we express our compassion or when we experience compassion from others. Our memories of compassion can help us to build the muscle of compassion and love for others. We could love others as ourselves, because we and others are inextricably linked. We could learn to be humane not because there is a crisis or an apparently extreme need, but because we are here to express love, to be love, to practice compassion and loving kindness. We may feel it as a gift to others, but it is actually a gift to ourselves. We may appreciate the gifts of kindness from others, but it is actually our opportunity to be the reason for loving kindness to be expressed. The powerful moments of love that we share are the divine music of our lives. We must remember the notes in times of struggle but also in times of peace.

October 11

Comparisons

Comparisons are a form of violence. When you believe
you are not good enough, you compare yourself to
others. – *Iyanla Vanzant*, Peace from Broken Pieces

Comparisons bring negative feelings along for our cosmic ride, so we must choose to abandon them. If we allow comparisons to enter our mind, we create an unhealthy separation from others. We may compare ourselves unfavorably to others sometimes leading to shame or self-hatred; or compare ourselves favorably from a place of insecurity. Either scenario is self-destructive. When we compare ourselves to others, we not only invite sadness into our lives, but we forget that we are magnificent.

If the daily experiences in our lives generate anything but love, they are misrepresenting misalignments that cause us to abandon awareness of the loving spirit that we are. Our love is complex, so we may not recognize it without mindful awareness. Love shows up constantly in our lives, flirting with our senses and our sensibilities.

Our love is as alive in nature as in a close-knit family. Music thrives on the energy of love and reflects the beat of our heart. Artistic creations touch us in tender places, opening our eyes and quieting our information-laden minds. Festival dances stir love within us, giving us rhythms and irrational bliss. Poetry and songs shake us away from routine paths and open new gates of connection to the inner stirrings of delight. The air we breathe metaphorically reminds us moment after moment that love is being gloriously alive; our individual expressions of life are so beautiful that breath fills us up so that we can continue to bless the world.

October 12

The Embarrassment

Hatred requires an exhausting commitment
to a theory. – *Ndidi,* Tea Leaves

A longtime member of the infamous religious community tweeted a trove of hateful messages on Twitter for years. The messages disparaged dead and disabled veterans, LGBTQ individuals, other races and anyone else considered a nonbeliever or infidel, particularly Muslims. The vitriolic tweets continued unabated until she realized that a world lay waiting for her beyond the imprisonment of hatred. She discovered that true freedom is not housed in judgments that shatter the peace of others, but in listening to other perspectives.

Hatred is an extraordinary embarrassment; it is a display of insecurity and a useless focus on something temporary. While we may intend to appear strong, as the story unfolds in a display of hatred, the energy devoted to delivering pain to another begins to weaken us. Nevertheless, we are then pressed to develop new ways to sustain the mental, physical or emotional assault on our object of hatred. The hated, objectified individuals or groups suck our energy, but we accommodate its desires by continuing to feed our obsession. Hatred is an embarrassment since it lays bare the thin argument our ego proposed to initiate our hateful actions or thoughts. The disingenuous ego convinces us that once we begin our assault we must continue until there is a winner, although the ultimate rewards become unclear. As time-space goes on, our thoughts begin to control us, robbing us of pleasure in the present moment. We want to end the struggle but winning is elusive, so we continue the weary game of misguided thinking, overreaction to imagined slights and unproven beliefs in the unworthiness or hatefulness of the hated other. Throughout this unfortunate charade the universe changes as it must, and old hurts soon seem out of place. Eventually, we become unclear about our original complaint, so our egos step in again to create new reasons to sustain the hatred. The entire story, based on a shaky premise of wrongdoing and assumptions, has now become a full-fledged embarrassment, a folly based on the belief that we can believe something long enough to make it true. We can turn away from our battle with ourselves and acknowledge our true self. Our confusion becomes clarity, and we become confident that we will survive being vulnerable. We are no longer embarrassed by the caricature of who we are and claim the true essence of joy and peace within our soul.

October 13

Good Samaritan

...for there is nothing heavier than compassion. Not even one's own pain weighs so heavy as the pain one feels with someone, for someone, a pain intensified by the imagination and prolonged by a hundred echoes."
– *Milan Kundera*, The Unbearable Lightness of Being

Showing love and compassion to those in need is an opportunity to fulfill our promise as human beings. Some states in the US are beginning to support the idea that people in need are our neighbors, not strangers who know how to survive challenges but simply refuse to do it. Our negative ideas about people without resources or good health are projections of our own fears. Like the parable of the Good Samaritan, those of us who know better, have been taught how to treat others, but don't always do what we say we believe. We may spend considerable time blaming people for their situation or dismissing their pleas for help as excessive whining or refusals to take responsibilities for their actions.

The thinking is usually linear, as if there is one cause and one effect in life situations. There are multiple causes and multiple effects arising sometimes simultaneously. The help we provide to others can be less about who they are and more about who we are. Our compassion and love are not commodities that can be bought and sold; we cannot locate love as an object, or compassion as a tool, because they are formless until their effects are felt. The significance of our lovingkindness is felt, not captured like a thing to be owned. Love exists everywhere in the universe; when we acknowledge love as who we are in our support for the well-being of others, we live our purpose.

October 14

Truth is Free

The magical, natural world inside us is free for
us to explore. – *Ndidi,* Tea Leaves

When the sunlight barely peaks up from the horizon, a photographer scopes out the area in a cove of trees for an upcoming photo shoot. She has opted to use natural lighting for the best photos; true lighting will allow the subject's inner light to meet the rays of the sun and dance with one another in her lens. The other option is contrived lighting and delicate manipulation of apertures to get a decent photo indoors. She wants the camera to capture the truth of her subject, the legitimacy that only nature can provide.

The truth of our lives is that we are powerful co-creators of our world. When we seek the truth in what we create we do so with the inspiration of the natural world. Our creativity does not come from the tools we use to generate a product; passion within us guides our hand, inspires our thoughts and opens our heart. Creativity is not something we do, it is something – unnamed and unseen – that we are. We become aware of the presence in the present moment, and are gently reminded of the passion that dances within. Out of nothing our creative energy, like the unexamined, unevaluated and inexplicable movement in nature, expresses the truth of our being. Our passion is beyond explanation, and voiceless; it follows no rules and has no goals, except its own continuation. When we immerse ourselves into the awareness of our true self, our passion bursts into creation, and our "work" becomes the play of the universe.

October 15

Heaven

If I adore you out of desire for Paradise, Lock me out of Paradise.
But if I adore you for Yourself alone, Do not deny me Your eternal
beauty. – *Rabi'a al–Basri*, in thesis by Margaret Smith (1928)

No one has ever seen the place, but most are convinced that it is prime real
estate. Many people want to move there for permanent retirement, but the
requirements for entering the community are varied based on what you
believe. There are rules to follow in order to qualify for admission, and
it seems to accommodate an exclusive residency. Some will be excluded
because they are deemed unreliable as believers. Some believe that they
are already experiencing the benefits now, although some people live in a
society that has denied them admission at birth.

Heaven is regarded as the place to be when we cease to be -- as the place to be
happy, so some of us defer our happiness to a time in the hopefully distant
future. The desire for happiness in a challenging world is understandable;
we want to live in that space now for immediate gratification, but some of
us are resigned to wait for happiness.

The place we crave is deep within the self, closer to us than we can imagine.
We search and search for happiness or resign ourselves to its elusiveness,
but it is with us while we search for it. Our inner happiness has the effect
of being free in the moment; free of pain and expectations. When we
understand that our chance for happiness exists right now in the present
moment, we experience what many call our heaven on earth.

October 16

Creative Guidance

Capture your joy and it will follow you
throughout the day. – *Ndidi,* Tea Leaves

Shepherds are well-known metaphorical characters that teach us profound truths because of the useful characteristics attributed to them. These caretakers feed the lambs, take them to abundant places to graze, maintain their grooming, and deliver new lambs. These expert guides lead the flock, encourage cooperation and togetherness, create a sense of community among the sheep, and guard them from likely predators.

When we release our creative energy into the world, we do so with the discipline of the shepherd. When we understand what feeds us, we return again and again to fill ourselves with joy. We may serve others, design a home or rear a child, but we continually recognize the inherent value in what we do and feel. We surround ourselves with people who nourish our spirit, and take care of ourselves in the process. We generate beauty in all that we do as compassionate beings, and receive guidance from others by engaging freely with them. We bring our true self to our creative energy and guard against establishing false boundaries that threaten our freedom. We are the caretakers of our heart and our loving nature. With the discipline of a shepherd, we create with joy.

October 17

Intuitive Creativity

Creativity requires the courage to let go of
certainties. – *Erich Fromm,* Man for Himself

Concentration may be an important component of mindfulness meditation, but the intuitive process of creativity arises out of chaos and pours itself into everything we do, say, feel or think. Creativity is experience released, pointing to reality. The mind that is free of definitions and thoughts concentrates with one-pointed focus. The clarity creates full awareness of life as it is. When the mind is clear we interact with our life in new creative ways.

Creativity has been described in a number of ways, but its origin is baffling. When we try to think about being creative, we lose the spontaneity of the experience. Creativity does not always begin with an idea, but the process breathes on its own and sometimes takes us to places we did not intend. The chi energy or life force energy compels us to create each moment, but we do not know if plans we construct will be altered on the path to a completed poem, musical composition or clay vessel.

No matter what we are creating, we are destroying something along the way in order to release what we are creating. The sculptor releases the object from the stone, and the writer spills words onto a page. Existing techniques guide us, but our intuitive self creates new rules. The mystery of creativity arises in a drumbeat, an improvisational dance or a landscaped garden. When we know who we really are the energy of creativity unfolds in our experience like a riderless horse. We jump onto its back and ride with it until there is no way to distinguish our self from the horse.

October 18

Seeing with Heart

Our creations are our legacy, the evidence
of life lived. – *Ndidi*, Tea Leaves

An artist does not see only with eyes but with the heart. Our senses are mere tools that we take with us on life's journey. Something much deeper, much more reliable compels us to create.

The eyes look for familiar patterns and think about how they fit in an existing scene in the mind; but the eyes see only within the limits of experience of color, shape, texture and light. Van Gogh was reportedly color blind and Claude Monet painted with failing eyesight, but their masterpieces are creative legends.

Our ears can detect the texture, tone and volume of sound, but we hear within a few decibel bands limited by the workings of the inner ear. In deafness, Mozart created music, even though his hearing steadily declined.

Lauren Anderson, a famous ballerina, had a physical challenge that did not thwart her drive to dance beautifully, and Misty Copeland defied naysayers as she overcame height concerns and racial barriers to become principal dancer at the American Ballet Theater.

When we reveal our creative passion, our entire body, mind and being-ness become the creation; and we create continuously out of the direct experience of our lives. Our thoughts are creating images, our legs, arms and head are creating our walk; our thoughts, body and senses are creating our feelings of well-being or illness. All of these personal signatures are given substance by the creative energy arising within us. Without our creative passion, nothing exists in form, so our passion to create in each moment of our lives is our contribution to life, our expression of joy.

October 19

The Evil Devil

The mind creates a fearful form so that it can justify being afraid. – Ndidi, Tea Leaves

We have created the devil to help us discern what arouses love in us and what arouses fear. We imagine a battle between good (God) and evil (Devil) where God is continually the victor. This continually victorious outcome assures us that God (Love) always wins, and with God on our side, we too will be safe from harm. When we look at the conditions in our lives that bring pain and suffering, we look for explanations, but often become frustrated or even doubtful that Love indeed will win. As life continues with ups and downs, victories and defeats, we surrender to a divine plan for emotional comfort. The mind at this point has successfully controlled us, and we become its servant.

The contest between good and evil draws important contrasts in our reality, but we must remember that these conflicts are ideas in the mind. In order to feel assured that we are fully experiencing life, our mind creates a protagonist and an antagonist for our life drama. The character of the devil encompasses everything fearful: physical harm, emotional distress, loss of control of life, illness, and death. God, Spirit or other concepts of divinity may on the other hand encompass everything that feels like love: well-being, happiness and contentment, the absence of stress, and eternal life.

We have difficulty experiencing love which we call good, without acknowledging the existence of evil. Tensions arise between the two concepts, creating a life of suffering with intermittent, fleeting periods of happiness. We may grow accustomed to life events that seem happy which are followed by disturbing events. We say that when we are happy, we're just waiting for the other shoe to drop. With continual swings from good to not good experiences of life, we live in constant anticipation of fearful events and see life as precarious and unstable.

When our expectations of life are shattered we blame these appearances on the devil, our embodiment of fear, but when we experience relief from suffering we say that God (good), Allah or Spirit has saved or protected us. In our scenarios, good (God) will always win over evil, but the contrasting concepts are inextricably linked; one cannot ever be released from its reflection. If love wins, or good triumphs, there must always be a vanquished opponent lurking in the background, ready to devise a new plan for our destruction. But if we think fear wins, we become immersed in depression, frustration and other aspects of suffering.

There is only one Love, even though opposites exist within the mind. As long as we rely on the imaginings of the mind, we will need to see opposing forces; but when we are aware that love is all there is because God is all there is, we taste the sweet nectar of liberation.

When we tame the fearful mind, we settle into the present moment of awareness and know that no fear is present. This state of awareness is without adversaries, and the ecstasy of Love is all there is. Fear and evil become mere stories we tell about our lives. With a mind that is free, we embrace all that arises in awareness, however it appears, and accept that our labels - good and evil, love and fear are aspects of the same story.

Love is All-That-Is; when we focus our attention on love, we will always "win" in spite of the fearful appearances in our consciousness. Relax into the present moment; we know that our true self is only Love.

October 20

Evolving Life

Creativity is the call of the universe to evolve. – *Ndidi,* Tea Leaves

Many know the cautionary story of the frog that is swimming in a pot of water, and does not notice that the water is slowly heating up, until it is too late. Our lives are continually heating up with our own passionate energy. The failure to recognize that energy can be depressing, even life-threatening. When we reveal our passion to create, we participate in the evolution of the universe. Some have a compulsion to procreate, like the desperately determined salmon that swim upstream to spawn; others have an idea or a solution growing inside them that must be given birth. Whatever we choose to be, our small footprint leaves an indelible imprint on the soul of the universe. We give purpose to our lives in the way we express the true self.

Every expression of gratitude and appreciation for our lives leaves a mark of love; and each act of compassion leaves a heart opened and warmed with tenderness. Every prayer for acknowledgement of healing sends light throughout the universe; each moment of stillness raises the consciousness of the planet for peace and understanding. When we answer the call, show up fully in the present moment, we bring joy into life and freedom from suffering for all of us. Our passion gives rise to new possibilities, and our special combination of ideas that take form direct the continual evolution of life on earth and beyond.

October 21

Luminosity

The view is clear, now that the light is shining
inwardly. – *Ndidi,* Tea Leaves

We often say that new information shines a light on a subject we are investigating or contemplating. Suddenly we see clearly something that perhaps moments ago seemed dense and complex. Often we attribute our new appreciation for a concept or data point to someone outside of ourselves, but our insight arouses out of nowhere, out of "no-thing." Potential or possibilities rest in consciousness, waiting to be illuminated in the mind or heart. This clarity is essential to our experience of life. The illuminated experience of life is not dependent on seeing with the eyes, but comes with awareness of the true self. We realize that relying on the senses or our thoughts and feelings to clarify events in our life, can still leave us in the dark.

Without this clarity, life seems confusing and frustrating, even though we live in a universe that is alive with possibilities. When we see clearly with the brilliance of awareness, we know the opportunities in challenges, the life in the midst of destruction, and the pervasive peace in chaos. Luminosity is not confined to what we see "out there" but also what we experience fully within. When we see our insecurities, our lingering disappointments, our frustrations and loneliness as thoughts we have chosen to cling to, we can decide how we want to respond. When we become conscious of the love that is our inner vision, we allow the light of our true self to release our grip on thoughts that lead to suffering.

October 22

Boundless

Your first love has no beginning or end. Your first love is not
your first love, and it is not your last. It is just love. It is one with
everything. – *Thich Nhat Hanh*, Cultivating the Mind of Love (2005)

If we look up to the sky, we are unable to find where it ends. We may
think that we are having a direct experience of the sky or the universal
expansiveness by just looking at it, but we cannot know it through our eyes.
Our vision only offers an impression of the sky based on our vision and
understanding of what a sky should be. We are observing the phenomenon
without consciousness of *being* that expansive boundlessness. Just as the
sky is boundless, so is our love. If we want to express boundless love that
extends to all beings in the universe, we must first have the experience for
ourselves.

Often we get trapped by the overwhelming desire to find the limits of our
experience so that we can know what we can control; we sometimes establish
those limits if none seem apparent. We say that we have preferences or make
choices that work for us, and feel confident that our self-determination
or self-control is the best path. Boundaries are our protective barriers that
assure us that we are safe from intrusion or violation. As long as life is
going well for us, the boundaries we place on the expression of love seem
to work, but this temporary satisfaction is an illusion.

Our true self has no boundaries; its expanse is endless, and so is love. If we
choose to set up restraints that control our expressions of love, we discover
that we are constraining our expression of who we really are. We are made
to love, to be love. When we are in a place of pain and anxiety, we can
sense more strongly our disconnection from others; suffering is denying

our potential for joyful connections, and resigning ourselves to be less than who we are. Our pain seems unique, but it is a proxy for the pain of others. We share a collective consciousness of thoughts and feelings, so when we find release from suffering, we do so for others who suffer from similar anxieties.

Boundaries dissolve as we feel vulnerable and desperate for relief; often our recognition of connection with others comes when we need their help or they request help from us. We come face-to-face with our inherent interdependence. If we go within to find strength, we may doubt our capacity, but if we stop to think of all the beings in the universe who have ever experienced the challenges we are currently experiencing, we can regain our strength.

With the boundless breath of Spirit, we can breathe in the pain of self and others, and then breathe out peace and calm for all beings. As we experience the connection and liberation of others, we know the healing energy deep within ourselves. We come home to awareness of the boundless universe, having a direct experience of boundless joy.

October 23

The Folly of Fate

Life is filled with lessons, not liabilities. – *Ndidi,* Tea Leaves

The morai of Greek mythology are white-robed incarnations of destiny sometimes also referred to as the Fates. They are said to have extraordinary powers to control our lives by spinning and allotting fateful events that cannot be altered.

As we journey through life, we realize that most events are not under our direct control, but sometimes our fears prevent us from responding in our best interests. It is easy to blame fate for the unfortunate or challenging events that stop us in our tracks, but we always have choices about how to respond to events, or how to think about them. We think our destiny is lodged in some nebulous future that we cannot imagine. If we allow ourselves to become mired in that cloudy future, we will miss the joy of our journey and make choices that may not work well for us. Pre-determination is only able to be acknowledged in hindsight. We say it was our destiny to experience or have something only after it is manifest in our reality. That's a bit like assuring ourselves that we were destined to win the lottery after cashing in the winning ticket. Our joy is not dependent on fate, but on the ever-present love available to us in each moment. Whatever happens in our reality, we will always have what is necessary to make choices about how to respond. Our responses can be based on the belief in the inherent love in all things, and the confidence in knowing that all is as it should be for us in this moment.

October 24

Virtue

I laugh when I hear that the fish in the water
is thirsty. – *Kabir,* The Kabir Book

A boy stands in front of two doors; one leads to happiness forever but requires that he give up any possibility of monetary wealth. The second door leads to great wealth, but requires that he give up knowing himself.

For many of us, the choice is clear, but for some of us, the idea of having to choose is the greatest travesty. Virtue demands that we make a choice in challenging situations, because our choices reveal our character. Our virtues are challenged when we try to balance gains and losses. We may wonder what the consequences will be if we make a certain choice. We will choose the option in any case because we think we'll feel better as a result.

Our desire to feel better is grounded in the thought that something is lacking. We may believe that something is lacking in us and that a deficiency exists that must be corrected; or we may try to make ourselves more appealing to others - more beautiful, attractive, respected or loved. We may be willing to risk reputation, relationships or repercussions in order to have a few moments of satisfaction. When we view our existence as lacking anything, we have entered a door of delusion.

We are loved beyond our comprehension, right now. There is no door that we have to enter, no test, and no loss. We are complete as we are; happiness is simply, joyously present however life appears to us. True virtue is awareness of the character of our inner truth. We must be still and know.

Roller Coaster

It is unwise to stop the world and ask to get
off the ride. – *Ndidi,* Tea Leaves

Everything in the universe moves. Even a rock, stuck in its spot is in continual motion, if we look deeply into its atomic structure. Life at its core is anything but stagnant or motionless. We are continually aware of this motion, since there are constant ups and downs in life's reality, like the motion of a roller coaster. When the roller coaster is at its lowest point on the route, it is preparing to climb to new heights; when the roller coaster reaches new heights, its descent is expected. Like the roller coaster, events in our lives eventually come to a resting point, but usually that point of balance is momentary. As soon as we recuperate from the thrill of the ride at rest, new thrills are attracted to us. When we are riding through life, enjoying the view at the high points, and resting at the low points, we experience the fullness of life. We let go of control, throwing our hands up in release, and have faith that everything is exactly as it should be. We need nothing but our awareness of now and an immersion into the experience of no control to experience joy. We relax, because nothing is under control. When we take advantage of the low points to savor moments of peace, and then allow the energy of the ride to flow freely, we soon realize that there is a constant state of peace at any point on the ride, and that the ride is our story, the way we are making sense of what we experience in our reality. When we let go we are able to see and feel the constancy of peace.

October 26

Realities

I am not who I think I am; I am much more. – *Ndidi*, Tea Leaves

We seem to exist in two realities: one is the world we observe as our life, and the other is our ultimate reality. We are continually negotiating the relationship between the two, shuttling between what is true and what is false. What we observe is our mind drafting compelling scenarios for us that either frighten or delight us. We react to the expected anxieties or temporary happiness, and resign ourselves to a life of appearances.

Our ultimate reality is a continuous state of well-being and love. Because the relationship between our two realities is so close we call it "my life," but we sometimes miss the subtle difference between the two. The observed reality comes and goes; it changes every moment with no warning about sudden unexpected variations, like Breaking News, during a dramatic television show. The news or variation is accepted as the dangers of living, and over time we become desensitized to the falsehoods and drains on our energy.

The ultimate reality is not observed but experienced as awareness of inner divinity. When we know who we are, we experience the universal peace and joy that sits reliably in the midst of our experiences, and realize that our potential is indefinable, and that our magnificence is a result of our formlessness within.

October 27

Clutter

To be full of things is to be empty of God; to be empty
of things is to be full of God. – *Meister Eckhart, as quoted
in* Men Who Have Walked with God *(1992)*

Hoarders are often an extreme reminder of the dangers of clutter, but
our lives are often not lived in extremes. Our closets, closed to visitors or
friends, are often cluttered with too many clothes, supplies or unused and
forgotten objects. We have forgotten the values or memories that material
objects conjure in our mind. We don't notice that we have unwittingly
attached our worth to many of those objects, and as a result we are often
reluctant to let the objects go.

Why then do we accumulate things, and then hold onto them, as if they
are important to us? And if we release them what remains? Will their
release create empty spaces in our living space or only in our hearts and
minds?

Each item is embedded with memories, some faint and some vivid. Somewhat
like rubbing the "Velveteen Rabbit," we believe that our love of these items
makes them and us *real*. Perhaps without our things - objects, people, work
and other "possessions" - we think we have no life signature, no definition,
or no uniqueness. That's why they are "our things."

The search for love is the real desire, since these objects are simply energy,
much as we are energy. We think we own the objects, and therefore have
love in our midst, but if we're not careful, we will allow our things to own
us, and when that happens, our things become the source of suffering
rather than the love we crave. Since everything is temporary, impermanent,

our clinging to clutter will ultimately lead to unreasonable expectations and disappointments. We begin to identify with what we "own," and define success or significance based on objects that cannot nurture us. Clutter is a disease of greed that denies us a sense of wholeness. When we release the clutter in our consciousness, we clear a space to see the fulfillment of our desires everywhere.

We are continuous, intelligent energy, expressing itself in this life space. There is nothing to gain or accumulate. Everything is already ours right now, but if we attempt to grasp for more, the experience is overwhelming. When we are at peace with our life as it is, our peacefulness allows joy to arise in us. We are more than the finite possessions we cherish; we are the universe in seamless union with unconditional love and abundance.

October 28

Disappearing Life

My death will be disappearance of a particular pattern in the water. – *Alan Watts,* Cloud–hidden, Whereabouts Unknown

We are all standing in the queue waiting to be called to enter a new phase of our eternal life. Some of us may choose to deny the eventual door that will open to eternity, because the experience of our current consciousness, although disappointing at times, is all we know.

The idea of death of this life is scary since we think we've had no experience with death. But we die every moment. All that we actually have to experience is now. We are also reborn every moment to begin again, to live fully again, and to love again. The last hour, minute, second is gone forever, living only in our memories, but we keep getting new chances.

We keep learning and allowing ourselves to be awed by the majesty of life. We smile at the giggles and coos of babies; we bask in the romantic glow of the sunset; and we cherish the devotion of our furry, adorable pets. Joy follows us around and shows up after every sigh, opens our eyes after sleep, and breathes life into our heart. Joy is a constancy that assures us of eternity, and it is transformative. It is unwavering in its promise to always be our essential nature, and is the consciousness of the undying love that pervades the universe.

We could reframe our concept of living, as part of a continuum of existence, where in this time and space, we enjoy a continuous adventure of contrasts and surprises, each of which startles us with the diversity of beauty and the constancy of creation. We could be aware of the moment by moment transformations that offer new opportunities for compassion and lovingkindness. We could be here now for the sheer joy of it.

October 29

Sculptors

Because you are alive, everything is possible. –
Thich Nhat Hanh, Living Buddha, Living Christ

Creative minds do not seek ways to be creative; they allow what is possible to appear. In a delicate dance of light and form, a sculptor starts with nothing and allows something to emerge. The images flood the awareness of the sculptor, but the selective eye and open heart bring a moment into static reality. Among the entire buffet of possibilities, the sculptor acknowledges the precise moment when life chooses to appear and allows it to take form. Sculpture is a metaphor for passionate creativity; it is responsive to a call, appreciative of the present moment, and zealous in its determination to express life fully.

We are all sculptors of our lives. When we reveal our creativity in response to what we experience in life, we appreciate life as it is, not as we want it to be. We release our judgments and find the beauty in the ordinary as well as the ordinary in the beautiful.

We love what is appearing in the moment, with no comparison with what has happened in the past. As life sculptors, the future is irrelevant, since the substance of our artistry is appearing now. When we are aware of our inherent presence in the forms of life we are creating, we no longer hide our talents. We develop the negatives in our lives with painstaking attention to what appears, with appreciation for the positive and negative spaces of each moment. And when the final masterpiece appears in its fullness, we realize that appreciating the beauty of our work has just begun. We see no need to frame it in static realities, but rather we see its fluidity, its nuances and inherent beauty.

Life is our creation, and the passion that simmers within us, wants to develop the story in all its shadows and lights. We must allow the full substance of life to unfold.

October 30

There is A Field

Out beyond ideas of wrongdoing and rightdoing, there is a
field. I'll meet you there. – *Rumi*, The Essential Rumi

When the world we have co-created seems chaotic, unfair and fearful, we
have a choice. We can live out the anxieties and even embellish them, or
we can get busy creating a different reality for ourselves. What we have
set in motion often has to make its mark on our lives, but even as the pain
intensifies, we can begin to turn our lives toward a less fearful path.

A Florida grand jury, deciding the guilt of a neighborhood watchman,
brought into bold relief what we humans can create out of fear and a belief
in our separateness. The more we see ourselves as separate, competing
parts of this universe, the more we act out our perceived differences. Our
perceptions of right doing and wrongdoing keep us separated and fearful.
We desperately seek ways to feel love, to feel special in some way. We create
an "other" that hopefully will set us apart as better and therefore more
lovable. Other-ness is an illusion that burdens us with continual efforts to
prove our worth and significance.

At the core of our being is all the love we need. There is a field that
breathes love, where that love erases the boundaries we have wrapped
around ourselves. We are free when we stay in the present moment of
peace, and know that we are spiritual beings, one energy, bathed in the
love of All-That-Is.

October 31

Happy for a Reason

Like smiles and yawns, happiness is contagious. – *Ndidi,* Tea Leaves

Freedom from wanting anything may be difficult to achieve in a world of materialism; we do have basic needs. We begin to suffer when our longing for material items disturbs our sense of peace. We make the material object, achievement or indicators of wealth our reason to be happy. The happiness is a byproduct of the thing we cherish, until it no longer makes us happy.

When we stake our happiness on something with conditional value, we are likely to experience disappointment. Since the happiness we've achieved is a temporary byproduct, we could invest in actions that have a longer shelf life, like compassion and lovingkindness. Being compassionate in service or in interactions with others has a two-fold possibility of happiness. When we are compassionate toward others, we are the primary beneficiaries, since what we do for others fulfills our own needs. If we want be happy for a reason, we could allow our natural loving essence to express joy in our lives; we could look for joy and let it direct our lives. Even though the expression of lovingkindness and compassion have benefits for us, we could let go of any expectation of benefits and experience happiness. Shared happiness is not really given away, it is invested with an immediate return of joy.

November 1

A Bundle of Twigs

Beavers do not build a sufficient dam with one twig. – *Ndidi,* Tea Leaves

Many teachers and guides have told us that we are never alone in this world, and we have been comforted by their counsel. We have assumed that not being alone meant that someone else exists to keep us company, or that even though we feel alone that there is always a divine presence to turn to in times of trouble. But the feeling of aloneness may persist if we believe that we are separate individuals with no connection to anything else in the universe. We may feel alone when we feel that there is nowhere to turn for resolution of challenges we face. When conditions seem overwhelming, or our own bodies become diseased or infirm, we may feel isolated.

Instead of experiencing aloneness, we could know the state of "all-oneness." Being alone is a false story we tell ourselves when fear takes over, shoving faith and love aside. Whatever we are feeling, someone else is feeling also. If we are aware of the interconnection of us all, we know that our sense of aloneness is a signal to us that someone needs a comforting presence. We can be that presence. When we reach out we reach inward; when we give comfort we are comforted.

November 2

Love Remains

Many waters cannot quench love neither can floods
drown it. – *Song of Solomon 8:7(KJV)*

If we forget about where we live, what we know, and where we work as
determining factors of our existence, do we have any significance in this world?
And will that significance mean that we are loved? Questions about love and
significance do not plague us everyday, but in times of crisis we may wonder.
We may settle on answers that either offer stability in our life or a sense of
mystery. But the answer has little to do with the limits of our life experience,
and more about the nature of our existence. We are love, beautiful and eternal.

Love is our ultimate spiritual essence that we express with strong emotions
and offer in acts of compassion. It has remarkable resilience since it remains
even after other emotions have cooled and declined, or when the feelings
of compassion have subsided. Love never leaves us because our essential
nature is our permanent signature; when fear makes an appearance in
the mind and disturbs the peace, love is still there. We cannot locate a
place where Love is not present, even though we may ignore or discount
its power. We acknowledge Love when we return to awareness of our true
self, after allowing fear to live with us temporarily.

The true evidence of the stability and sustainability of Love is that it
remains when the conscious experience of life in this time-space has ended.
Our physical consciousness is Love's expression but not its limit. If any
conditions are placed on love, they obscure its truth, since love does not
exist in a conditional universe; it is unconditional. The grace of Love is
the unexplained, relentless presence in our lives that peels away the sadness
and despair that obscures our real nature.

November 3

Ministers, Mentors and Masters

At some point in life we must find our own
way to self. – *Ndidi,* Tea Leaves

Although our teachers and guides encourage us to pay attention to our lives with stories, parables and examples, we already embody the answers we seek. When we deny our own wisdom and experience, we forfeit the peace and happiness that is already available to us. When a teacher shares a story that resonates with us the effect is an awareness that is already inside us, but we give praise to the teachers who have clarified for us what was living within us.

Our inner wisdom is always here now, but we cover it in layers of false stories and self-limitations. Our ministers, mentors and masters are artful reflections of us, who show up in our awareness not to teach us who we are, but to show us what we already know about ourselves. Our guides are mirrors showing us a clear image of our essential nature.

When we listen and pay attention to what we feel in the moment of clarity, we will get a spiritual glimpse of who we really are. But if we depend upon those teachers and guides to hold the keys to our self-knowledge, we may be disappointed. We will discover that conceptual or historical information may attempt to point to the truth of our being, but truth can only be found within. When we resonate with what we are paying attention to in the words of our teachers, we are touching our divine spirit. In an instant, we can touch the messages from an eternity of wisdom; if we stay with that awareness in the moment, we learn the powerful lesson of our true reality.

November 4

Atonement

We are completely "at one" with the universal
presence. – *Ndidi,* Tea Leaves

At times, the etymology or history of a word sheds light on its intended use and meaning. Words are like living organisms that take on meanings that serve the times and conditions. The Christian meaning of atonement is the reconciliation with God through the sacrificial death of Jesus the Christ, but the word and meaning can have value for us in another context. Our divine teachers often provide lessons in the metaphor of their life experiences. Siddhartha Gautama used teachings to display his path to realizing the four noble truths of life. The Prophet Muhammad demonstrated the power of inspired words to bring people together in love and compassion. Lord Krishna demonstrates the wisdom of elders in tough situations during his counsel and comfort to Arjuna in the Bhagavad Gita. Each divine spirit has taught reconciliation, the expression of love and compassion that comes from unity, whether the union is with God, the true self, Allah or a supreme deity. Separation is demonstrated as a stressful reality with conflicts, suffering and destruction. We are encouraged to love one another, practice compassion and be devoted to divine love. The word "atonement" has a history that traces a transformation of meaning from unity to reconciliation. When we realize that we are one spirit, one love, we can be in a state of atonement. Our "at-one-ment" becomes a state of completion, a final return to the true self, after wandering aimlessly in the dense forest of separation from our divine origin. Joy brings us back to ourselves.

Dough Will Rise

I believe that every single event in life happens in an
opportunity to choose love over fear. – *Oprah Winfrey*, as quoted
in Oprah, in Her Words: Our American Princess (2008)

Many of us have been present when parents or grandparents have made
bread. The flour and salt are combined with other ingredients, including
yeast or baking powder or soda. Combining the acidic yeast or soda and
the flour mixture creates a chemical reaction that releases carbon dioxide.
The bubbling reaction causes the dough to rise. A baker often presses the
dough down to make it rise higher, because multiple rises create better
flavors. The yeast does not die until the heat during baking cooks the
gluten and the dough solidifies.

During the course of our lives, the mixture of life conditions can cause
different reactions, some volatile. We may descend into the chasm of fear
and linger there for longer than is healthy for us. Events in our lives can
leave us flattened from the shock and awe of them. We may be laid off
from a position we enjoy, or experience a severed relationship. We may
experience financial hardships or declining physical health. Like the dough
of the baker, we may feel pressed down, deflated or less vigorous, but our
spirits can always rise higher to create different and better experiences.

We recognize the truth that whatever goes up must come down, but also in
the depths, creativity will rise. In the deflation of our lives, our creativity
expands and with a resilient spirit, we rise to new possibilities. When we
are pressed and flattened, we reveal new creative energies that allow our
transformed self to emerge, and solidify our dreams into new realities.

November 6

Peace from Panic

Breathing in, I calm body and mind. Breathing out, I
smile. Dwelling in the present moment I know this is the
only moment. – *Thich Nhat Hanh*, Being Peace

A young woman had a difficult childhood with experiences of physical
abuse. When she finally distanced herself from her abusive father, she
thought she would have peace, but the dreams of her destruction came
crashing into her sleep whenever she had to interact with her father again.

Every experience of our lives is an opportunity. Past events that we bring
into our present moments have the power to snatch peace from our hearts.
The events may be devastatingly painful or simply uncomfortable, but
as past events, they have little news to reveal. Even when we enter new
relationships or try new skills, we may experience initial discomforts. Our
unsteadiness may interfere with the confidence we could show.

Sometimes the situation we are facing generates panic in us for no known
reason. If we try to use reason to explain panic attacks we are sometimes
at a loss, but we are familiar with the feelings of fear and helplessness
in panic. If we allow the panic to grow, we can become overwhelmed
by it; if we fight the feelings of panic, our feelings fight back to assert
themselves. But, if we make friends with our panic, explore how if affects
us, and the messages it brings to us, we can begin to put panic in its
place. If we pay attention to our breath, slowly moving to deeper breaths,
breathing in through the nose and out through the mouth, we begin to
relax and are able to observe our own process. We can scan the body for
places of tension, and breathe deeply as we concentrate on those points of

tension. As we begin to relax, we grow stronger in spirit and recognize the transformative power of peace.

We may believe that old patterns are difficult to change, but neuroscientists are convinced that our brains are changeable; they call it neuroplasticity. The new thinking suggests that our brain is able to reorganize itself throughout our lives, including after injury, disease or other environmental changes. From a psychological or spiritual perspective, our brains need clarity out of the maze of confusion and stress that we experience. We want peace with ourselves so that peace with others can be a possibility.

Being still is a start. Another way to acknowledge the sudden intrusion of panic into our consciousness is to be still in a state of meditation. In that stillness we can repeat to ourselves the word "peace" over and over again, with every out-breath, until the panic of the moment dissipates. The cooling breath of stillness makes thoughts and fears simply a part of the way things are. We can make peace with that. We can let go of the desire for the situation to be something other than what it is; and accept what is without longing for what is not. We can rest in the awareness of our core self and ultimate reality. We can know who we really are and realize that we can have peace from panic now and always.

November 7

Walking in Love

Leave only footprints of love on your path. – *Ndidi*, Tea Leaves

There is a difference between knowing a path and walking the path. Devotees of many religious belief systems know the writings and teachings of spiritual leaders, but sometimes forget in their living of life to merge what they believe with what they do. The path is always ours to walk, and sometimes we have to make a path where none exists in order to accommodate the spirit of the teachings. As long as the path is love expressed, the journey is probably in concert with the prescribed teachings. If the path excludes other sentient beings or pushes them aside as unfit to travel with us, we have stumbled upon a rock, a painful judgment. Although we may think the path is straight and narrow, such boundaries are sure to make it difficult for some to be included.

Every path is a series of curves and turns; life itself is a striking example of the circuitous nature of the path. If we intend to know the ultimate truth of our being, we must be willing to walk uncharted terrain, because there is no map for the territory. Each of us is trying to find our way; our beliefs are sometimes excellent outlines of a map, but we alone can fill in the roads. Ultimately, there is no destination, and the roads can be tricksters along our path. We are already where we want to be, when we walk in love.

November 8

Imagination

Reality is a collection of images that have caught
our attention. – *Ndidi,* Tea Leaves

About 60-65% of people think in images rather than words. Imagination,
our ability to transform thoughts into things is one of the mental activities
that helps us to create our sensory reality. According to the great scientist
Albert Einstein, imagination is more important than knowledge.
Imagination has the capacity to open new gates and expand boundaries
because it broaches them with impunity. Without a prescribed structure,
imagination invents and invokes new patterns and views that can resolve
problems and create new challenges. As thinking beings, we are in an
enviable position in the universe to think about ourselves and our lives. We
can use logic or rely on our intuition but our imagination brings different
realities to us.

During guided meditation, we may be invited to imagine ourselves in a
place of peace, another space, or another state of being. We relax and let
our minds take us there, but when we return from our trip into images, we
return with more than we had available before the journey. Imagination
creates more of what we can experience through the voicing of words alone.
Yet, the writing process or building project also creates from a place that is
inspired. Although the imagination can be prompted as in guided imagery,
it arises from an unknown place, but that place can be accessed again and
again. Whether we think in pictures most of the time or in words, our
imagination is a door to our inherent state of being. We can experience
joy in being our creative self.

November 9

Aspiration

Joy is in the breath. – *Ndidi*, Tea Leaves

An aspiration is either a strong ambition or the act of breathing in. In either case, we are allowing our life force to be directed toward fulfillment. Although most of us would agree that ambitions are useful in the sensory reality of careers and desires, fulfillment can be achieved in other ways.

We may believe that there is something that we must *do* in order to feel complete, but our sense of satisfaction is dependent upon who we are *being*. If we are being thankful for things as they are in the moment, we are breathing inward; we are settling comfortably into the present experience of peace. We are aspiring with love.

Intense ambition, on the other hand, leaves us impatient with the present and focused on an unrealized future. The pull of the uncertain future can be unsettling because it is an unknown experience, not yet realized. Ambition is a statement not only of a desire for more, but also a sense of not having enough right now.

Everything we need or want is already available to us, but we are often out of spiritual alignment with it. When we are grateful for what is our current reality, we make room for what can be. The only time is now, so all is present now, even if we're not fully aware of it. When we embrace the love and peace in the present, we are soaked in the loving spirit of All-That-Is. There is no-thing outside of that awareness.

The feelings of lack or incompleteness are assaults on our spiritual contentment. What we desire is already done at the moment we desire it. When we are uplifted in the thought of the manifestation of our desires without trying to control the details of the manifestation, we can breathe in peace. In the state of peacefulness, we exhale and aspire with love.

November 10

We are That

A human being is essentially a spirit–eye. Whatever you
really see, you are that. – *Rumi,* A Year with Rumi

Technology has become so familiar in our tools for living that many of us
hardly remember a time when a cell phone or computer was not available.
The information superhighway, otherwise known as the internet, has made
information accessible in an instant. We are comfortable knowing more
than a moment ago. Additional information may assist in completing
whatever we're doing, but more information does little to add to our being.

We are creating what we see; whether it's Wikipedia or other sources and
resources on the internet, we collectively create it. Then, in awe of our
creation, we marvel at the scope and details of our creation as if we are
simply receivers and not creators of the reservoirs of data and information.

We essentially "know" everything collectively, but we know little
individually; our independence is an illusion. Our collective energy sits
below our conscious awareness of life; with the eye of spirit, we see into
the totality of being. The experience can be overwhelming, unless we rest
in knowing that we control nothing as an individual; and the information
is a shallow representation of our ultimate awareness. What we actually
know exists far beyond our conceptual knowledge or understanding. We
are what we are creating; we are potential, expressing continuously in the
universe. Our creations connect and configure new understandings, but
we do not rest on what we have created. We are compelled to create more
and more each day, each hour, each moment.

When we live fully in the present moment, we flow with the steady, relentless evolution of the universe. And we begin to feel resistance when we cling to a moment that has passed, or a thought that we want to hold onto. As long as we are aware that creating is our purpose, we continue to see things as they are, as we are. We experience life as a moment-to-moment opportunity to appreciate what we are seeing, and to observe and respond to the thoughts that have become things. We will have reactions to what we have created at times, and that's an indication that we have begun to cling to a thought. But if we simply respond without judgment to the information and images we are seeing, we realize that what we see is temporary, so we let it pass away. What we can really "see" is the constancy of our true self. Who we really are does not pass away; it remains because it has never been created, with no beginning and no end, it is infinite.

November 11

Outside Is Inside

What is the body? That shadow of a shadow of your love, that somehow contains the entire universe. – *Rumi*, The Essential Rumi

Sometimes after vigorous exercise we look into the mirror and notice the inner glow radiating on our faces. The exercise could be a brisk walk, a morning run, yoga or tai chi. Whatever the form of exercise is, we can feel the upsurge in energy that floods our body; what we see on the outside is also inside, we can feel it. Just like the surge of life force that pervades our being after exercise, the pervasive stream of thoughts that flow through our consciousness can be felt throughout our body. Our thoughts can direct tension and stress that can lead to *dis-ease* and disorders of the body.

Blockages of our natural energy flow cause parts of our body to get stuck and stop working properly, like a break in electrical current causing a power outage. When we allow what we see as conditions in our reality to direct our thoughts we may become fearful of an impending loss of security, relationships or our life.

The outside world can influence the well-being of our inside world. Our responses to what we see are displayed in our walk, our speech and our nonverbal communication. What the mind controls will be displayed to our outside world so we become what we think.

When we decide to tame the mind, and to allow the free flow of energy throughout our bodies, we discover that our internal well-being is the source of all that we need to respond joyously to the challenges in life. We discover that confidence in the way things are is the requirement for a sense of liberation, and that our surrender to what is occurring as the way things are now, is our true source of well-being.

Selective Attention

If a tree looks the same every time you look at it, you're
not paying attention. – *Ndidi,* Tea Leaves

What we pay attention to is the result of habitual views and perspectives. We constantly miss aspects of our world that we are not accustomed to seeing. It is not so much that we have no interest in seeing things as they are, our lens is colored by our habitual thoughts that become beliefs.

For some of us, anything that does not fit our habitual way of doing something or seeing something can be rejected forcefully when the different experience is brought to our attention. The cognitive or visual dissonance can be a cause of our biases or bigotry; if it doesn't align with our habitual thinking it is deemed unsafe, unclean, or unworthy. We find a sense of safety in our habitual ways of seeing things, and often believe that any departure from the norm is a threat to our sense of safety and well-being. We may begin to feel frightened of fear itself, and become more and more entrenched in our limited view of our world as a mode of survival.

When we begin to realize that our broadened awareness, our expanded consciousness of what is, actually lessens our sense of vulnerability, we begin to loosen our grip on false ideas. When we feel safe we are open to new experiences, but when we felt vulnerable, we closed our minds and our hearts.

The more we experience the diversity in life, the more we know that we always have what we need to thrive. Our egos, ideas in the mind, continually threaten us with the possibility that we will be injured, humiliated, or even worse, killed. We believe the stories of our demise, and try to protect ourselves from harm. The problem for us is that the ego uses fear to protect us; and fear itself harms us in many ways. Fear causes us to miss so much of our life, since we spend time protecting ourselves from past hurts or anxieties. Moments pass quickly, so time unfulfilled is quickly lost.

Love is the antidote to fear, and it's a healthy alternative to the corrosive effects of living in fear of death or harm. While love offers an infinite experience of peace and calm, the frightening ego offers a life of dramatic, untrue stories of vulnerability, striving for significance, and persistent discomfort.

We could pay attention to the beauty of the moment, the unfolding of life's majesty, instead of the fantasy of control. When we choose to love each moment, fear falls away like an unnecessary veil.

Salt

There is nothing heavier than the weight of
unrealized creativity. – *Ndidi,* Tea Leaves

Few substances carry such significance to our survival as salt. Without air, water and salt we could not survive. Long ago, salt was the means of preserving food, and in many ways salt has survived as a metaphor for our worth – "the salt of the earth" or "worth her weight in salt." In the Christian tradition, a person who loses his "saltiness" is worthless, a powerful metaphor for commitment to beliefs and faith. Mohandas Gandhi launched a successful protest march against the British salt tax, because he correctly reasoned that everyone needed to have salt to replenish the bodily loss of salt in the heat. There is usually solidarity in collective loss.

We could see salt as another metaphor – the seed of creativity, "a pinch of salt" that if present can flavor the way we express ourselves in the world. The creative salt, essential to our being, is always there in our ultimate reality, ready to create our new perspectives, and an opening to joy. If we choose to hide our creative selves, we deny who we are and we might as well "trample that seed under our feet." Of course, the seed cannot be destroyed, but it can be transformed, continually. We are the salt that flavors our reality. We are the opportunity for joy to appear.

November 14

Loving-kindness

Through my love for you, I want to express my love for the whole cosmos, the whole of humanity, and all beings. – *Thich Nhat Hanh*, Teachings on Love

An automobile sitting still may have the capacity to move, but its energy must be ignited by the fuel in the engine. The engine does not cling to the fuel; that would be dangerous and explosive, but the fuel does flow through the auto so it can move toward some new place. Since the journey from one place to another is as important as the destination itself, having enough fuel is important. Our spiritual fuel is love; it has no destination but is present everywhere. It is the beginning, middle and end of our journey; and its presence is relentless and omnipotent.

Loving-kindness is the tireless act of love moving toward all beings. Using the flow of love and the knowing that all of us are made of the same star dust, the energy of our universe, loving-kindness moves inclusively and intentionally, without clinging or arrogance. Love is complete as it spreads joy and peace, yet it demands nothing in return – no applause or praise. Unlike the auto, it moves continuously, and is fueled by the inexhaustible energy of All-That-Is, asking for nothing but an opportunity to love again and again. Every act of loving-kindness is an opportunity to express the truth of our identity, and to appreciate the shared reality of all of us. Loving-kindness assumes that we are all one spirit creating and experiencing the challenges and triumphs of life. It is the balm for our bruises and the joy in relationships.

November 15

No Way Out

Embrace the joy in life that shows up unexpectedly; it is
what the moment demands. – *Ndidi,* Tea Leaves

In Jean Paul Sartre's famous play, *No Exit,* incompatible people are
trapped in an elevator with a door that will not open. After the failed
attempts of the people to open the elevator door, and when there is finally
a feeling of surrender to the situation, the door to the elevator suddenly
and mysteriously opens. The trapped people, although still not compatible,
fear the unknown so much that they are frightened of walking through
the open door.

We may sometimes feel as if there is no way out of a life challenge or
condition we are observing. If we identify strongly with the challenging
conditions, we will become so comfortable with the challenges that we will
become reluctant to embrace new possibilities. If we are not careful, we
will believe that the temporary conditions are permanent or the problems
are insurmountable. We may begin to describe ourselves in terms of
the conditions: I am unsuccessful; I am sick; I am totally alone; I am
unworthy. Soon the perspective of "no way out" becomes "dropping out."
Our resignation is then a new challenge that we have placed on ourselves.

We could avoid the descent into despair if we see our conditions as
impermanent aspects of life, and observe the emergence and dissipation
of challenges, without identifying with them. We could resist the tendency
to believe what is happening now will persist, and know that nothing will
persist unless we cling to it in our minds.

If the door we desire does not open immediately, perhaps it's not our door. Soon a door inevitably will open and we will know that in order to step into a new reality, we must be confident that we will have the love and peace necessary to embrace new experiences. Before the next door opens, we could practice resting in a space of peace now, so that we can become accustomed to the joy that lies ahead.

November 16

Priceless

Love—like kindness, compassion, and peace—is not a thing that money can buy, because it is never in short supply. – *Ndidi,* Tea Leaves

A young child enjoyed visiting her grandmother because of her grandmother's beautiful flower garden. Each day that she visited, the young girl plucked many flowers and presented them to her grandmother lovingly in the afternoon. Every morning she noticed that the flowers had wilted but her grandmother was always smiling broadly. She wondered why her grandmother was so happy.

If we believe that love is a commodity, we believe that it is in limited supply. There are no reports of success in measuring love, because it is immeasurable, infinite. Attempts have been made to place conditions on the expression of love. We say we are loved if certain behaviors are present, and unloved in other instances, but love at the core of our being is unconditional. We often label a show of affection as love, but love is not affection based in desire or a transactional relationship. Love is not a feeling or a reaction; feelings are temporary and changeable. Love does not diminish if it is shared from our core, because it is not a thing with form and substance. The love we seek cannot be explained or weighed in contrast to other aspects of our existence. If we look for love we will not find it, because it is not a thing to be found. Love is inexplicable, defying description.

We become frustrated in finding love because we are looking for clues that point to it, and yet it lives everywhere within and around us. We call love many false names: devotion, sexual attraction, obedience, being chosen or protected. Each false label leaves us disappointed and incomplete.

We can know love only in the effects of its presence. We find peace and we know love is present. We feel inconceivable joy and we know love is the reason. We sense the love in others and recognize it as a reflection of an awareness deep within. Our search for love is a search for our true self; we are what we are looking for.

The great love that we are is boundless, infinite, and inexplicable. If we search for love, we miss it, because we expect it to be somewhere other than within our soul.

November 17

The Presence

I wanted to be loved, and then discovered my existence
<u>as</u> love was my only purpose. – *Ndidi,* Tea Leaves

Throughout our lives we have a sense of personhood; we are certain that our breath and body make us real. But just as we are certain of our existence, as we develop and mature, we realize that something else is present. We give it a name with the help of religious leaders or sacred texts. We have a sense that even when we are physically alone, we aren't really alone. We may feel anxiety or frustration but we know that the experiences arise out of something. We call it God, Jesus, Allah, Krishna, Ultimate Reality, Infinite Intelligence and many other names. We have faith that it will stay with us as long as we are conscious and breathing. We long to know it intimately and fully, but sometimes feel distant or disconnected from it. We become so invested in the concept of our individual self that we may forget our existence within the Presence. We adopt rules, laws, customs and rituals to keep the Presence in mind and soul, but sometimes we fail to live up to the standards that have been set for us. We blame ourselves for our failures and weaknesses and say that we are sinners or miscreants. In spite of all the ways we beat ourselves and others up about behaviors and transgressions, we cannot shake the Presence that remains. Then, one day we stop and rest in stillness and know. We are overjoyed with the love that we feel, the liberation from all our doubts. We remember that this life is an expression of the divine presence and that it is up to us to make the best of it, to be the best expression of love that we can be.

November 18

Peak Experiences

You can find something truly important in an ordinary
minute. – *Mitch Albom*, For One More Day

"Be all you can be" is a compelling invitation from the United States
military recruitment program; the promise is fulfillment of potential – a
peak experience of completion and purpose. But we need not join the
military to have the promise of expressing our potential. In a dramatic
world, we may expect a peak experience to be accompanied by intense
emotion that stands out from the ordinary, but the peaks exist in the
ordinary.

Every moment can be a peak experience; every breath can express our
potential to be a loving spirit. When we look for the joy that exists in every
experience of our lives, we can have a continual peak experience. When
we are expressing our compassion or appreciation, we can have a peak
experience. When we hold a baby, rub the top of a pet's head, gaze at the
stars, allow the moonlight to fall on our cheeks, or read a favorite poem to
a precious senior lying in a hospital bed, we experience the peak experiences
of life. The conditions do not create the experience, our responses to
the gifts in our experience are peaks for us. In a constant state of peak
experiences, we rest in a state of ultimate reality; we realize that the only
valleys are ones we have created. We can find joy in the ordinariness of life.

Undefeated

When it comes to Love, failure is an unrecognizable
option. – *Ndidi,* Tea Leaves

Many human interest stories report the indomitable spirit of people
who have overcome obstacles to not only survive but thrive. We may
be encouraged by their determination or resilience, and marvel at their
strength of character and refusal to be defeated by an injury or challenge
to their life or livelihood. We praise them for having goals and sticking
to them, and applaud their courage, their heart and strength. The stories
of triumph are understandably inspiring, because defeat is regarded as a
failure, a flaw. But failure is never part of the plan; it is simply a detour
along the road of life.

Victory is not an individual accomplishment; it is available to everyone,
and is always a collective effort. Whether we admit it or not, we are
interdependent beings; nothing we do is completed without a supporting
cast. When we are undeterred by conditions, and believe in our inherent
connectedness, we all thrive.

If we believe that an individual has had success, or has defeated a challenging
condition, we make our selves vulnerable to comparison; but we all survive
when any one of us survives. We are in relationship with all others in
this life, even those who are different from us in many ways. When we
are excited about the accomplishments of others, and participate in their
celebrations, we also experience the joy of the moment. If we cannot be
joyful with others we cannot feel the joy within ourselves.

Often we are challenged in life and struggle to make a choice that will not end in defeat; but we do not fail, we receive valuable feedback from our choices. We may believe that we alone must overcome the challenges.

If we believe that an "individual" achieves anything alone, we have begun to enter a deluded state. The paralyzed woman who walks had the help of many in physical therapy and pharmacology; and the once-impoverished millionaire had a number of supporters and sympathetic ears for her invention. Persistence, focus and faith were important for the sense of victory, but the alignment and awareness of All-That-Is makes the expression of completeness and healing a reality. Love is the source of our being; and we are its continuous expression of victory.

November 20

Unconscious

Your joy is your sorrow unmasked. – *Kahlil Gibran*, The Prophet

Creativity is often an unconscious process. In a trance called "flow" we release spiritual energy in novel ways to advance the evolution of the universe. We are here to be unconsciously competent creators of beauty and love. We are here to express our gifts, the momentary ways in which we splash as a wave upon the shores of life. Artists may not have a goal in mind; the creation emerges of its own accord, not at the artist's direction. Musicians caress the notes and the silence between them; and the painter obeys the internal rhythm that spreads itself on the canvas. A furniture maker loses herself in the craft, and the chef pours her imaginative combinations of flavors onto a plate. Poetry writes itself, stirred by a memory or a wish; and music emerges not from a combination of sounds but from a sense of rhythm and drama deep within the soul. A disciplined dancer practices for long hours then loses himself in the flow of the dance, or the beat of his own heart. A writer enters a cave of images, feelings and ideas and emerges with a combination of words never before expressed.

"Magic" heats us like molten lava, deep within. The stirring creation seems haunting until it is released from the barriers of doubt and fears of disapproval. We create even when we are unaware of our offerings; we are natural creators often hiding our crafts in the back rooms of our lives. When we open to our passion, we authentically appear, and the sorrow is transformed into a new expression of our creative souls.

November 21

Winds of Change

Storms move on and so should we. – *Ndidi,* Tea Leaves

During the harsh winters on the tundra, communities of penguins huddle to keep warm, and to protect their young or newborns. They take turns moving to the outer ring of the huddled mass so that the brutality of the cold is shared. Although there are casualties, the majority of the community survives the winter.

We sometimes have our own storms to weather, often with few members of the community to take turns facing the brunt of the winds and cold. In the darkest of times, a warm breeze will blow through our challenges, giving us encouragement that the temporary storm will eventually pass. We sometimes say that we brought on the storm ourselves; the more we focus our attention on the self-recriminations and regrets, the longer the storm stays with us. Like the penguins, we've seen the storm before, and we've weathered it, but we may forget how we managed the challenge previously.

If we allow what we see as challenges to define our lives, we will eventually grow weary, drained from investing so much energy in what we see. What is happening before our eyes is a remnant of something now in the past. Our anxiety about what we see is a belief that it will linger too long and we won't be strong enough to hold on. The illogic of those fears is that what we see now will disappear in the next moment. Subtle changes are occurring continuously.

We are not experiencing in this moment what we experienced a moment ago. Impermanence is a loving friend, so we can rest in knowing that the pain will not last. The only consistent and stable reality for us and with us is the love of All-That-Is. That presence is the strength of the storm, the warm breeze that calms us and the healing love that rests within us. We can remember that truth, and release our winter of suffering.

November 22

Inherited Memories

Our total experience of reality is one moment
in time. – *Ndidi,* Tea Leaves

A five-year old girl walks into the bathroom one morning, looks into the mirror and says to the image she sees, "Good morning world!" Her mother gasps with surprise as she passes by the open bathroom door, overhearing the child's exclamation. The mother was also five years old when she first uttered the same joyful announcement.

If we pay close attention to those we meet and love, we will recognize ourselves in them. We will hear and see evidence of our inherited memories. Carl Jung was a psychoanalyst who advanced the idea of inherited memories. According to Jung, we inherit certain memories, feelings and ideas as part of a collective unconscious. Although some scientists may question the plausibility of inheriting intangibles like feelings and information, our direct experience keeps the dialogue open. Some curious occurrences may convince us that we have inherited ideas or feelings, but we can rest assured that we are expressions of All-That-Is and as such nothing is impossible.

We are heirs to love that never ends and knows no boundaries. One major challenge in this life is to remember that our connection is real. From time to time we get post-it notes from the universe encouraging us to remember that our inheritance is here now. We don't have to earn it or wait until someone makes a transition; our inheritance is assured. We don't have to petition for our portion or hope that we are remembered in the universal will. Our treasures are here right now.

November 23

Passion as Sorrow

What hurts us is what heals us. – *Paul Coelho*, Aleph (2011)

The famous Michelangelo marble sculpture called *La Pietà,* is a stunningly beautiful depiction of passion and sorrow; the sorrowful mother of Jesus of Nazareth holds his dead body in her loving arms. The entire depiction reeks of the intense feelings generated when a person suffers, but also how we can suffer with another in that intensity. When compelling, strong feelings emerge within us, that energy can flow in uncontrolled directions. We can feel a whole spectrum of emotions: fear, anger, sadness or love. The power of the passion is stronger than our thoughts or motivations; we are overtaken by the exhilaration we feel and the sense of wonder as newness unfolds.

Many throughout history have tried to control passions and its creative energy; the frightening effects of uncontrolled passion have led leaders and their followers to restrict, reject and destroy misunderstood expressions of creativity. When we face our passions, see them as a part of who we are. We allow passions to express as love and realize that our passions *are* love. Love lies at the center of our existence expressed, desired or unexpressed. Our fears are a desire for love and anger and a response to not feeling loved. When we are sad, we turn away from the possibility of affection, and embrace an internal anger. From a place of restricted emotions, buried underneath shame or regret, we smother our creative energy. But it cannot be silenced.

Bursts of creative energy can be mistaken for aggression, depression or uncontrolled ecstasy, but the source of the energy is love. Our creations arise from a clear soul basking in universal love; and the thrust of creativity is the conscious awareness of joy. When we create with the loving spirit that we are, we allow our creative energy to be a testament of soulful release. We show up in the world.

November 24

Projections

Keep knocking and the joy inside will eventually open a window
and look to see who's there. – *Rumi*, A Year with Rumi

We walk out of movie theaters and other entertainment venues buoyed by the performances we have just enjoyed. It's easy for us to see the experiences as scenarios that have nothing to do with our lives as we are living them, but they do. Our buoyancy is recognition. We embrace the projections and metaphors of our lives, and deny that we live with the dreams, frustrations, challenges or triumphs. The plays we observe are rehearsals, but we know that our life is a live performance. Because the messages sometimes feel uncomfortably familiar, we laugh or cry in response to dramatic displays of our life.

Although movie theaters display entertaining dramas, comedies and horror films on giant screens to the delight of audiences, the images come from a projector usually positioned at the rear of the theater. What we experience starts with us as we co-create our world, like the projector at the rear of the theater beaming onto the giant screen. We are the experiencers and the ones who project our experiences.

When we disown what we have co-created, we tend to believe that something or someone is creating our life drama, and that we are simply members of the audience. We are human projectors, casting our light on the world we know; we are both audience and cast.

Clinging to the idea that we are defenseless victims in a world of hurt and danger absolves us of any responsibility for conditions in our lives. There are parts of our humanness that we regard as favorable so we guard those

412

attributes as wholly our own. We have some past mistakes that haunt us, so we happily part with the pain and rejection we feel, and give those failures to others.

The false self is composed of the behaviors and masks that we deny in ourselves. These qualities and failings as so different from how we see ourselves that we unknowingly cast them onto others as judgments. When we disown ourselves, we allow our egos to control us, and concede control to a false identity.

The true self is not a performance or a regret, but pure joy, relishing the adventure of life as it is. When we own all the aspects of ourselves that we know and discover, we can shed the false self, propped up by our ego. Shedding the false self does not leave us vulnerable, as the ego wants us to believe. Without the false self, we discover who we really are, and we see the performance of our life play as a passing story of joy.

November 25

Uncountable Blessings

Most of what we call valuable is uncountable. – *Ndidi,* Tea Leaves

The abundant blessings of the universe are like the leaves of a 30-year old oak tree. Although we may think they are countable as individual leaves, the task is daunting. If we were to begin the process of counting the leaves, we could become frustrated since the nature of the abundance is continuously changing, with new growth and withered leaves falling to the ground.

On a clear night, we may enjoy the stars, but if we start to count them, we become overwhelmed. We have organized some stars into constellations, but the stars we see are only visible because their light has finally found us. The number of stars is essentially uncountable.

We could reasonably attempt to count most of the things we see, and in some cases, those objects would be countable. But how do we count faith, trust or love. Are these experiences real if we cannot count them? Some phenomena in our world are real only because we believe them to be so. So, what prompts us to measure the love in our life? We say there's not enough love in the world, or he loves me so much, or so little. We may attempt to count the truth of love by keeping score, leading to resentment, shame or a sense of abandonment. Love is uncountable.

We may attempt to measure the success of one person or another. External markers of success are part of the masks of the false self. True success is an internal sense of loving spirit, realized through service to others. We may attempt to measure success by the amount of money a person has accumulated, or the degree of celebrity a person can show. If we attempt to use external measures, we will become frustrated, because loving spirit is known by its effect on others. When we love one another, each one of us benefits; the effects are uncountable.

Whether we are witnessing the uncountable diversity of the natural world or the many effects of kindness, our abundant life is like a tree with so many branches, leaves and blooms that we cannot begin to know them all. When we realize that abundance is uncountable because it is constantly expanding and changing, we also realize that scarcity is a falsehood.

We can be confident that there will always be more than we can imagine, more than we can count. The universe is a cornucopia of potential, emerging in our reality from seeds of love and joy. When we are appreciative of what we experience now, in the present moment, we are able to be present for the inexhaustible abundance that is already ours.

November 26

Shadowboxing

A shadow is present because of the light. – *Ndidi,* Tea Leaves

Odysseus survived mythical monsters as he floated through treacherous waters during his exile. His hero's journey is a metaphor for the ability to not only survive but to thrive through troubling waters of life. There are choices that must be made, but each choice simply leads to another choice. As long as we live, we will choose. If we choose to regret our choices, we have missed the point.

Prometheus endured his suffering, chained to a rock, as punishment for enlightening humanity with the gift of fire. We don't always appreciate those who open our eyes to the truth of our being. Often our first thought is to punish the messenger, until later when we recognize the value of the messenger's truth-telling. We are then eternally grateful for being brought out of the shadows and into the light.

Job moved from patience to frustration to resentment and then triumph as he endured the suffering of physical, emotional and economic disasters. Like Job, we know how to suffer. We cling to what we think is the real story of our lives, lived in the past or the future. If we look closely, we will experience life as shadowy, impermanent events and conditions that always come and go. The warmth of truth is what we seek.

Stories ancient and modern provide vivid pictures to stoke our fears. We believe the shadowy stories of our vulnerability as humans. Our thoughts are reinforced by news of disasters and hateful acts against one another. When we face our true self and discover the power of love, we come out of the shadows and into the light-- strong, humble and compassionate.

When we face our fears with the fortitude of love, like Job we survive the onslaught of challenges in our life, and discover that we are stronger and more alive than we at first thought. If we let go of preparing for the worst, we stop shadowboxing with our imagination. We suffer because we depend on our beliefs alone to sustain us through troubles. When we open our hearts to Love, we allow our opened hearts to release us from our self-imposed burdens, and realize that our thoughts have convinced us that something is lacking – peace, safety, connection. We must emerge from the shadows into loving light; love shatters our insecurities and lights the way to truth.

November 27

Universal Harmony

Complex music of the universe is always
harmonious. – *Ndidi,* Tea Leaves

If we allow ourselves to be drawn into the news of the day, we may begin to see
the world as a disharmonious place where conflicts are the norm, and peace is
an illusion. It is true that appearances give us the impression that we will never
agree, and that harmony is elusive. Our individualized view of the world may
be influenced by local or world news but the truth is subtle and synchronous;
everything works together in a way that is order in chaos – *chaordic.* We have
evidence of the chaordic nature of the universe in phenomena like Fibonacci
numbers or fractals, but also in the evolution of our lives. We may be faced
with a challenge that seems insurmountable, but after some unnecessary
worry, doubt and frustration, we overcome the challenge. Often in hindsight
we realize that we had no need to worry, but when we had no idea what to do
or that we had no control, the challenge was threatening. There is harmony in
the universe that has the quality of creating order from chaos and something
from what seems like nothing. With a series of complex causes and effects, in
a web of possibility, the universe creates with loving energy.

In a state of meditation, we know deeply that all is well, and that a pattern
of stability always lies beneath the constant movement toward something
new. In the stillness where our breath is the point of concentration, the
constant motion of our lives becomes less prominent in our awareness.
During meditation, we surrender to the true self, stillness itself, unbounded
love. Deep abiding peace pervades our consciousness, and we allow
our spirit to just be. In the state of present awareness, we experience
participation with the unfolding universe, and deepen our faith in its
harmonious progression from the present moment to the next.

November 28

Sacrifice

Don't grieve. Anything you lose comes round in
another form. – *Rumi,* A Year with Rumi

We often understand sacrifice as giving up something cherished that we
possess. We say that soldiers who are killed made the ultimate sacrifice, or
that parents make sacrifices for their children. We talk about sacrificing
beliefs or desires in the interest of the greater good, and remember our
spiritual leaders who were martyred as they sacrificed their lives for their
beliefs.

A sacrifice is a sacred act, unassailable because it is an act of love. When we
sacrifice out of love, we are liberated from pride and desire for approval. But
when we seek acknowledgement for our sacrifices, we expose our selfishness
or greed. Mother Teresa sacrificed her comfort working tirelessly for the
poor in India; and Nelson Mandela sacrificed his freedom for 27 years,
so that others could be free. When people we revere give up so much, our
daily sacrifices seem to pale in comparison. But sacrifice is more than
heroic events.

Ultimately, sacrifice is the process of agreement to lose in order to gain;
we lose the ego's sense of the world and gain a strong sense of the true self.
We notice that loss is both dreaded and expected, and that growth and
change happen quietly regardless of our efforts to maintain the familiar
status quo. The two experiences of life - loss and gain - happen regardless
of our plans or attempts to control circumstances.

The interplay of loss and gain is central to the transformation that
continues life. Trees sacrifice leaves in order to make room for new growth.

A caterpillar loses the safety of the cocoon in order to become a butterfly. Some of us are willing to explore uncharted paths in life in order to open new opportunities for others. A writer loses herself in the writing to allow the emergence of new concepts or stories. We say that when one door closes another opens, but it is the closed door that makes the opening possible.

When conditions in life seem like a dark tunnel of despair, and all who seemed supportive fall away in fear, we know that our loosened grip on those conditions is a necessary sacrifice. Whatever is lost is reborn, renewed in another form. The necessary sacrifice is the false self, since it is a mere caricature of who we really are, and facing it allows us to come home to our true self.

Love waits outside the fearful confines of the desperate tunnel of delusion, and leads us to new beginnings. When we sacrifice the fears that plague us, we emerge from the tunnel into the glorious light of love. And with love, nothing is lost forever.

November 29

Following the Love

If we take a good, long look at our lives, we can notice
one thing: in spite of many challenges the universe
continues. – *Ndidi,* Finding Joy–Finding Yourself

When we are young, we are encouraged to follow the rules or suggestions of our parents or the significant adults in our lives. We rely on their experience as reliable information about what is important to pay attention to. If we are looking for answers that will keep us safe and secure, we are eager to rely on someone outside of ourselves whom we trust.

As we grow older, we decide that there are decisions about our welfare that are within our own capacity, so we make independent choices. We go through a series of challenges and unsuccessful ventures and once again question our individual efficacy. We seek answers to difficult, inexplicable questions, and become frustrated with insufficient answers; so we decide to follow someone's guidance in order to be assured that we are on the right path. We have been conditioned to see the path as something outside of ourselves.

We question our purpose and the meaning of life; or question the differences between the life we live and how others live, for better or worse. We wonder about fairness and equality or equity in our lives, and blame others for not correcting the conditions that fuel inequities. We fall deeply into judgments of others without noticing the mirror continually positioned in front of us.

As we grow wiser, we know that we have always had a guiding light within us; we may realize that with that light, we have been on the path to joy all along. When we overthink the path we separate ourselves from the joy of it. The source of our lives is within, and the evidence of our inward presence is lived outwardly. Love is our guide, so when we allow love to lead us, we are never misguided on our way.

November 30

Bat Wisdom

The world needs you to be who you are. – *Ndidi,* Tea Leaves

Bats are the only mammals capable of sustained flight because of their thin webbed forelimbs. They travel in darkness and shield themselves from the light of the day in roosts, typically hollows, crevices, foliage and caves. Their foraging for food, typically insects is facilitated by a process called echolocation. Bats emit sounds that return an echo that aids in detecting, localizing, and classifying prey. Present all over the world, bats are flower pollinators and seed dispersers; they are critical to agriculture and life on earth.

The bat uses her skills to stay alive and in doing so influences the lives of us all throughout the world. The bat is equipped with all he needs to be a bat; he does not think about being a bat, or dwell on memories of unsuccessful foraging events. He rarely flies in the rain because it interferes with his echolocation. He knows that there are times to move out of the cave and times to stay where he is. She is not afraid of the darkness, but instead makes use of her gifts.

When we realize who we are, we can fly through our challenges with blissful appreciation of life. We don't ignore conditions or pretend they don't exist, we simply make adjustments in our plans, or rest in the awareness that conditions are not permanent but temporary.

We can appreciate our differences as essential to life's expression and continuation. We understand that our worthiness is not dependent upon what others think. We know that our existence is sufficient testimony to our value. When we are less concerned with how we look and more focused on who we are being in the moment, we move freely with life. We are not afraid of darkness because we know that living in the spotlight is not always a comfortable place to be.

When we know who we are, we know that we are complete and perfect beings who are being what life needs us to be. We have bat wisdom.

December 1

Gratitude Now

Joy is the simplest form of gratitude. – *Karl Barth*, as quoted in Finding the Magnificent in the Mundane

As the plane approached the runway, she looked out of the small window, knowing that within an hour she would be home. The business trip had been long and difficult with challenges she had not fully expected. She was eager to sleep in her own bed instead of the uncomfortable hotel bed she had known for three days. She had gotten off track with her new eating plan, so returning to healthy eating would be a welcome change. She was going home.

Being at home is so much more than being in a personal space. Our space is filled with our presence, and the nurturing power of familiarity. But home is also a state of mind; it is knowing what to expect, and where everything is in our space. We want home to be the same as when we left it. We want it to be unchanging. We want to know one place that we can depend on to be ours and feel secure within the boundaries of that space. We want to feel sheltered from harm.

It is not the place, space or familiarity that comforts us; who we are at our core, creates the warm energy of home. Who we are is pervasive and constant; our true self is complete freedom, like the freedom we feel in familiar surroundings. When we go home we go into our true self. We experience the joy of appreciation.

December 2

Companions

The God who dwells in our inner sanctuary is the same
as the one who dwells in the inner sanctuary of each
human being. – *Henri Nouwen*, Here and Now

An angry pillar of salt who considered himself superior to others went for
a walk and noticed a calm lake just beyond a clearing in the woods. The
closer the pillar came to the lake the more it experienced a sense of peace.
The mesmerizing reflection of the trees on the placid lake produced a
strong and unfamiliar attraction for the pillar of salt. He couldn't imagine
what would produce such a peaceful feeling, so he jumped in to find
out. As he dissolved into the peaceful lake he was awakened to his true
connection to life.

We are sometimes resistant to the idea that we are one spirit, companions
in the process of change; how we appear in life is a playful expression of
All-That-Is. We adapt to change but the natural world flows freely with
the self-organizing interplay of conditions in life.

Fire and water are companions, not enemies; they express what is true for
them. Water extinguishes fire leaving it smoldering and quiet, but when
the fire is extremely hot, the water becomes steam and dissipates into
droplets. We could say that their relationship is transformational.

The soil settles on the face of the earth but is constantly perforated by the
eager seeds bursting forth from its bed. Their relationship is supportive to
growth and creativity. We could say their interdependency is critical to life.

The volcanic mountain stands majestically but sometimes cannot control the molten lava boiling inside; the lava produces richer soil and lush landscapes. The relationship between the mountains and the lava is volcanic. We could say their willingness to allow destruction is the basis for a richer life.

The trees spread their power and claim their presence in the forest but a bolt of lightning severs a limb or reduces them to charred fertilizer for the newest trees. We could say the relationship between the trees and the lightening is volatile but the trees have transformed to a new form of energy.

We are not immune to change; we are companions in the process. When we realize the creative power in change we joyfully enter the infinite flow and reveal our own passionate relationship with life.

December 3

Self-Love

You yourself as much as anyone else deserve
your love and affection. – *The Buddha*

As he walked out of the door, never to be seen again, he said, "I really love you, but I'm not in love with you." Through tears and the pain of an opened heart that was closing with hurt, she struggled to comprehend his words.

We search throughout our lives to understand the experience of love, or to capture the essence of it in another person. We want to have it, to be certain that it will remain with us, but it continues to be elusive. We attempt to define love, so we can know when we've found it, but our definitions are fruitless. We struggle to recognize it when we see it, so we search for clues, and even though we grasp for it in desperation, it does not want to be possessed.

In our frustration, we try to remember when love has appeared in our lives, or when we have expressed it. We may have felt affection for our parents as children, or significant adults as we grew to maturity, but we may have been disappointed in a return of loving-kindness, if those adults did not know their true self. Love is patient and kind but does not look for itself.

We may see love in our children or family, but we soon realize that we don't have sole ownership of that love. But we find joy in the relationships, the happiness that lies between us. We may seek love from one, special adult relationship, but we soon realize that we may sing in harmony, but we still have our own tunes. Love is not an exclusive essence; it is universal.

We continue to seek love outside ourselves from other people, but at the suggestion of teachers and counselors, we try to love ourselves. We may think that loving self comes from being satisfied with how we look, or from what we are able to accomplish, but we will soon become disappointed again. Love has no conditions.

Loving our true self is awareness that we are love expressing itself in the world. It has been with us during all our seeking and not finding. In the stillness of the present moment, we stop seeking love outside ourselves; we remember that we are love and that it has always been closer to us than we could ever imagine.

December 4

Dreams

Stop acting so small. You are the universe in ecstatic
motion. – *Rumi*, The Essential Rumi

Langston Hughes warned us about the consequences of a "dream deferred."
All dreams are deferred in our consciousness, waiting like thin veils in the
future. Nothing is clearer than the present moment, where the experience
of life encompasses all that is important to us. If we become frustrated
because our dreams are not immediately realized, we will open ourselves
to anger and resentment. But sometimes we feel as if our dreams have
shriveled up and died, before we have a chance to enjoy the happiness
we hope they will bring. We are never satisfied with the status quo, the
existing state of appearances. But what appears to us is only temporary.

A dream that is realized will soon remind us that we don't have everything
we want; we will then think of something new to want, assuming that it
will bring us happiness. The sense of happiness is experienced when we face
conditions as they are; knowing that events are constantly changing. When
we *don't* get what we want, we are exposing ourselves to new possibilities.
No realized dream is final; a dream is a stop along the road to eternity.

The present moment is not good or bad, but simply the only time that
is real; it is fleeting, but so are all the things we don't want. It seems
contradictory, but when we make friends with reality, our vibrations
increase in intensity and we participate in the creation of what we want.

Longing for unrealized desires can turn ugly. The longing gives attention
to what we think is lacking, so when there is no immediate gratification,
we lose patience with the present and doubt the future. But when we rest

430

in the present moment, we realize that every moment gives us what we need to be happy. Our gratitude for what is focuses our attention on what we have now that is life-affirming. Feeling thankful in the present creates space for what is already waiting for us; all that we desire is given without question, but often the gift comes packaged in a way we least expect. When we trust the true nature of our being, we realize that we lack nothing at all.

December 5

Awakened Heart

Wisdom comes from those who learn nothing, unlearn everything. – *Anthony de Mellow*, One Minute Wisdom

With few exceptions, virtually all of the spiritual leaders we turn to for guidance have embarked on a journey based on the conditions that emerged in their time. They responded with an open heart, caring less about their own welfare and more about the suffering of others. Their compassion was in teaching us to look deeply into our life and give up superficial differences that ignore our collective divinity. They encouraged us to lift the veils of confusion that blurred our view of meaning in life. They used artful communication, verbal and nonverbal, to send fear running from our consciousness; they showed us light where we could see only darkness.

We learned after some time with their presence touching our soul that we could remove the filters of anger, resentment, pride, hatred, and delusion. With their loving hand over our hearts, we chose compassion, loving-kindness and joy as paths out of our destructive illusion of control. With their example, their sacrifices and clear guidance, we can push through the pain, let go of what we think we want, and let drop from our tired shoulders the heavy cloak of suffering. We can discover that without doing anything, just being love in our relationships with others, we can discover the truth in life.

December 6

Last Words

I would hurl words into this darkness and wait for an echo, and
if an echo sounded, no matter how faintly, I would send other
words to tell, to march, to fight, to create a sense of the hunger
for life that gnaws in us all. – *Richard Wright,* Black Boy

Parents may wait impatiently for a baby's first words; when the tiny
utterance is heard, they smile with joy. As the child grows, parents are
amused, proud, and sometimes shocked by what comes out of a child's
mouth; words can be powerful agents.

As we grow older, our words are noticed for different reasons. Our words
can offend, perplex or encourage; we are frequently evaluated based on our
words. In the minds of others, our words carry an image of who we are.

But when our days are coming to a close, our last words are rarely
remembered; the curiosity about last words is reserved for the famous or
infamous. But our words can guide, inspire, comfort and enlighten; words
are creative energy.

The Buddha is reported to have counseled his bhikkhus, monks, to
remember that life is ever changing and disappointing, and that they must
be vigilant in gaining their own salvation. One report is that the Prophet
Mohammad in anticipation of being in Paradise with Allah, said as his last
words, "O Allah with highest companions." A dying Moses, the deliverer
of Jewish people, inspired the Israelites to continue their journey without
him as his last words. Jesus of Nazareth delivered guidance in his final
hour, uttering his seven last words or phrases. The last words of the Christ
were like a journey from a human experience to awareness of divinity -- a

demonstration of the transformative nature of faith. The divine presence of these leaders touches us with revelations about the spirit of words.

We never know what will be our last words to others; every utterance could be our last. What we have created in our lives, how we have lived our purpose, how we express joy, will be our true last words, our legacy. What we reveal to the world through the creative energy of our lives will always be the last word, the last love, the eternal joy.

December 7

Sexuality

We seek in another an ecstatic reflection of our love. – *Ndidi,* Tea Leaves

Throughout history, sex has been a trigger for emotions and opinions leading to laws and restrictions. Our fears have convinced us to prohibit, restrict and destroy individuals or groups, because of their sexual behaviors.

Opinions about sexual morality ignite base fears that divide communities, families and religious people around the world. Sexual repression and oppression exist throughout the world as a form of control and separation; cultures, communities and countries establish societal or legal sanctions that limit sexual expression.

Individual sexual expression is complex; it defies labels. We have tried to segment it for eons, but often individual expression collides with established norms or identifiers. We live in our labels and identify ourselves according to whatever feels right for us, and most of us hope that we will be accepted for how we express as human beings in this world. But cultures and communities demand conformity, and tend to punish those who do not conform to arbitrary standards. An inherent spirit does not have labels; those symbolic identities are for the outside world we call life. What we are seeking in sexual expression is a reflection of the love we are - love reflects love.

We may think that sex is love or approval, or a promise to end a sense of loneliness; sex is passionate expression, but love is spiritual presence expressing itself without limits.

One aspect of sex is the emergence of creative energy. We may think sex is only for procreation, or that sex should not be an expression of love, but all of life is an opportunity to express love. We may think the pleasures of sex are reserved for the young, and that as we age, sex is unreasonable and unnecessary; but we cannot set aside our authentic loving self. When we came into this time and space, we intended to express life fully. Joy is found in all expressions of our humanness, including sex.

A long history of guilt and shame about sex cannot change who we are or how we express ourselves in life as human beings. Sex is a reminder that we are not separate spirits, but one spirit aware of the transformative energy of sexual union. We are already connected in spiritual love but able to join physically in the ecstatic experience. In sexual union, we are looking for ourselves in another, but we have never been lost to one another.

December 8

Losing the Self

Sit like mountain. Flow like water. Shine like sun. – *Zen saying*

When a Zen master sits zazen for many hours, he may lose consciousness of time, space and his own body. Becoming one with spirit, he is aware of the formlessness of ultimate reality. In the stillness, the master basks in the light, and releases suffering.

The true self is formless, so the lack of boundaries makes anything possible. When we say that the universe creates out of nothing, we know that there is "no thing" that creates, and yet that lack of constraints from form, makes anything possible. Divine energy makes everything new because of its lack of form and restrictions. As the potential of the universe, our loss of self is necessary to gain the full abundance of life.

When we express our creativity, we have a similar experience. We simultaneously lose the self and find our true creative self. When we lose the self, there is a spiritual connection between the mind and the spirit; and the body creates without the sense of being principally involved in the production. The artwork paints itself onto the canvas; the book writes itself, and the dance moves of its own accord. We are not the ultimate doers, only the channels for what must be done. As channels, our love flows freely making everything new. There is no right way to create, there is only creation. There are no unequally created people, just expressions of the light of divine power. A flower or tree is not right or wrong, it is a possibility realized.

Released from responsibility for performing correctly, we allow our perfect spirit to express itself to the world. We become liberated from our self-assessments and standards. The creations heal us with their originality, breaking through barriers of redundancy. With each new feast for the eyes in art, splashes of notes in music or twists and turns in dance, the impassioned soul of life is enriched. With each crying newborn, peak of the sun behind the clouds, or chirp of spring robins, we see unapologetic creation. Out of nothing a new creation emerges to bring joy to the world.

December 9

Spontaneity

Carry a flame to ignite your own soul. – *Ndidi,* Tea Leaves

Spontaneous combustion occurs when internal heat ignites an object. Our spontaneity emerges from a different kind of latent heat, the heat of creativity erupting from a planned way of doing things. Unlike spontaneous combustion, human spontaneity may be sparked by excessive boredom or the rejection of routine. Boredom according to Paul Tillich is "rage spread thin." The energy of rage can generate spontaneous solutions that complacency would never consider.

As loving spirits our spontaneity can take on new meaning. When we love boundlessly, we can spontaneously connect with others in unplanned joy. We may meet the eyes of someone on the street and smile, or pay for a stranger's meal as a random act of kindness. We may visit a senior center and read poetry, or call a loved one because we think about her. We could drive down a different street to get to work, or take the stairs instead of the elevator, not because of a plan, but because it stirs us. Our lives are filled with potential; we can notice the heat stirring within us and allow our spirit to fly freely. When we allow the flames to ignite our curiosity, our passionate potential is released. When we recognize the infinite possibilities in our life, we can create a life of boundless love and unfettered beauty.

December 10

Worldly Possessions

Love bears all things, hopes all things, and endures all things. Love never ends. – *I Corinthians 13:7–8 (KJV)*

The tomb of Tutankhamun contained exquisite funerary objects intended to accompany the young king on his journey after death. In Western societies, funeral proceedings may be less elaborate in maintaining worldly possessions but the usually well-dressed body of the deceased suggests that there is preparation for an afterlife, and possible resurrection in the future. In some Eastern cultures the deceased may be cremated in recognition of the uselessness of the body after death, and the belief that the spirit will be reincarnated in a different form.

Whether we believe we can take it with us or not, our worldly possessions hold our energy. The transfer of energy into inanimate objects may seem strange to some of us, but objects themselves are just energy. Our visual perception of objects convinces us that the objects have boundaries, and that there is no possibility of movement of energy within a solid object. But the microscopic examination of objects confirms that there is energetic activity at the atomic and subatomic levels of existence. The universe is alive, and we are contributing to the aliveness.

What are our spiritual possessions? What do we own that money cannot buy? As spiritual beings we are heir to an infinite intelligence and the grace of eternal life. We don't have to worry about whether we can take it with us, because it does not disappear with a body. The grace of All-That-Is is awareness of the abundant energy of Love. The incomprehensible durability of love assures us that our inheritance will always be there for us, because it is already our true reality. Love never ends; spirit never ends. When we know unequivocally that love is who we are, we release our attachments to our worldly possessions, and glory in the sheer magnificence of being alive in the present moment. We realize that what we hold in our spiritual awareness are the keys to freedom from fear, and an end to suffering.

December 11

Acknowledgment

Each friend represents a world in us, a world possibly not born until they arrive, and it is only by this meeting that a new world is born. – *Anaïs Nin*, Diary of Anaïs Nin, Vol.I

If we look at a tree and see only the trunk, branches and leaves, we have missed the tree. If we do not see the miracle of the tree that converts carbon dioxide into oxygen, and buds into leaves, we are not paying attention. If we miss the presence of life in the tree, and our own connection to it, we have missed the ultimate reality of our being. If we miss the plentiful flowers that bloom in our world, not because they owe us their beauty, but because they are being what they are, we have failed to sniff the fragrance of love. If we could appreciate the rush of a wave, crashing on the shore in a momentary death because its turn had come to dazzle us, then we could know the relentless rhythm of the universe. If we could love the sunset so completely that it filled our heart and not just our eyes with its orange-yellow canvas, we could know the cycle of life and death in all its glory.

If we could imagine a world where there is peace, we could know the truth of our existence. If we could feel the tender hope in the eyes of a defenseless child, we could touch the heart of compassion. If we could hear the desperation stuck inside a homeless man, we could resolve our own aimlessness. When we perceive with our hearts in the mirrored reflection of others, and appreciate the miracle of a dynamic world, we acknowledge the everlasting love of All-That-Is.

December 12

Sleeping Lion

The real shame of life is to withhold our magnificence from the world because we believe our history is our future. – *Ndidi,* Tea Leaves

Shame is like carrying a sleeping lion on our chest. The shame is based on a story that gets more deeply ingrained in our minds and hearts as the months and years accumulate after we have experienced painful, sometimes horrific events in our lives.

The story may sound like this: Someone failed to meet our expectations, perhaps they deceived us. Perhaps we were abandoned or betrayed; maybe we were physically or sexually abused by a parent or we witnessed a horrible crime that took away a loved one. We were both disappointed and shocked by what we experienced; so we could not forgive the person who ruined our life. That unforgivable act began a series of difficult challenges. The theme of our life experience remained unchanged; there were just different conditions that challenged us. We kept searching for resolution in education, material possessions or get-rich schemes, but nothing helped us to release our continually stressful existence. We became convinced that we are unworthy of peace.

In spite of gifts and talents we possess, our shame prevents us from sharing them. We dream of being successful, so we can remind the perpetrators of our worth; but we see ourselves as longstanding victims of seemingly insurmountable problems, and a group of people called "they" are the source of persistent irritation. Our innocence becomes buried under the shame we experience, so we continue to believe that we cannot realize our dreams. We avoid the truth of our magnificence, because we believe that another person's opinion of us is more valid than the truth of who we are.

443

When we believe untrue stories of our worth, we mortgage our lives to suffering. We become oblivious to the one thing we want so desperately: love. When we begin to see the past, painful events in our lives for what they are -- feelings and reminders that have clung to our chest, scratched and clawed us into thinking we are unworthy and shameful --we begin to feel our core innocence.

We could begin to look deeply at our lives and give thanks for all the love that sits in the background, waiting to be felt and experienced fully. And then in time, we can recognize that we were vulnerable but not shameful; and then we could change our internal response to what has happened, and face the repetitive challenges that have consumed us, because we have not changed our responses to pain. The change could be easy if we know that we're not forgetting anything by changing our response; we are rewriting the long-awaited ending. We could begin to forgive ourselves for holding onto shame. We are not what has happened to us; we are love expressed in this time-space reality, and our light must shine.

December 13

Surprise

Joy is allowing yourself to be surprised. – *Ndidi,* Tea Leaves

One of the entertaining aspects of a mystery novel is the sense of uncovering the unknowns as the story unfolds. The expectation of surprise is tantalizing as we attempt to outsmart the writer with our deductions about who is guilty. We are most impressed when our best guesses prove inadequate, as the writer weaves a plot that exposes information that we had not considered, or had no way of knowing.

Fiction may imitate life at times. Surprises are part of the substance of ongoing life. They are like cosmic laughter entertaining us as it flirts with change and complexity. We live continually with surprises: the changes in weather, societal events, losses and gains. Not knowing what is going to happen in the future can be an enormous gift. Instead of being concerned about the future that we cannot control, we can enjoy the present moment.

Present moment surprises are temporary but can be dramatic. Without the changes that surprises offer, the universe would cease to create, at least in our eyes, and would suffer from sameness. Such a scenario is hard to imagine in a continually changing universe. Each moment is a new experience, because of the continually surprising changes in our life story.

December 14

Intelligent Love

When the wave rises, it is water; and when it falls, it is
the same water again. – *Kabir*, Songs of Kabir

Infinite intelligence is transforming life in every moment; we are that
life. Our main faith in this intelligence is based on the consciousness that
it has always existed and will continue its flow into infinity. We're in a
committed relationship with this presence, infinite intelligence, and there
is no way that our true self can be separate from it. There is no reason to
doubt this power, since its creativity is the reason that we exist.

Universal intelligence is defined as an intrinsic tendency for things to self-
organize, in others words, to continue to change and grow in complexity
based on prevailing conditions. We are in the waves of self-organization,
continually moving toward order.

When we surrender to the power of the flow, without resistance, possibilities
open up to us. It seems contradictory, but the more we let go, the more
life opens to us. The response is dramatic; what we have wanted, prayed
for, comes to us, not in the limited way we imagined it, but in a way that
loves us. We are unfolding our purpose within the complex movement of
the universe. We breathe in a giving universe.

Although surrender may be a great idea, we are continually responding
to the conditions created in our mind, some of which are not loving. In
our personal identification with Infinite Intelligence, we may believe the
words of Jesus of Nazareth that if a person asks for something, it will be
given to her, "Ask and it is given, seek and ye shall find, knock and the
door shall be opened unto you." (Matt.7:7) We often are disappointed,

since our faith may be burdened by continual thoughts of not having what we want. Asking is not enough, believing is required, and in the believing a strong vibration or energy is intentionally released. But whatever we intend is already done. Whatever we ask for is realized when we have a strong sense of peace and gratitude now. The mind cannot describe or comprehend the truth of our being. Our faith must extend beyond reason, and beyond time and space. The intelligent universe is like a circle without a circumference and a location that is everywhere. We live and breathe in an infinite universe, unfathomable with our limited minds, but we are not innocent bystanders, simply victims of circumstances.

We have a role to play in our created stories, and we can change the story at any time.

Buddha recognized why we suffer in the world; we hungrily grasp for more than we have, believe that we have no connection to our "neighbors" and become deluded by false ideas. For the Buddha, infinite intelligence was within, and the tamed mind would lead us to peace.

If we believe Lord Krishna in the Bhagavad Gita, we must let go of our mortal fears and recognize that God is all. Fear distracts us from our own power, and sometimes makes us oblivious to the love in our midst. When we shake it off, we realize that fear itself is our greatest threat to peace and well-being.

Infinite Love is the infinite intelligence of the universe. The universe is committed to us because we exist in its image as an expression of all that lives and breathes. When we are being who we are we live the fullness of love.

December 15

Surrender

The snake does not hold onto the old skin as the
new skin appears. – *Ndidi,* Tea Leaves

The struggle to hold onto anything that is temporary inevitably leads to loss; impermanence is a universal law. We are getting practice for the ultimate surrender all the time as we observe the ongoing changes in our lives. Surrender to sleep is preparation to wake up in a new day. We surrender the day as the night approaches; and over time we surrender years as we gracefully age. With so much daily practice we can become comfortable with surrender because we are assured of our ongoing renewal.

We do not just surrender to change; we flow with the inevitability of it. We do not resist the light of the morning sun, but welcome it. We do not curse the darkness while we hold our own lamp. We only surrender what is here for a short time; the permanent self remains. The essence of who we are does not disappear with the night, or suddenly appear as we awaken; the true self never gives up its unchanging essence.

Many spiritual leaders have assured us of the promise of everlasting life, and offered themselves as examples or models of how to prepare. The message has always been similar, in spite of differences in their delivery and the cultural or political contexts of their life on earth.

We have learned that we must surrender the false self in order to clearly experience the true self. All that we thought we were falls away in the surrender, so some say we become enlightened or born again. With surrender, we become who we have been all along; and come "face-to-face"

448

with the eternal love that we are. Our new awareness requires that we acknowledge a new reality.

Becoming something new means that we must monitor our thoughts, and change the way we respond to events in our life. Instead of reacting with fear, we begin to respond with love. Instead of judgments, we look into our own mirror, and change our own views. Instead of pushing away anyone with whom we disagree, we embrace their inherent innocence and listen. We welcome new opportunities to surrender, with the awareness that every moment will be new for us, but our true self will continue to be what it has always been.

December 16

Movie Life

The eye is meant to see things. The soul is here for
its own joy. – *Rumi,* A Year with Rumi

Our lives are like a long running movie with no beginning and no end.
We believe we are guest actors with small parts, but without us the play
would have to be cancelled. The script is improvisational, so we craft new
lines for each daily performance. We interact with the audience, sometimes
as if we are witnessing a tragedy that requires compassion and listening,
and at other times as if we are in a comedy that requires a sense of humor.
Sometimes the movie gets scary, but that happens whenever we lose faith
in the intent of the movie. We may forget our lines and believe that the
movie will end badly, or that someone may steal our lines. From scene to
scene, we have as our major goal to continue the movie, because we realize
early in the performance that we are doing it for the joy of being in our role.

Then one day our spirit realizes that there are no more lines to craft, no
jokes to tell, and no cameras. So we quietly rest from the daily surprises
and alterations in the script, and sit in quiet repose. Our spirit is aware of
the dreamy part we have played, and appreciates the breaths that made it
possible.

The true self shows itself as the producer of the movie, and takes credit
for all aspects of the production. It was the sun for bright lighting and the
moon for the moody scenes or compassionate roles. It was the stars for soft
lighting and a camera in the eyes of one community of beings. Thunder
made occasional appearances for commanding sound like a drum roll, and
gentle rain gave spirit misty scenes for the sad tales. The wind blew in to
stir things up when the scenes were too long, and the breezes flowed when

the heat of passion needed to be cooled. The waves crashed the after-parties but soon departed, and the oceans stood like worried parents waiting for the waves, as if they had run away from home. The birds provided music every morning, and if necessary throughout the long days, and the animals watched with adoration as if spirit was speaking only to them.

Now as the movie continues, spirit hands over the parts to understudies who will continue the production. Awareness convinces us that there is only one story, one movie, one love, and that it will continue forever.

December 17

It's All Right

If you feel the soft—strength of love surround you, it has
bubbled up from within. – *Ndidi,* Tea Leaves

Love in our lives makes life worth the adventure. It is not a mystery to be
solved, or a commodity to be traded. Love is not a momentary feeling,
or a gushing throb in the heart. Love is the unmistakable knowing that
everything is all right, even when we face inconceivable loss and tragedy. In
its humble understatement, love sits with the hurt we feel, and encourages
us to cleanse our mind and heart with sobbing. Love does not judge us for
our doubts or continual visits to the past. Love stands with open arms to
welcome us back to the present with every new inhalation.

When we fall into fear, love lifts us into our true selves, assuring us that
what we fear is an illusion. When we are ready to give up, love surprises
us with a joyful moment or the kindness of a stranger. When our personal
reality leaves our mouths gaping with disbelief, love transforms our shock
into compassion. When our body aches with lingering fears, or unresolved
suffering, love takes us by the hand and leads us into awareness of the full
expanse of who we are. When we think all is lost – friends, family, career,
health or money – love reminds us that everything changes and that all
is well, always.

December 18

Sacred Witness

Deep reality is that place in the center of our being where we experience our existence in an unlimited way. – Beatrice Bruteau, Radical Optimism

Our courtrooms rely on witnesses to complete the picture of what has happened in a case. Often the testimony of a witness is the difference between believing what is claimed or what is known. But in our spiritual realities, truth is the witness. The true self is the sacred witness of the universe.

Within any struggle lies the sacred witness, the conscious awareness that is anchored in truth. The divine within us bears continuous witness to the reality we are creating. As material witnesses, we can easily feel responsible for what we are seeing, and engage with a reality we are creating. When situations erupt into pain or difficulties, we may feel guilt or anger. The story we create about how the situation occurred and who is to blame are powerful reflections of our belief in the mind's images. Stories from the past and fears of the future are the main ingredients in what we witness as pain and suffering. Our devotion to 'then and there' instead of "here and now" can wreak havoc with our sense of peace.

But when we are sacred witnesses, conscious awareness of our true self is the canvas for our visions, and the present moment holds every element of potentiality that we need to move beyond pain. As sacred witnesses, we are aware of no separation between what we are seeing and who we are. We know that the perceiver and the perceived are one. We recognize a strong affinity with all that exists in our consciousness and become grounded in a limitless experience of life. We see ourselves in others; and recognize the innocence in others as our own. We realize that the sense of isolation and disconnection from the agony we see in the world is not possible, but we also feel empowered to change our experience. We witness the comings and goings of our negative emotions, and resist the tendency to identify with them.

We are careful as witnesses to complete the statement "I am…" in a way that honors our wholeness. We understand that the "I am" is a statement of conscious awareness, and a revelation of truth, so we prefer to describe what is actually true for ourselves in our "I am" statements. We say "I am loving," or I am thankful," instead "I am sick" or "I am a failure." As sacred witnesses, we are compassionate energy, venerating the truth of our existence in loving consciousness of All-That-Is. We experience through our sacred witnessing that all is well, and that our longing for the meaning of life is found in awareness of our unlimited self.

December 19

Strength to Be Love

The sheer beauty of the universe should make us weep. – Ndidi, Tea Leaves

The root origin of the word, universe, is *"uni"* meaning one and *"verse"* meaning to turn, so we could say that the universe is turning as one. Awareness of the oneness of the universe makes love a necessity rather than an option. Since we are connected to everything else in the universe, we become aware of the awesome power of that turning.

The bodhisattvas of the Buddha or disciples of Jesus the Anointed One are revered for their model of spiritual purity. What spiritual leaders have shown us seems impossible to achieve in our lifetime, because we may see ourselves as inferior to the divinity of the leaders, or we may feel incapable of miraculous works. We prefer to give away our potentiality to others and often deny our own power.

We may continually deny our true selves to stay true to our reverence for those we respect or worship, but we are not weak and broken. As conscious beings, we are aware of our thoughts, behaviors, desires and created reality. We can look deeply within the story of our lives and clearly appreciate how, when and where we are right now. We can model joy in life so that others will feel its loving essence. When we understand our interdependence with everything else, we exert our power for good and pay attention to the way our life influences others.

We can express love for others in our lack of judgments. We can bask in the contentment of the present moment; and smile at the abundance that appears in our world daily as smiles, laughter, flowers and fauna. We could raise our arms in praise for the stars and feel the energy of the universe course through our veins. We are strong enough to love.

December 20

In Our Time

Without birth and death, and without the perpetual
transmutation of the forms of life, the world would be
static, rhythm-less, un-dancing, mummified. – *Alan Watts,*
The Book on the Taboo of Knowing Who You Are

We are all standing in a queue, waiting to be called. We say that our
number is up, or our time has come; and we have developed horrific
images and characters to dramatize our fears. We talk about a Grim
Reaper or the Dark Knight to further catastrophize our fear of death. We
talk depressingly about how life is short or cruel and full of suffering. Our
continual preoccupation with the end of our life causes us to miss the joy
in it. In a weird irony, when we perceive death as an end to life, we focus
most of our precious time on an uncertain time in our future.

Every moment is an opportunity to enjoy life, but so often we cling to
debilitating anxieties about what will happen in the future instead of
celebrating what *is* happening in our lives right now. We reminisce about
the way things were, and dream of better times in the future, while the
present moment slips by without notice.

When we are aware of the nature of our being --that we were never truly
born --we relax and enjoy being here now. When we are aware that we
existed in some form before we were conceived as human beings, and will
continue to exist as the true self, when we transition for a new adventure,
we begin to be less in a hurry to accomplish everything right now. We
know that we have all the time we need, so we slow down and savor each
moment.

December 21

We Have Overcome

We are not broken; we are limitless Love. – *Ndidi*, Tea Leaves

During the 1870's and 80's a theme-based author named Horatio Alger portrayed teenage boys rising from "rags to riches" through acts of courage, honesty and hard work. Often the key to their rise was the beneficence of a wealthy man who repaid the boy for his honest gesture or hard work. The Horatio Alger stories live on in the minds of many in developed countries as the formula for success; the stories of people who have overcome suffering have become attractive in many societies.

The lack of "success" may be seen as a flaw, even though many of us have no known benefactor. We may ignore the talents and skills that lie dormant in our consciousness and intuition, because we have no one holding up the mirror. We crave someone who "gets us," who understands our potential and the self that gets obscured by conditions. We may ignore honesty in the homeless teenager, or the courage of an impoverished mother of three children. We may underestimate the wisdom of a precocious eight-year old or the clear seeing of the blind. We may discount the innovations of the rapper or the skill of an Irish step dance.

We could look at the stories that appear in our lives differently. Everything we will ever need in this life is available to us and others. If we experience "dis-ease," there is an herb, grass, tree or other substance that can bring relief. Some herbalists believe that there is an antidote to everything that disturbs our well-being.

We exist in the complex web of humanity; if we are experiencing difficulty in relationships there is someone else who is experiencing a similar challenge. Online dating sites, self-help books, and popular television series depend on the sense that our life experiences are similar and that we want similar changes in our lives.

If we are struggling financially or in our careers, there is someone who understands the strategies to improve. Our counselors, coaches and consultants are our benefactors, providing the questions that we must answer. We will always have what we need when we know who we are.

But Alger delivered something more valuable as a compelling story; he taught us that in order to overcome the appearances of lack in our lives, we must know our unlimited potential. We could rejoice in who we are and be free of self-judgments about what we should be or have. The universe is waiting for us to ask, so that the forces of love can respond, and we can begin to overcome the limits we place on ourselves.

December 22

Our Part

Each of us has a unique part to play in the healing of the world. – *Marianne Williamson,* The Law of Divine Compensation: Mastering the Metaphysics of Abundance

A poem emerges out of nowhere on the pages of the poet's notebook. She is not expecting the inspiration. Her mind opened up and triggered the thought; the power of the poem took over, poured itself onto the notebook page in a fury of passion. When the poem had written itself, the woman settled back into herself and sighed. The call of the spirit faded into stillness.

We are all called to be who we are, loving spirits. As creative spirits we respond to the calling. We say that we are finding our talents or establishing our niche. We are inspired with the gifts of the universe and are compelled at times to deliver them. We are orators, facilitators, coaches and inventors. We find ways to inspire youth and develop new technologies to make access to information easier and to reduce complexities. We are teachers and lawyers, preachers and poets solving problems and illuminating minds. We are healers and physicians, strategists and implementers of plans.

We are like a field of flowers of different hues and shapes, but with fragrances that are both captivating and necessary. When we are called from the depths of our soul, our hearts open and we come to life. No matter whether our intention is to create new expressions or products, creativity is the fuel of the universe. When we answer the call we experience joy and the evolving universe thanks us.

December 23

A Pearl

Through the irritation of sand, the clam
creates a pearl. – *Ndidi,* Tea Leaves

Throughout our lives we are creating a pearl from the contrasts and conditions that bring clarity to our existence. The pearl is our joy that has emerged from the challenges. Our pearl is fashioned into a perfectly crafted summary of the life we have lived; it is our imprint and legacy, evidence of a life we have lived fully.

Everyone we meet is a teacher for us, so we owe them our gratitude. They fill in the gaps of our life experiences with guidance and leadership. Reportedly during the last days of the Buddha's life, he taught his followers to seek refuge in his teaching that included the four noble truths and his sutras. The Prophet Muhammad instructed his followers to treat others well and to be kind to future messengers, and Jesus of Nazareth entreated his followers to love one another as he loved them.

The life we live is a model for those who live on when we are transformed; it is a living memory of the love and joy we have experienced. Our lifetimes are precious testimonies to the beauty of the world. In the enjoyment of our present moment we can know that our thoughts, feelings and actions are continually delivering instructions to those we meet. Our loving spirit announces our intentions and our compassion fulfills our loving promise. When we embrace the true self as who we are, we are creating a legacy of joy. We are allowing love to replace our fears, and meeting others in peace. When we allow life to unfold as it should, we experience it as the perfect pearl that it is.

December 24

Revolution Within

Spiritual revolution is the by–product of a struggle between the past and the future, when the present consistently wins. – *Ndidi,* Tea Leaves

Even for revolutionaries, the temptation to run away from the pain of rejection and being misunderstood can be almost unbearable, but they continue because their intentions outweigh their fears. The causes for revolt are far less tumultuous than the revolutions within us. We are tempted to retreat from confusing messages of life: the different belief systems that seem to be in conflict, the attractiveness of the real world that constantly changes, or the elusiveness of peace in a conflictual world. We can become ensconced in the mire of a fearful mind, and begin to believe that life is only a struggle with an uncertain end.

When we realize that there is no opponent, only our fearful mind offering competing ideas, we can begin to experience the triumph of life. When we experience directly the love in relationships, the wisdom of constant change, the temporary nature of pain and the release of suffering, we can be open to life. Joy is knowing that distress is not permanent, and neither is victory. When we know that joy is the only stability in life; it is our purpose and our saving grace. Our revolution is the Shiva-like destruction that creates new beginnings. The surrender to love and joy is a settlement with life, a commitment to our true self. The revolution within is recognizing that without surrender to what is, there can be no peace.

December 25

Refuge

Taking refuge is alignment with truth. – *Ndidi,* Tea Leaves

Jesus of Nazareth taught that the kingdom of God is within. Whether we are remembering the story of Buddha, Jesus or Mohammed, reports of their ascensions into heaven or paradise are instructive about our own life's promise. They asked that we follow them, and in so doing follow their examples. But the kingdom is not a place out there or up there, it is outside our conscious awareness. It exists in our heart every moment; not in the organ that beats continually, pumping blood into our vascular system, but the heart that is aware of the universal soul.

Glimpses of the kingdom routinely flood our awareness in many ways; we simply have to shift our awareness from what we perceive externally to what is always present internally. The "kingdom" of All-That-Is is on display for us to see in the colors of a rainbow; the broad smile of a proud parent; the power of the wind in the desert; and mindfulness of the present moment.

We have "entered" heaven when we are being love, offering compassion, expressing appreciation and being grateful. We are settled into the refuge of truth when we take the journey inward. Our hearts are gateways to the essence of our true selves. When we are aware of our essence, fully conscious of the majesty of being, we realize that we have been in "the kingdom" all our lives, and will be for an eternity.

December 26

Transformation

Everything changes. – The Buddha

Unless we observe the gradual changes in children as they grow older, we may miss the continual transformations that are part of their growth. Many changes in life are nuanced and gradual, so they occur without our awareness. Every moment is a metaphor for continual growth and transformation. Every in-breath is new and every out-breath has been transformed. The natural environment presents numerous examples of transformation; nothing in life remains the same.

We may not notice subtle changes, but dramatic changes happen all the time. People have epiphanies that change their perspectives. Communities respond to losses when tsunamis or hurricanes ravish homes and claim lives. The glaciers crash into Glacier Bay, and wild fires race through forests.

Change can be terrifying until we realize that the temporary nature of life is the reason life continues. If everything we perceive in our world were to remain the same, we would not experience the changing of the seasons, the splendid display of flowers, the births of babies, the beginnings of friendships or the end of suffering. Change is a constant we can embrace, as long as we don't allow ourselves to get too attached to whatever or whomever comes into our life. We heal from those losses when we begin to accept and align with changes in our lives, and know that all that we experience is as it should be. We grieve the loss of loved ones or friends because we have caught a glimpse of ourselves in them, and in losing them we believe that we lose a part of ourselves. Nothing has gone anywhere, because the only real place is here, now. What we think we have lost continues to exist in a form we no longer recognize.

What we describe as loss in our lives is difficult to reconcile at times because of our tendency to think we possess what we connect to in our lives. We think our children belong to us, or our parents exist to support and understand us like no one else. We may believe that we own our material possessions, or that a spouse or partner belongs to us alone. Each of these relationships can be transformed as conditions change. We are connected to everything else in the universe, but the nature of our connections is continually changing. When we are comfortable with change, we align our hearts with the transformative nature of reality.

December 27

Fire

No one must die in order for us to live forever. – *Ndidi,* Tea Leaves

Explosions on the sun release heat and light and reaction particles; the heat and light stimulate growth and maintain life on earth. We are warmed beside a fire or gather around a fire pit, but fire as a metaphor takes on less positive connotations. We say that determined people have fire in the belly, or we terminate people and say, "You're *fired!*" We talk about the destruction of *wild* fires, and the downsides of *blazing* arguments. We describe impassioned speech as *fiery,* and we describe strong ambition as having a *burning* desire.

It is no wonder that a metaphorical place for eternal punishment would be a lake with fire and brimstone, a lemon-colored stone now called sulphur, that gives off noxious fumes when it is burned. Anger and fear demand retribution for broken social agreements, diverse perspectives, and misguided actions. Judges sort through what is punishable based on prescribed rules and laws. The verdict, difficult to enforce, is death of the soul. In an eternal universe of transformations, the true self always remains.

When we focus our awareness on love instead of punishment, we adopt new metaphors. When we have conscious awareness of our potential, we experience life as love, the eternal *flame* of forever. We become grateful for life as it is, and pray that all beings experience happiness. The fire in our belly is loving-kindness and passion, and the embers of love and compassion are easily stoked in service to the well-being of all others. We appreciate the life-giving fire storms on the sun that continue to generate heat from the rays. We remember those who have transitioned as keepers of the flame, and celebrate their lives in this space and time as bright and warm. We say that when we are full of love our hearts are aglow. When we expand our awareness of who we are in relationship to life, love and other sentient beings, we know that life is an adventure that can be continually warmed by the fire of passion.

December 28

Reunion

We never lose our loved ones. They accompany us;
they don't disappear from our lives. We are merely in
different rooms. – *Paul Coelho*, Aleph (2011)

Many believe that transition from this life to the next experience will bring a reunion with those who have gone before us. We may cling to the idea that we are our bodies and without them we are non-existent, but we are not our bodies; we are much more. Many religious traditions have described the arduous journey of the soul after it departs the body; after a challenging life experience, another struggle is promised, especially for many of us, who have led less than stellar lives. The message is that we must work to be liberated, accepted, or allowed to be reunited with spirit in eternal life.

We wonder about what we must give up in order to stay alive for an eternity. Our faith communities provide guidelines, but we are sometimes not fully convinced that we will qualify. After all, we have created an identity for ourselves that we call "I."

Clinging to the sense of "I' obscures our true essence, the self that will not die. There is no "place" for the essence of who we are to disappear. We may believe that when the body withers and grows cold that the essence of who we are washes away with it, because we so closely associate who we are with our bodies. But we cling to our bodies and brains as our only definition of living.

The reunion we seek is with our true self, but we do not have to wait until we leave our bodies to bring about that reunion. Like a wave, and the sea that it encompasses, we are never cut off from the source of our being; there is no place where the water of the earth does not exist in some form. Like water, the essence of All-That-Is pervades our being and expresses as one spirit.

The bond with Presence is already a reality; we are not separated from our true self. We are complete as spirit, needing nothing to make us whole. But the struggle in life that we sense is our resistance in the mind to our true identity.

We are not our limited bodies, although we may be most familiar with the body during our lives. Our ultimate reality is so much more than a body can contain; it is a vast space with no beginning and no end. All that we are, have been and will be is that space.

We may wonder how our loved ones who have transitioned will know us without our bodies after death. But how do we know someone if we speak to her by phone or in an email? What is our sense of someone in a "different room?" The essence of who we are is not bounded by what we can see or even hear. As pure essence, we are known without labels or boundaries.

We desire a "reunion" so that we can remember who and what we are, and become aware that our bond has never been broken.

December 29

The Death of Fear

Fear points to something unresolved and unopened. – *Ndidi,* Tea Leaves

Decades ago, children played a game where they were blindfolded and asked to find their way along an obstacle path. They walked with uncertainty, stumbling and bumping into obstacles, but relying on what they could touch to guide them to the end.

Life can feel like an obstacle course, where unexpected rocks along the journey get in our way. We do all we can to avoid the "rocks" but at times it's difficult for us to find a smooth place on the journey. We stay in a constant state of fear or dread, assuming that the next challenge will come soon, and that the final challenge will come too soon. We rely on the mind to help us and believe that if we prepare and protect ourselves, we will be able to manage whatever occurs. We may come to believe that whatever we can touch, taste, see or hear is real, even though a life ruled by the senses can be deceiving.

We quickly realize that the mind is stressed, trying to make sense out of whatever is happening in our lives. We know that we cannot believe everything we think, so the path to truth can become frustrating, even after we have given a lot of thought to a situation.

We may pray for guidance, but the "answers" we receive require a different kind of listening. We discover that we can close our eyes and see more than we could with eyes open. Our hearts are "touched" in a way that defies explanation when a loved one listens to us or recognizes who we really are. We say that we have "tasted" victory when we achieve a goal; or we taste the love in the cooking of a grandmother, cousin or father. As if our senses were only pointers to reality, we become aware of the thoughts in our lives that shape our stories and experiences, but we also come to know that some things are inexplicable.

With the reliance on an inner knowing, a faith in the grace of the universe, we no longer live in a painful past or a frightful future. Awareness of our essential nature, our true self releases us from the fear of death. When we know that we can listen to a voice that does not use words, and yet it touches us so deeply that we stop breathing for a moment, we are free. When we know that we are never stuck in a situation, because everything is changing, we let go of suffering. We come to realize that stumbles along life's journey have been mid-course corrections, sometimes leading us out of danger, or forcing us to face pain that we have been avoiding. When we know that there is no death, we are freed from the crippling arms of fear. Our awareness, bolstered by faith in our true nature, transforms us from living moment to moment with the fear of death to relaxing in each moment with the death of fear.

December 30

Resurrecting Love

The goal in life is to transcend it. — *Ndidi,* Tea Leaves

From the resurrection of Osiris by Isis, rejoining his many forms and pieces into a whole, to the resurrection of Jesus of Nazareth, promising eternal life, we have been encouraged by the force of love to achieve the freedom of spirit and eternal life. We have been comforted by the notion that life does not end with our last breath, but continues in its sweet way in awareness of All-That-Is. In the ancient near east, observers of the changes in the length of days associated the seasonal changes with Tammuz, a god of the Babylonian pantheon. The life, death and rebirth of Tammuz was consistent with the seasons. The Greek god of beauty and desire, Adonis, is linked also with the seasons of vegetation in a metaphor of life, death and rebirth. Krishna, a reincarnation of the Hindu god Vishnu, is killed, his body burned but then he ascends to heaven.

From the historical to the mythical, the stories of resurrection have provided powerful messages of the cyclical nature of existence, or the promise of eternal life. The cycles send the message of continuation of life as spirit or a transcendent consciousness; the promise of eternal life pays homage to peace. Resurrection is a testimony to the omnipotent presence of peace and love in the universe. It was Love that drove Isis to the ends of the earth to resurrect Osiris. Inner peace and love of others without judgment even in dire circumstances is the peaceful message of Jesus the Anointed One. Whether we believe in mythical gods or historical spiritual leaders, the message is consistent. We can transcend the limitations of our life experiences. We can overcome challenges with love rather than hatred, faith rather than fear, and conscious awareness of our divinity rather than a continual dependency on the false self. We could resurrect our sense of joy and peace. We could be love.

December 31

Ending is Beginning

Forever is a promise to us from a loving universe. – *Ndidi,* Tea Leaves

"It is finished," is the famous sixth expression reportedly uttered by Jesus of Nazareth as he suffered crucifixion on the hills of Golgotha. For many Christians the statement is an announcement of triumph. An ending is a triumph because it is followed by a beginning; the endings make beginnings possible.

Conditions we face in life are a series of events that will arise out of nothing and disappear into nothing. We know when the appearances are no longer with us, when it is finished. Before the next phase can be experienced in its fullness, we must let go of what we have seen, felt, done, or experienced. We must open ourselves to what is here now in this moment.

We could pay attention to the pain as it arises in us, look deeply at it, and watch it subside and move away. We could welcome each new moment in our lives, as the gift that it is. We could be grateful for all that we are in this universe and know that suffering does not continue unless we refuse to let go. We could remember that suffering does not mean that we are alone in our struggle, and in knowing that we could nurture the vision of peace in the world for all beings. We could celebrate our being love incarnate in this life. "It is finished," could be expanded to "It is finished so that we can begin anew," as we acknowledge the cycle of life. We could rejoice in the opportunity to be joy and peace for an eternity.

Acknowledgements

Thank you to my grandson, Michael Cooper, for reminding me that I matter; and thanks to nieces, nephews, cousins and friends whose emotional support cannot possibly be repaid.

I express sincere gratitude to Mary Alice Saunders, Miriam Robinson, Nancy Brown-Jamison, Andrea Briscoe, Rosa Green, LaTanya Hicks, Jarvis Cooper, Dr. Stephen Middleton, Ralph Hume, Linda Bain, Sandra Hayes, Thomas Ashford, Tara Brown, Swami Gyankirti, Elizabeth Jende, Myque Harris, Gail Jarrett, Diane Hill, Delores Hooks, Gloria Sylvester, LaFern Batie and many colleagues for caring about my spiritual journey.

Thank you also to members of the Friday meditation group:

Diane Carter, Theresa White, Kim Gladden, Marina Thomas and others for their energy and inspiration.

Thank you to Bobby Miller, Ahmad Karriem, Patricia Reid, Darlene Jamison, Ruth Porchia and other members of the Virtual Village who have provided a forum to discuss life's important questions.

Without the work of my editor/proofreader, Anita Diggs, the book would not be complete.

Special thanks to Denise Agard for her photography and friendship.

Contributors Index

Many wise men and women contributed quotes to the *Daily Sips*. The names of contributors are listed alphabetically with their origins, work/ genre and life dates. Ndidi is the author's pen name and is the author of two books of quotes, *Tea Leaves* and *Finding Joy-Finding Yourself.*

A

Achebe, Chinua – Nigerian novelist, poet, critic -1930-2013

Adyashanti – spiritual leader, author – b. 1962

Aesop – Greek storyteller – 620-564 BCE

Angelou, Maya – American author, poet, inspirational leader– 1928-2014

Albom, Mitch – American author, journalist, playwright – b. 1958

Aristotle – Greek Philosopher – 384-322 BCE

Aurelius, Marcus – Roman emperor, 121-180

B

Baldwin, James – American author, novelist, poet, playwright, activist – 1924-1987

Barth, Karl – Swiss theologian -1886-1968

Basri, Rabi'a al – Sufi mystic and poet – 717-801

Beckett, Samuel –Irish novelist, playwright, poet -1906-1989

Beckwith, Michael B. – American New Thought minister, author – b.1956

Bible – a collection sacred texts in Judaism and Christianity (KJV)

Blake, William – English poet, painter and printmaker – 1957-1827

Bonta, Vanna – Italian-American writer and actor - d. 2014

Borge, Victor –Danish-American classical pianist, comedian – 1909-2000

Bradbury, Ray – American science-fiction writer – 1920-2012

Brown, Brené – American author, researcher/ professor – b.1965

Bruteau, Beatrice – Author, philosopher – 1930 - 2014

The Buddha – Ascetic and sage on whose teachings Buddhism was founded – 563-483 BCE

C

Campbell, Joseph –American mythologist, writer and lecturer – 1904-1987

Chinmoy, Sri –Indian spiritual leader – 1931-2007

Chödrön, Pema – American Buddhist nun – b. 1936

Coelho, Paul – Brazilian novelist and lyricist – b. 1947

Cohen, Leonard – Canadian singer, songwriter – b. 1934

Covey, Sean - American author, speaker – b.1964

D

Dalai Lama XIV – Tibetan Buddhist head monk, teacher – b.1935

Desai, Panache – Inspirational leader and visionary – b. (info not available)

Dickinson, Emily – American poet – 1830-1886

Dogen, Eithei – Japanese Buddhist priest, writer -1200-1253

E

Eckhart, Meister – German theologian and philosopher – 1260-1328

Einstein, Albert – German-born theoretical physicist – 1879-1955

Ellison, Ralph - American novelist, literary critic – 1914-1994

Emerson, Ralph Waldo- American essayist, lecturer, poet – 1803-1882

Epicurus – Greek philosopher – 341-270 BCE

F

Finley, James, PhD – American Clinical Psychologist and former Trappist monk – b. (info not available)

France, Anatole – French poet, journalist, novelist -1844-1924

Frank, Anne – German diarist – 1929-1945

Fromm, Eric –Psychologist, author – 1900-1980

G

Gandhi, Indira – Indian prime minister – b. 1917-1984

Gasset, Jose Ortega y - Spanish liberal philosopher, essayist – 1883- 1955

Gibran, Kahlil – Lebanese-American poet, writer, artist – 1883-1931

Bhagavad Gita – 700-verse Hindu scripture in Sanskrit, part of epic Mahabharata

de Grasse - Tyson, Neil– American astrophysicist, cosmologist – b.1958

Gyankirti, Swami – Founder, Medissage Centers, inspirational leader – b. 1954

H

Hanh, Thich Nhat – Vietnamese Buddhist monk, author, activist – b. 1926

Hay, Louise L. – Motivational author and founder of Hay House - b. 1926

Hicks, Esther with Jerry Hicks– New thought leaders – Esther b.1948

Hosseini, Khaled – Afghan- born American novelist – b.1965

I

Ingersoll, Robert- American lawyer, political leader -1833-1899

J

Jamison, Judith –Dancer, choreographer – b. 1943

K

Kabir – Indian mystic poet and saint – c.1398 -1448

Katie, Byron – American speaker, author – b. 1942

Keating, Thomas – American Trappist monk, Cistercian order – b.1923

Keller, Helen – Author, political activist, lecturer -1880-1968

Kierkegaard, Søren – Danish philosopher, theologian, poet, social critic – 1813-1855

Kundera, Milan – Czech- born, French-naturalized writer –b.1942

Krishnamurti, Jiddu – Indian speaker, writer – 1895 -1986

L

Lipton, Bruce – American developmental biologist – b. 1944

Wadsworth Longfellow, Henry - American poet – 1807-1882

M

Marquez, Gabriel Garcia –Colombian novelist, journalist – 1927-2014

McLeod, T. Scott – American cartoonist, comics theorist – b.1960

de Mellow, Anthony – Indian Jesuit priest, psychotherapist – 1931-1987

Merton, Thomas – American writer and monk – 1915-1968

Montaigne, Michel de – French writer, philosopher – 1533-1592

Morrison, Toni – American novelist, poet – b. 1931

Muir, John –Scottish-American naturalist, author -1838-1914

N

Nasmyth, James – Scottish engineer – 1808-1890

Nin, Anais – French novelist and diarist – 1903-1977

Nouwen, Henri – Dutch Catholic priest, writer, theologian -1932-1996

O

Osho – Indian mystic and teacher – 1931-1990

P

Palahniuk, Chuck –American novelist – b. 1962

R

Rilke, Rainer Maria – Bohemian-Austrian poet – 1875-1926

Roosevelt, Eleanor – American first lady, activist, author – 1884-1962

Rowling, J.K. –British novelist – b.1965

Rumi (Jala ad-Din Muhammad Rumi) – Persian poet – 1207-1273

S

Salzberg, Sharon – American author, teacher, meditator – b.1952

Sanderson, Brandon – American science fiction & fantasy author – b. 1975

Schulz, Kathryn – American journalist, author – b. (not available)

Schweitzer, Albert – French-German theologian, philosopher, physician -1875-1965

Seneca –Roman philosopher, orator – 4 BCE -65 CE

Socrates –Greek philosopher, orator – 470 -399 BCE

T

Tagore, Rabindranath – Bengali poet, novelist, essayist– 1861-1941

Teresa, Mother – Albanian-Indian nun – 1910-1997

Thurman, Howard – Author, philosopher, theologian, educator – 1899-1981

Tillich, Paul – Philosopher – 1886-1965

Tolle, Eckhart- German spiritual teacher, author – b.1948

Tripathi, Amish – Indian author - b.1974

Tubman, Harriet – American abolitionist – c. 1822-1913

T'san, Seng – Chinese author – 529 – 606

Twain, Mark – American novelist and humorist – 1835-1910

Tzu, Chuang –Chinese philosopher – 369-286 BCE

Tzu, Lao – Chinese philosopher – 604-531 BCE

U

Upanishads – Sacred Hindu treatises in Sanskrit c. 800-200 BCE

V

Vanzant, Iyanla – American author and speaker – b.1953

W

Walker, Alice – American novelist, poet, activist – b.1944

Watts, Alan – British philosopher – 1915-1973

Whitman, Walt - American poet – 1819- 1892

Wiesel, Elie – American Jewish writer – 1928-2016

Williamson, Marianne – author, inspirational leader – b.1952

Winfrey, Oprah - American media personality – b.1954

Wittgenstein, Ludwig – Austrian-British philosopher -1989-1951

Wordsworth, William – English poet – 1770-1850

Wright, Richard – American author,
poet, novelist -1908-1960

Y

Yutang, Lin – Chinese writer,
philosopher – 1895-1976

Z

Zolli, Andrew – Contemporary
author – b. (info not available)

CPSIA information can be obtained
at www.ICGtesting.com
Printed in the USA
LVOW12s2102120717
541117LV00006B/416/P